American Public Address

ALBERT CRAIG BAIRD

American Public Address

Studies in Honor of
ALBERT CRAIG BAIRD

Edited by Loren Reid

University of Missouri Press • *Columbia*

Foreword

THE proposal for a volume of studies in honor of Albert Craig Baird goes back many years. In 1948, Lester Thonssen, H. Clay Harshbarger, and Orville Hitchcock were appointed a committee to investigate the possibility of such a publication. Later Otto Dieter, W. Norwood Brigance, Carroll Arnold, and Ota Thomas Reynolds were added to the group. At the annual convention of the Speech Association of America in Chicago in 1956, the manuscripts were presented to Professor Baird at a ceremony in connection with the State University of Iowa luncheon. In 1959, Loren Reid of the University of Missouri was designated to assume the final task of preparing the manuscripts for publication.

Generous financial assistance from friends and students of Professor Baird in all parts of the country has facilitated publication.

The editor and contributors are grateful to the following persons and companies for permission to quote from their publications:

Abingdon Press for permission to quote from Ralph W. Sockman, "The Minister's Work as Preacher," in J. Richard Spann, ed. *The Ministry*.

William Jennings Bryan, Jr. for permission to quote from *Speeches of William Jennings Bryan*, published by Funk and Wagnalls.

City News Publishing Company for permission to quote passages from issues of *Vital Speeches*.

Columbia Broadcasting System, Inc. for permission to quote excerpts from broadcasts of Edward R. Murrow over the CBS radio network.

Harcourt, Brace and Company for permission to quote from Oliver Wendell Holmes, *Collected Legal Papers*.

Harper and Brothers for permission to quote from Harry Emerson Fosdick, "What's the Matter With Preaching," in *Harper's*

Magazine, July, 1928, and from the same author's *On Being Fit to Live With.*

The President and Fellows of Harvard College for permission to quote from *Speeches of Justice Oliver Wendell Holmes,* published by Little, Brown and Company.

Fola La Follette for permission to quote from *La Follette's Autobiography, A Personal Narrative of Personal Experiences,* published by The Robert M. La Follette Company.

The Macmillan Company for permission to quote from Herbert Croly, *The Promise of American Life,* copyright 1909 by The Macmillan Company; from Belle C. and Fola La Follette, *Robert M. La Follette,* copyright 1953 by The Macmillan Company.

The Editors of *Newsweek* for permission to quote a comment by Edward R. Murrow reported in the March 29, 1954, *Newsweek.*

Fleming H. Revell Company for permission to quote from Donald Macleod, ed., *Here Is My Method.*

Charles Scribner's Sons for permission to quote from Clarence Darrow, *The Story of My Life;* from Theodore Roosevelt, *Autobiography,* and from the same author's *The Works of Theodore Roosevelt,* National Edition.

Ralph W. Sockman for permission to quote passages from his sermons, broadcast by the National Broadcasting Company over the National Radio Pulpit.

The Viking Press, Inc. for permission to quote from Irwin Edman, *Candle in the Dark.*

The H. W. Wilson Company for permission to quote various passages from A. Craig Baird, *Representative American Speeches.*

L. R.

Table of Contents

SOCIAL AND POLITICAL ISSUES

Albert Craig Baird

ORVILLE A. HITCHCOCK*

THIS volume of studies in American public speaking is dedicated to Dr. A. Craig Baird, Emeritus Professor of Public Address at the State University of Iowa. The authors and most of the members of the editorial board were guided to doctor's degrees in speech by Dr. Baird. His influence on us and on his other students is almost immeasurable. The book is meant to express our affection and respect.

Albert Craig Baird was born in Vevay, Indiana, on October 20, 1883. His father, William J. Baird, also born in Vevay, was of Scotch-Irish extraction, and his mother, Sarah Hedden, came from an English family who settled in New England before 1630. Vevay was established in 1801 by French-Swiss pioneers. By the second half of the nineteenth century it had become a cultural center, its people greatly interested in literature and current issues. William Baird was editor of the Republican newspaper, the *Vevay Reveille*, for more than forty years, and local postmaster during part of that period. His son thus grew up in an atmosphere of writing, working as a printer's devil in his father's shop, and sorting mail in the post office.

Baird once said that his early life was one of "endless books, and the discussion of political and historical affairs." He and his parents read the works of Dickens, Scott, Shakespeare, Emerson, and others, and kept up with the newspapers from nearby Indianapolis, Louisville, and Cincinnati. Chautauqua was at its zenith at this time, and political campaigns also reached into Vevay, giving the Bairds opportunity to hear William Jennings Bryan and Albert J. Beveridge,

---

* Orville A. Hitchcock (B.A. Pennsylvania State College, 1931, M.A. 1932, Ph.D. 1936, State University of Iowa) is professor of speech at the State University of Iowa.

and such local products as Congressman Francis Griffith. William Baird's position as a Republican editor in a Democratic county brought him vigorously into the great debates of the day. Craig Baird wrote on one occasion: "I grew up hearing endlessly, and discussing, the pros and cons of Bryan and free silver, high tariffs, popular election of Senators, the merits and demerits of Cleveland, Harrison, T. Roosevelt, McKinley, the pros and cons of the war with Spain, and the issues of free Cuba, the Philippines, imperialism, agricultural depression, control of railroads, and the other issues of the period—oh, yes, and the waving of the bloody shirt."

Baird attended school in Vevay, where his favorite teacher was Miss Julie Le Clerc Knox, who presided over literature and Latin. As one would expect, he participated in the school's declamatory exercises and other speaking activities. His graduation oration, "Hoosier Quills," concerned the famous Indiana writers, James Whitcomb Riley, Booth Tarkington, Maurice Thompson, Lew Wallace, and Edward Eggleston, the latter another home town boy.

Baird was graduated from high school in 1902. That year his parents moved to Ohio, settling for a short time at Hubbard and then moving again to nearby Youngstown. The young high school graduate accompanied his parents and spent a year working in local mills, the National Tube Works and the Youngstown Sheet and Tube Works. He was employed first as a tester of line pipe and later became a shipping clerk and night time-keeper. His year in Ohio enabled him to earn money for his college education and introduced him to some of the industrial problems of the time. He learned about long hours, low pay, poor employee protection, and accidents—and reacted strongly against them. Later, in college, he was to speak and write of these experiences.

Baird entered Wabash College, at Crawfordsville, Indiana, in September, 1903. He selected Wabash, he says, because it was a small college for men only, with significant literary traditions. There he studied languages (Latin, Greek, German), literature (including Anglo-Saxon), social studies (history, political science), psychology, philosophy, and science (zoology, physics, astronomy, mathematics). His professors included Henry Zwingli McClain (Greek), Arthur B. Milford (English literature), Norton Adams Kent (physics and astronomy), Charles A. Tuttle (political science), President George L. Mackintosh (psychology and philosophy), and Rollo Walter Brown (rhetoric). The freshman English text was John F. Genung's *Practical Elements of Rhetoric*. Professor Brown, to whom Baird became assistant in his senior year, favored the Harvard pattern of teaching rhetoric, with daily themes and formal speaking exercises.

Like many other young men of his day, Baird worked his way through college. He fired furnaces, sold aluminum utensils, inspected pipe, and even raked leaves for General Lew Wallace, while, as he puts it, "the General marched to and fro with proper military bearing." Still he found time to be active in the extracurricular programs. He was class historian and literary editor of the *Wabash*. He also took part in the annual Mock Day program, and in his senior year was "elected" president of the college. In addition to his school activities, he engaged in boys' work in the poorer districts of Crawfordsville.

His training in speech at Wabash began in the Calliopean Society, one of the student literary organizations. Baird took a prominent part in its extensive program of speeches, debates, and discussions. Debates were presented not only at the closed meetings of the group, but also before the student body at large. As Baird later observed, "We had many sound wrangles."

Intercollegiate debating was inaugurated at Wabash during Baird's junior year. The members of the team were selected through a series of tryout debates in the college chapel. Baird entered the competition and was successful in making the team. That year he and his colleagues had one major campus debate (against Parsons College—Wabash won), and took part also in the program of a small Indiana debate league. In his senior year Baird was on the team which met Earlham College, and this time his side lost. He also participated in the Baldwin Oratorical Contest, a major event at Wabash, with a speech entitled "The Open Shop." He made speeches too at the Class Day and Mock Day exercises.

Craig Baird was an outstanding student. He was elected to Phi Beta Kappa, and, upon graduation, was invited to remain at Wabash to teach English. He declined the offer, however, preferring instead to continue his studies. He entered McCormick Theological Seminary, in Chicago, in September, 1907, but transferred at the end of that year to Union Theological Seminary, in New York. At Union he studied history, theology, philosophy, languages, and rhetoric. He was greatly influenced by Julius Bewer (Hebrew), President Francis Brown (Old Testament), and above all, by Arthur McGiffert (church history, history of religious thought). His speech instructors were Francis Carmody (oral reading, voice), Harry Emerson Fosdick (preaching—"We made many outlines and talked them off"), and Henry Sloane Coffin ("formal sermons in the Chapel, with sharp criticism"). Baird was at Union for two years, receiving his B.D. degree, *magna cum laude*, in 1910. "At Union," he later declared, "I received my education."

Baird took courses in English at Columbia University while he was still a student at Union. After his B.D. degree he continued his work at Columbia in the summers until 1915. There he came under the influence of Brander Matthews (world drama), John Erskine (advanced English composition and literature), Harry Emerson Ayers (middle English), Charles Sears Baldwin (attended his seminar, but without credit), and Ashley Thorndike (English literature). Baird received a Master of Arts degree in February, 1912. His thesis, entitled "The Sources of Chaucer's Man-At-Laws Tale," was done under the direction of Professor Ayers.

The years in New York were rewarding ones. Baird saw many plays, remembering particularly the acting of David Warfield, Maude Adams, and E. H. Sothern. He was greatly interested in religious speaking and made a special effort to hear the leading preachers of the day. Among those he heard were Charles Parkhurst, S. Parkes Cadman, Newell Dwight Hillis, Rabbi Stephen Wise, and John Haynes Holmes. He also attended political gatherings, and even spoke himself at one such meeting, on behalf of Charles Evans Hughes. The speech was delivered on New York's east side, to an audience sympathetic to Hughes's opponent. Baird stated later that he made "a splendid failure." Baird also had charge of a community church at Teaneck, New Jersey, for a short time, and did some speaking there. In the summers he directed a vacation school on 118th street. Norman Thomas followed him in this "neighborhood house" project.

In September, 1910, Baird accepted a position at Ohio Wesleyan University. Here he taught English composition and English literature. Professor Robert Fulton was in charge of courses in speech. Baird judged debates, but did not assist with the coaching. Ralph Sockman was in his senior year at Wesleyan at this time, and Baird remembers hearing him in a debate. He also remembers hearing William Jennings Bryan deliver his famous lecture on "The Spoken Word."

Baird moved next to Dartmouth, where he taught for two years, from 1911 to 1913. Craven Laycock, of the O'Neill, Laycock, and Scales debate text, was dean then, but was still active in the speech program. Warren Choate Shaw was the director of debating activities. One of his debaters, later to become chairman of the speech department at the State University of Iowa, was E. C. Mabie. Baird heard Mabie debate against a team from Williams College. Another person who was to occupy an important position in the speech field, James O'Neill, also was at Dartmouth during part of this period.

Bates College was Baird's next teaching assignment. He moved to Bates in 1913 as professor of argumentation and rhetoric, and remained there for twelve years. His main assignment was to teach a required course in argumentation for sophomores. The textbook for this course for many years was William Trufant Foster's *Argumentation and Debating*. Baird also taught advanced composition and related courses and had charge of the intercollegiate debating program. This program was closely allied with courses in argumentation, always a central point in Baird's philosophy.

Debating was an important activity at Bates, and Baird's teams were unusually successful. Among the colleges debated were Harvard, Yale, Pennsylvania, Cornell, Colgate, Toronto, Clark, Bowdoin, and Colby. The debates were looked upon as major events and attracted large audiences. The debaters, three on each team, usually wore tuxedos. The judges, also a panel of three, were prominent men, sometimes even senators, college presidents, or state judges. The audiences were partisan and enthusiastic, at times "engaging in much organized singing," as Baird once recalled.

While at Bates, Baird organized the State of Maine Debate League (1914) and initiated the international debating program (1921). The latter came about because one of the Bates debaters, John Powers, became a Rhodes scholar at Oxford, and persuaded Oxford to invite Bates to send over a team for a debate. The *Lewis-*

ton Journal promoted the project, raising enough money to send not only the debaters, but also the director. Oxford came to the United States on its first tour soon after, and later, under the sponsorship first of the National Student Union, and then of the Institute of International Education, visits of foreign teams became an annual event.

The trip to England in 1921 led indirectly to Baird's move to the State University of Iowa. Glenn Merry, head of the speech department at Iowa, and then president of the National Association of Teachers of Speech, asked Baird to speak at the New York convention of the Association on his experiences with British debating. Shortly after this meeting Baird was offered a position at Iowa, but turned it down. When E. C. Mabie became head of the department at Iowa a short time later, he renewed the offer, and this time Baird accepted.

At Iowa Professor Baird has been the heart of the program in public address. His interest in argumentation and debate continues and has followed much the same course as at Bates. He took over the direction of the Iowa High School Forensic League upon his arrival and continued as its guiding spirit until 1948. He brought international debating to Iowa, and became a leading figure in the Western Conference Debate League, where, as he once said, he worked his soul out "with wonderful coordinators—Rarig, Weaver, Woolbert, Dennis, Lardner, O'Neill, and others—a great coterie for speech." Always, Baird has kept debating anchored to courses in the department. His book, *Public Discussion and Debate*, was a pioneer text in the field, and in recent years he has become even more interested in this phase of public address. He has been active in Delta Sigma Rho, honorary forensic organization, for many years. At this organization's Golden Jubilee meeting in Chicago in 1956 he was cited among those members "who have made outstanding contributions to the welfare of their fellow man through the ethical and effective use of speech."

At the graduate level Professor Baird has devoted his energies mainly to the history and criticism of American and British public address. Since 1925 he has directed more than a hundred masters theses and some fifty doctoral dissertations. His influence has reached out also to hundreds of other students who have sat in his graduate classes.

When World War I came, Baird was scheduled to go to Europe with the YMCA, but was called back to Bates at the last minute because of the serious illness of the head of the English department. At Iowa, during World War II, he was in charge of the communications course for the premeteorology students of the Army Air Corps, director of Wartime Services and Information for the eastern half of Iowa, and director of the Johnson County Speaker's Bureau. He taught at Columbia University in the summers of 1924, 1925, 1931, and 1937. In 1939 his colleagues in speech elected him president of the Speech Association of America. He was awarded a Doctor of Literature degree from Wabash College in 1932.

Professor Baird has written many important books. His *College Readings in Current Problems* appeared in 1925. *Public Discussion and Debate* came in 1928 (revised in 1937), and *Essays and Addresses Toward a Liberal Education* in 1934. *Discussion* was published in 1942, and *General Speech*, written with Franklin Knower, in 1950 (revised in 1957). A shorter version of the latter book, *Essentials of General Speech*, also written with Knower, was published in 1950 (revised in 1959). He collaborated with Lester Thonssen on *Speech Criticism* in 1948. *Argumentation, Discussion and Debate* appeared in 1950, and *American Public Addresses: 1740-1952* in 1956. From 1937 to 1959 he edited the annual volumes, *Representative American Speeches*, for the H. W. Wilson Company. His educational speeches and articles have appeared in the *Quarterly Journal of Speech, Central States Speech Journal, Southern Speech Journal, Vital Speeches of the Day*, and other periodicals.

In 1952 Baird became Emeritus Professor of Public Address at Iowa. Since then he has taught full time at his home university during first semesters, and has been much in demand at other universities as a visiting lecturer in second semesters and summer sessions. In 1953 he taught at the University of Missouri, the Richmond Area University Center (in a project sponsored by the Rockefeller Foundation), and the University of Southern California; in 1954, at Florida State University and Michigan State University; in 1955, at the University of Mississippi; in 1956, at the University of

Washington; in 1957-58, at the University of Missouri; in 1959-60, at Southern Illinois University; and in 1960-61 at the University of Illinois. In 1952-53 he served on the Development Committee of the Fund for Adult Education of the Ford Foundation.

Professor Baird was married to Marion Peirce, in Lewiston, Maine, in 1923, and has one daughter, Barbara, now Mrs. John Rees, Jr.

Professor Baird has always been first of all a teacher. His primary interest is in making students better communicators and thus more effective members of society. He is concerned with the whole range of public address but particularly with discussion and debate. He looks upon discussion and debate not as games or busy-work activities but as educational tools, as meaningful practice situations in which young people can learn how to analyze problems and to work with others in arriving at solutions. Hundreds of undergraduates have profited from his instruction, and through the graduate students he has trained, he has influenced thousands more.

Professor Baird has contributed much to rhetorical theory through his work in forensics and his analysis of British and American oratory. His fundamental position, essentially Aristotelian, is that "rhetoric for the speaker exists to give effectiveness to truth." This leads him to emphasize knowledge, analysis, and integrity. Throughout his speaking and writing he stresses the importance of "thorough understanding of the . . . problem under consideration," "careful analysis of the issues and survey of the major arguments and supporting evidence," and "careful testing of each argument pro and con." The cornerstone of his philosophy is an ethical principle. In a speech to a forensics group at the State University of Iowa in 1954 he summarized his point of view in this advice to the debaters: "First, you are to have genuine intellectual integrity. . . . Second, we expect you to have social integrity and outlook. . . . Thirdly, your personality reflects moral . . . integrity. You are on the side of truth."

He is fond of quoting rhetorical theorists to support his belief in the ethical basis of effective communication. Several years ago he told me that the more he reads and studies, the more he realizes the importance of Aristotle's contribution. He frequently quotes the Greek philosopher's statement that "We yield a more ready and complete credence to persons of high character." He also refers to Aristotle's writings to establish other fundamental points in his philosophy, such as his belief that the aim of communication should be to forward truth and, in the last analysis, "to exalt human nature itself," and his belief that good will and a desire to cooperate are essential characteristics of the effective communicator. He also draws upon Cicero and Quintilian, and such later writers and speakers as John Milton, Richard Whately, John Stuart Mill, Albert J. Beveridge, and Woodrow Wilson.

The view which Professor Baird takes of communication is a broad and fundamental one. He has a great concern for free speech and individual expression. Speech teaching, he thinks, should have as one of its central tenets the idea that "communication is for the preservation and progress of a free society and for a good society." In short, he says that we should "identify communication with political freedom under law and with sound ethics." He agrees with Walter Bagehot that "ours is a government by talk," and would add that our whole society is one which operates through talk. This to him makes communication one of our most vital activities. Because of its importance, he wants this communication "permeated with these values, these individual and group standards of intellectual integrity, good will, and high character."[1]

This, then, is the man to whom this book is dedicated: a man enthusiastically interested in rhetoric, particularly discussion and debate; a man with a deeply rooted faith in education—liberal education, political education, mass education; a man with a strong belief in philosophical and ethical approaches to communication; a man with a great concern for free speech and individual expression. He has reached and touched many lives. We honor him as teacher and leader in the field of public address.

1. Henry L. Ewbank, Sr., A. Craig Baird, W. Norwood Brigance, Wayland M. Parrish, and Andrew T. Weaver, "What Is Speech? A Symposium," *Quarterly Journal of Speech*, XLI (April, 1955), 146-147.

American Public Address

THE LAW

The Public Speeches of
Justice Oliver Wendell Holmes

OLIVER WENDELL HOLMES, JR. *(March 8, 1841–March 6, 1935). Son of Amelia Jackson Holmes, daughter of Charles Jackson (an associate justice of the Massachusetts Supreme Judicial Court), and Dr. Oliver Wendell Holmes, professor and author; prepared for college at Dixwell's Private Latin School, 1851-1857; attended Harvard College, 1857-1861; studied writing and speaking for three years under Francis J. Child, Boylston Professor of Rhetoric and Oratory, and James Jennison, instructor in elocution; contributed essays and book reviews to* THE HARVARD MAGAZINE *and the* UNIVERSITY QUARTERLY; *studied philosophy with Francis Bowen; read widely in classical and English literature and in philosophy and the history of art; officer in the Union Army from 1861-1864; studied at Harvard Law School, 1864-1865; continued reading law in the offices of Robert Morse, 1865, and of Chandler, Shattuck and Thayer, 1866; admitted to the bar, 1867; active law practice with Shattuck in Boston, 1867-1882; attended meetings of the Metaphysical Club, 1870-1872, where principles of pragmatism took shape; with Arthur Sedgwick edited* AMERICAN LAW REVIEW, *1870-1873; edited the twelfth edition of Kent's* COMMENTARIES ON AMERICAN LAW, *1873; in the winter of 1880-1881 gave series of lectures on "The Common Law" at Lowell Institute in Boston; member of the Supreme Judicial Court of Massachusetts, 1882-1902; chief justice, 1899-1902; appointed by President Theodore Roosevelt to the Supreme Court of the United States in 1902 where he remained until his retirement in 1932 at the age of ninety.*

The Public Speeches of Justice Oliver Wendell Holmes

DOROTHY I. ANDERSON*

IN 1923 Justice Oliver Wendell Holmes said in a letter to Dr. John C. H. Wu: "A man's spiritual history is best told in what he does in his chosen line. Life having thrown me into the law, I must try to put my feeling of the infinite into that, to exhibit the detail with such hint of vista as I can, to show in it the great line of the universal."[1] This "hint of vista" is the distinguishing mark of Holmes's legal opinions. Felix Frankfurter says that the Justice's approach to judicial problems was inseparable from his consciously wrought notions of his relations to the universe, that specific controversies were seen in the context of larger intellectual issues.[2]

To discover the intellectual framework reflected in his opinions, philosophers, jurists, and social historians turn constantly to Holmes's public speeches. Most of these messages, to laymen, to college students, and to members of the bar on memorial occasions, are printed in the little volume called *Speeches*. The collection was first published in 1891, revised several times, and printed in its final form in 1913, 1918, and 1934. In these twenty short speeches, and in four more printed in *Collected Legal Papers*,[3] Holmes discussed his major premises about the infinite and the universal, about life and living, that he sometimes hesitated to include in his judicial opinions.

Although Holmes was in active law practice for sixteen years and served as a judge for almost fifty, he appeared infrequently as a public speaker. He disapproved of the "itch for public speaking" and believed that the best service for one's country and for oneself was to see and feel so far as possible the great forces behind every

* Dorothy I. Anderson (B.A. 1928, M.A. 1931, Ph.D. 1944, State University of Iowa) is associate professor of speech at the University of Colorado.

detail, "to hammer out as compact and solid a piece of work as one can, to try to make it first rate, and to leave it unadvertised."[4] He gave only a few speeches other than those printed in *Speeches* and *Collected Legal Papers*.[5] The Justice talked informally at times when no records of his words were kept, but even if his every utterance to the public were recorded, the volume of his occasional addresses would be small for a jurist with almost seventy years of active professional life.

In spite of his infrequent public appearances, Holmes was recognized as an effective speaker. Two of his speeches are included in volume eight of *Modern Eloquence* (1902). A review of these volumes in the *Chicago Tribune* quoted Holmes's speech to the Bar Association of Boston in 1900 to illustrate the gift of "natural eloquence."[6] But most vital to this eloquence is the thought, the ideas which helped his listeners think clearly about man's persistent problems. What Holmes called his "chance utterances of faith and doubt" printed for a few friends (*Speeches*) and the "fragments of [his] fleece that [he] left upon the hedges of life" (*Collected Legal Papers*) continue to be important to members of professions who wish to pursue their callings greatly. Max Lerner, in the introduction to *The Mind and Faith of Justice Holmes*, says: "Holmes is a great man regardless of whether he was a great justice. He will probably leave a greater effect on English style and on what the young men dream and want than upon American constitutional law. . . . The greatness of Holmes . . . will stand up as long as the English language stands up, as long as men find life complex and exciting, and law a part of life, and the sharp blade of thought powerful to cleave both."[7]

THE IDEAS

The phrase, "chance utterances of faith and doubt," is more than a whimsical expression; it is an important clue to the beliefs which formed the core of Holmes's occasional addresses. The philosophy expressed in his speeches is precisely a combination of faith and doubt—doubt enough to motivate thinking, faith enough to motivate action. The Justice frequently referred to himself as a "bettabilitarian," willing to bet that for his time and place his fundamental beliefs were sufficiently valid to warrant his using them even though he could not prove them to be cosmic and ultimate truth. He said:

"It does not follow that without . . . absolute ideals we have nothing to do but to sit still and let time run over us. . . . there is every reason for doing all that we can to make a future such as we desire."[8] Thus intellectual doubt and activating faith were combined to make a vigorous view of life.

Holmes's preoccupation with discussing his "bettabilitarianism" in his speeches is but a reflection of his constant effort to discover "the great line of the universal" and to bring philosophical principles to bear on his professional activities. From the winter of 1866-1867 when as students at Harvard he and William James "were deep in a continuing metaphysical discussion"[9] to his last summers at Beverly Farms, he used his leisure time "to enlarge and enrich [his] view of life and the universe." He read the work of men of all philosophical persuasions, from Plato to the Pragmatists.[10]

The Justice's constant examination of all kinds of philosophies did not lead him to modify his own basic view of life. He preached a kind of sentimental rugged individualism[11] from his first Memorial Day Address in 1884 to his last short radio speech in 1931. Neither did Holmes's minute examination of the philosophers make him feel that he should present his own philosophy systematically and completely. His speeches stated conclusions vividly, but they did not carry the listener through all the steps in his thinking. Evidently he thought that the greatest contribution of the speaker, like that of the philosopher, "was a lot of penetrating *aperçus* that are quite independent of all his spider work" and the "laying out of life on an architectural plan."[12] Each of Holmes's occasional addresses includes one or another, and sometimes the whole set, of his *aperçus* about (1) the nature of the cosmos, (2) the search for truth, (3) the nature of life, and (4) the source of its value. A particular subject or occasion might bring a change in the pattern of emphasis or mode of expression, but each speech was a poetic statement of his working beliefs.

The unimaginable whole

Holmes's philosophy began with his theory of reality, the nature of the cosmos. In 1929 he wrote Laski, "I begin by an act of faith. I assume . . . although I can't prove it—that you exist in the same sense that I do—and that gives me an outside world of some sort . . .

so I assume that I am in the world not it in me."[13] He thought the best image for man was an electric light: "the spark feels isolated but is really only a moment in a current."[14] Holmes expressed this idea fully in his Commencement Address at Brown University in 1897:

> The difference between the great way of taking things and the small—between philosophy and gossip—is only the difference between realizing the part as a part of a whole and looking at it in its isolation as if it really stood apart. . . . [A man must learn] that he cannot set himself over against the universe as a rival god . . . but that his meaning is its meaning, his only worth is as a part of it. . . . It seems to me that this is the key to intellectual salvation, as the key to happiness is to accept a like faith in one's heart, and to be not merely a necessary but a willing instrument in working out the inscrutable end.[15]

In a speech given in 1911 at the fiftieth anniversary of his graduation, he repeated what he had so often said before, that "our only but wholly adequate significance is as parts of the unimaginable whole."[16]

The search for bettable premises

Out of this act of faith grew Holmes's concept about the way to find bettable premises. He called his premises about fact and value his "can't helps." As a part of an unimaginable whole he accepted the fact that truth as he saw it might be only the system of his own intellectual limitations. To Laski he explained (January 11, 1929): "When I say that a thing is true I only mean that I can't help believing it—but I have no grounds for assuming that my can't helps are cosmic can't helps—and some reasons for thinking otherwise. I therefore define truth as the system of my intellectual limitations—there being a tacit reference to what I bet is or will be the prevailing can't help of the majority of that part of the world I count. The ultimate—even humanly speaking, is a mystery. . . . Absolute truth is a mirage."

Holmes used many of his speeches to combat any intellectual lethargy or reliance on emotional or intuitive action which might result from believing that the quest for changeless and immutable truth was useless. He thought that no man had earned the right to intellectual ambition until he had learned to "lay his course by a star which he had never seen,—to dig by the divining rod for springs which he may never reach."[17] Because he thought that curiosity felt in the face of the mystery of the universe was man's most human appetite and the satisfaction of it was as truly an end in itself as self-preservation,[18] he encouraged his listeners to seek bettable premises through intellectual struggle, through a constant effort to see one's work in relation to the whole of things: ". . . if you don't see the universal in your particular, you are a manual laborer and it doesn't matter."[19] Intellectual examination of problems should also guide our judgments about a course of action. Holmes reminded members of the New York Bar Association (1899) that they could avoid judgments which were simply traditional, fashionable, or intuitive by having a knowledge of history and by observing accurately and thinking clearly about the social desires of the community.

In a lecture, "The Profession of the Law," given to undergraduates of Harvard in 1886, Holmes spelled out this way of arriving at the bettable premises:

> All that life offers any man from which to start his thinking or his striving is a fact. . . . every fact leads to every other by the path of the air. . . . your business as thinkers is to make plainer the way from some thing to the whole of things; to show the rational connection between your fact and the frame of the universe. If your subject is law, the roads are plain to anthropology, the science of man, to political economy, the theory of legislation, ethics, and thus by several paths to your final view of life. It would be equally true of any subject. The only difference is in the ease of seeing the way. To be master of any branch of knowledge, you must master those which lie next to it; and thus to know anything you must know all.[20]

In his letters, opinions, and essays—though not often in his speeches—Holmes discussed another way of discovering bettable premises—the way for which he is widely known: to square one's beliefs with the "can't helps" of others—or at least "with the majority of the world which counts." To Pollock he said that a sensible man would recognize that if he were in a minority of one he was likely to get locked up.[21] In his essay on "Natural Law" he said that an early statement of his, "truth is the majority vote of that nation that could lick all others," was correct in so far as it implied that a test of truth is a reference to either a present or an imagined future majority in favor of our view.[22] The Justice believed that principles of conduct were only the outcome of particular habits in a community, that morality is social in character.[23] A statement he made in the opening pages of *The Common Law* is frequently quoted, "The life of the law has not been logic; it has been experience,"[24] and it implies that judicial decisions could not be considered rigid and infallible but could only embody the preference of a given body in a given time and place.[25]

Questions about this last way of testing truth are bound to arise. In the first place what is "that part of [mankind] that we are to take into account?" How does one decide whose opinions are relevant on a given question? Holmes never says, but he certainly implies that he held a criterion of some sort. In the second place how does Holmes arrive at the conclusion that truth is the majority vote of that nation that could lick all others, or, that even more widely quoted conclusion, that truth is what is accepted in the marketplace? One can understand the testing of one's senses and one's judgments of fact and value by comparing them with the senses and judgments of others. But accepting this idea does not lead directly to accepting the notion that truth can be determined by majority vote or a show of power. Such votes or demonstrations of power do not necessarily involve the intellectual processes required for a responsible testing of ideas. In view of Holmes's regard for science as disciplined inquiry, it is surprising that he was not more explicit about the rational methods of testing judgments. Perhaps, as Max Lerner suggests in the introduction to *The Mind and Faith of Justice Holmes*, the Justice had more faith in the influence of the intellectual processes than we now have because in his lifetime the art of manipulating human opinion had not produced such frightening results. A little more "spider work" on Holmes's part could have clarified this for us, but, as usual, he gave us only his *aperçus*, vividly expressed.

Although Holmes did not think that any rigid set of moral principles could be established, he seemed constantly preoccupied with the study and discussion of how man could improve his judgments. He welcomed philosophical studies of the ultimate question of worth such as Morris R. Cohen's *History Versus Value*, and *Reason and Nature*. He thought Dewey in *Experience and Nature* had a feeling of intimacy with the inside of the cosmos that he found unequalled.

To live is to function

The most distinctive part of Holmes's philosophy and the general proposition that he used most frequently in his speeches was that man must act on tentative premises. Life was to act to the full extent of one's powers: "If we believe anything is, we must believe in that, because we can go no further. We may accept its canons even while we admit that we do not know the truth of truth. Accepting them we accept our destiny to work, to fight, to die for ideal aims."[26] Since life was too short to discover an articulate answer to every question, Holmes saw no reason for not doing our job "without waiting for an angel to assure us that it was the jobbest job in jobdom."

Holmes's enthusiasm for this idea led to the criticism of his Memorial Day speeches. The "Soldier's Faith" was called "war-mongering." Although the economic views hinted at in the "Soldier's Faith" irritated the critics, they were even more irritated by Holmes's attitude toward war.[27] What Holmes was trying to do was to dispel the idea that war was always wrong and to show that in retrospect one could see that war did provide opportunities for men to act with enthusiasm and faith, with high and dangerous action, to go somewhere as hard as they could even though they might not be able to foresee exactly where they would come out. On reading the "Soldier's Faith" now one feels that Holmes emphasized action without bringing into operation the stabilizing effects of the other principles of his philosophy. His reaction to the criticism was that people forgot that the speech was designed for Memorial Day and not for December, 1895, when it was published in the *Harvard Graduates Magazine*. By December of this year the tension of relationships with England had increased so that any talk of war would have received an ominous interpretation. However, the speech was a sincere reflection of Holmes's opinion that his service as a soldier had helped to crystallize the realization "that the joy of life is living, is to put out all one's powers as far as they will go."

That Holmes was leavened with "the will to act," which he called the Puritan ferment, is obvious. There is scarcely one speech in which he did not mention either directly or indirectly the joy which came from the release of spontaneous energy toward the attainment of some ideal. He said that law provided that opportunity,[28] that the experience of other men corroborated his doctrine,[29] and that the highest duty of the schools was to help students to "make good their faculties."[30] Holmes seemed loath to leave a speech without saying that the end of life was life itself—to vent and realize the inner force.

Ends outside ourselves

Holmes was convinced that if a man could see himself as "a leaf of the unimaginable tree" and could define his place in "the great line of the universal," he would inevitably work for ends outside himself. He thought that nature took care of our altruism for us and that "a man who thinks he has been an egotist all his life, if he has been a true jobbist, . . . will find on the Day of Judgment that he has been a better altruist than those who thought more about it."[31] He was fully aware of the motivation of self-interest, vanity, love of power, but he believed that for the jobbist these superficial ends became submerged and the work itself became the important thing.

At the dedication of the Northwestern Law School building in 1902 Holmes said that although the unselfish expenditure of energy in art, philosophy, charity, and the search for the North Pole did not bring economic success, the effort expended was nevertheless justified because it gratified "an appetite which in some noble spirits is stronger than the appetite for food."[32] At other times Holmes reminded his listeners that happiness could not "be won simply by being counsel for great corporations and having an income of fifty thousand dollars"[33] nor by the acquisition of "immediate forms of power."[34] He had no ambition for public office for himself, and he praised those members of the legal profession who inconspicuously helped "the mysterious growth of the world along its inevitable lines towards its unknown end."[35] He urged college audiences to develop their unselfish interests and aims because he thought that comparatively few imaginations were educated to work for ends outside themselves.[36]

These beliefs about the nature of the cosmos, the search for bettable premises and the principles by which man lived were the themes of Holmes's occasional speeches. He seldom talked about immediate economic, political, or professional problems. The Justice was less interested in the machinery of education, economic controversies, and political nostrums than he was in bringing home to people a few fundamental truths about life and living. These themes he thought most practical. For only the incompetent did the study of theory and general ideas mean an absence of particular knowledge. For the competent it simply meant getting to the bottom of the subject.[37]

The use of these general views of life as the core of every speech led William James to comment that O. W. H. seemed "unable to make any other than one set speech which comes out on every occasion."[38] But the "great line of the universal" was the theme in which Holmes was most interested and which he thought the most appropriate for his audiences. His constant effort was to make clear to his hearers that as parts of an unimaginable whole they must reconcile themselves to the fact that the truth was not absolute, that in spite of this they must expend every intellectual effort to discover premises on which they were willing to act, and that having discovered these premises their joy would come from acting on them as hard as they could.

The Development and Arrangement of the Ideas

Just as Holmes's ideas were free of the mark of any one man or book, so also was his method of developing and arranging them. He exercised an independent spirit here as he did in all personal or professional decisions. For such a spirit, the training in rhetoric which Holmes had at Harvard would be important, not because it gave him bits and pieces of technique, but because it stimulated his interest in rhetorical principles. This interest continued throughout his life. In 1906 he told Pollock that reading Fowler's *The King's English* made him miserable over his own legal style. In 1922 he found Willis's *The Philosophy of Speech* rewarding, but Quiller-Couch on the *Art of Writing* "barely repaid the reading."

Whether by natural inclination, training, or experience, Holmes knew the value of striking directly to the essential point and disregarding the remotely related bypaths. The evidence in his speeches was not elaborated in great detail, nor were his arguments long and complicated. He believed that since time was ever short one had to try "to strike the jugular and let the rest go." In a letter to Wu he said:

> The great thing is to have an eye for the essential. If a boy gets his finger pinched between two inward revolving wheels, it probably will only distract attention and bore the reader to describe the machinery. If I am right in remembering Croce . . . as saying that all experience is art, I am inclined to add all art is caricature, that is, it emphasizes what the artist wants to call attention to at the expense of other elements that may have a cosmic equality but that are not relevant to what he wants to make you see, feel, or think. Such insight, which of course has different directions in different men . . . is an inborn gift. . . . I think it the great human gift.[39]

Holmes's eye for the essential characterized the development of his ideas.

Since so many of his short speeches were simply statements of his philosophy with only briefly elaborated lines of proof, the listener's opinion of Holmes's character was an important part of the effectiveness of his speaking. For most of his audiences his reputation for intelligence, integrity, and independence was well established. When he talked at Northwestern University in 1902 shortly after President Roosevelt had submitted his name to the Senate as a justice of the Supreme Court, "the audience sprang to its feet in welcoming applause that was prolonged for several minutes."[40] Though he made no direct attempt to establish himself in the eyes of the audience or to answer arguments against his beliefs or opinions, his speeches reflected his principles of living. His frequent reference to writers of history, literature, and law, to artists, and to incidents in his own life revealed Holmes's wide knowledge and experience. He was sensitive to the common experiences of men and recognized the "loneliness of original work," the danger of the *cul-de-sac*, the dependence of those too modest to seek appreciation, the disappointment of unfulfilled dreams, the pleasure of feeling that one has done one's best, the misery of power denied its chance.[41] He talked like a man more keenly interested in telling you how he felt about things than in trying to convince or persuade. In his first published speech he told the audience that he could not argue a man into a desire. He could only express his feeling in the hope that desire might be imparted by contagion.[42] His sole concern when he prepared and delivered his speeches was to make the ideas clear and vivid. He said: "If you want to hit a bird on the wing, you must have all your will in a focus, you must not be thinking about yourself, and equally, you must not be thinking about your neighbor; you must be living in your eye on that bird. Every achievement is a bird on the wing."[43]

Most of Holmes's public speeches were delivered on Memorial Days, at university commencements, reunions, banquets, dedication ceremonies, or in commemoration of colleagues. Such occasions demand a thoughtful consideration of man's basic values rather than polemics on current problems. The Justice spoke of man's desire for honor, power, and happiness. But always the mind of the audience was directed toward ultimate rather than immediate honor and power, and toward happiness through mental security and self expression. He drew examples of the effectiveness of living with high purpose from his actual and vicarious experience. His Memorial Day speech of 1884 was a series of brief descriptions of soldiers he had known whose "hearts were touched with fire," for whom life was "a profound and passionate thing," and who knew only duty and accepted their fate generously. In his address to the Harvard Law School Association in 1886 he listed the names of professors—Greenleaf, Stearns, Story, Parsons, Washburn, Langdell, Ames, and Gray—whom the audience would recognize immediately as men incapable of mean ideals and easy self-satisfaction. In "The Soldier's Faith" in 1895 he listed briefly a series of incidents from his own experience to show that a soldier's pride in discharging his duties honorably was more important to him than his life. He frequently mentioned the lives or work of such men as Bacon, Hobbes, Descartes, Milton, Kant, Wordsworth, Nansen, Correggio, and Dürer as well as names of reputable men in the law to illustrate his concepts of honor, power, and happiness.[44] These illustrations were presented briefly as if he were only reminding the audience of the vitality of the desires of men, of the significance of the broad principles of human conduct held in common by the speaker and his listeners.

A section of the Justice's speech at the dedication of the Northwestern University Law School shows his ability to illustrate his ideas concisely and exactly:

It might be said, as I have often said, and as I have been gratified
to find elaborated by that true poet Coventry Patmore, that
one of the grounds of aesthetic pleasure is waste. I need not
refer to Charles Lamb's well-known comments on the fallacy
that enough is as good as a feast. Who does not know how his
delight has been increased to find some treasure of carving
upon a medieval cathedral in a back alley—to see that the artist
has been generous as well as great, and has not confined his best
to the places where it could be seen to most advantage? Who
does not recognize the superior charm of a square-hewed beam
over a joist set on edge which would be enough for the work?
To leave art, who does not feel that Nansen's account of his
search for the pole rather loses than gains in ideal satisfaction by
the pretense of a few trifling acquisitions for science? If I
wished to make you smile I might even ask whether life did
not gain an enrichment from neglected opportunities which
would be missed in the snug filling out of every chance. But I
am not here to press a paradox. I only mean to insist on the
importance of the uneconomic to man as he actually feels
today.[45]

Analogy was another method of elaborating ideas which Holmes
used frequently and effectively. Occasionally he developed a speech
through the use of an extended analogy as he did in speaking to the
Suffolk Bar Association (1885) about "our mistress, the law." At
the anniversary of the First Church in Cambridge (1886) he described how history burned away what was individual of both the
Crusader and the Puritan, leaving them only as symbols of passion,
courage, and devotion. Graduates of Brown University were told
how he had found his way through the ocean of the law. The
speeches do not seem to bristle with short analogies as the correspondence does, but the comparisons he used are always original and
striking:

His [Daniel S. Richardson's] long career is spanned by the reports between the seventh of Metcalf and one of our latest
volumes. It is strange to think of that monotonous series as a
record of human lives. I have seen upon the section of an ancient tree the annual rings marked off which grew while the
Black Prince was fighting the French, while Shakespeare wrote
his plays, while England was a Commonwealth, while a later
republic arose over the western waters, and grew so great as
to shake the world. And so, I often think, may all our histories

be marked off upon the backs of the unbroken series of our reports.[46]

Although a typical Holmes speech is only a succession of vivid variations on one or another of the themes composing his philosophy of faith and doubt, he did reason with his audience when it was appropriate to do so. In his speeches to the Boston University law students on the "Path of the Law" and to the members of the New York Bar Association on "Law in Science and Science in the Law," Holmes took care to show how he had arrived at his conclusions. He drew example after example from his knowledge of the history and practice of law to show the distinction between morals and law, to show how tradition obscured the social ends of law, to show how a study of the history of law revealed the development and transformation of human ideas into legal concepts. Bare facts may have bored him, but Holmes was fully aware that his generalizations were simply strings for the facts and that only a combination of the two could produce the valuable theories. Statistics, however, he never used. His reply to Brandeis's suggestion that he read reports of textile industries in Massachusetts is well known: such reports are "not the essence of salvation."

Although the form of the thought in much of Holmes's speaking was inductive, he often made swift deductions at the beginning of a speech to relate the specific theme to his basic philosophy. In his speech at the 250th anniversary of Harvard University (1886) he established quickly that a law school's business, like that of all other education, was not merely to teach the law but to shape the interests and the aims of the students. The rest of the speech showed how Harvard had produced great lawyers by following this method. In "The Soldier's Faith" Holmes explained first that living greatly meant a struggle for life rather than freedom from all pain and that war was only an aspect of the larger struggle. Then he gave examples of the opportunities for living greatly in a war. Although the steps in syllogistic reasoning were never laboriously spelled out, Holmes did succeed in keeping his ideas about specific problems firmly tied to his major beliefs about life and living. "Although practical men generally prefer to leave their major premises inarticulate," he said, "yet even for practical purposes theory generally turns out the most important thing in the end."[47]

The parts of Holmes's speeches, like the steps in his reasoning, never stood out in bold relief. In some of the longer speeches on days of commemoration, his first words served only to catch the attention of the audience. He begins "The Soldier's Faith" by saying: "Any day in Washington Street, when the throng is greatest and busiest, you may see a blind man playing a flute. I suppose some one hears him. Perhaps also my pipe may reach the heart of some passer in the crowd."[48] But most often, as in "The Use of Colleges," he captured the attention and introduced the theme in the first paragraph: "At every feast it is well to have a skeleton. At every gathering of the elect, the doubting spirit must be allowed to ask his question. In these days all the old assumptions are being retried by the test of actuality, and at a feast in honor of a college, at a gathering of the elect of Yale, the question will arise, What is the use of colleges, after all?"[49] The customary mechanical signposts, the transitions to relate an idea with what has gone before, the preliminary analysis of the ideas to be presented, the summaries at the ends of ideas or of the speeches are seldom present. Rather his speeches are compact units in which the meanings are so logically related that he does not need to call attention to the relationship. Only in the longer speeches, "The Path of the Law" and "Law in Science and Science in the Law," is the form obviously used to contribute to the understanding of the speech. And in truth these may be the only ones in which such methods are necessary, because the ideas in the other speeches are immediately clear. Here again, his method reflects his beliefs. In a note to Wu (September 20, 1923) he wrote: "A further thought occurred to me with regard to the forms of thought. Whatever the value of the notion of forms, the only use of the forms is to present their contents, just as the only use of a pint pot is to present the beer (or whatever lawful liquid it may contain), and infinite meditation upon the pot never will give you the beer."[50] He objected to the German method of over-systematizing and wrote to Pollock (March 1, 1918) that systems are forgotten—only a man's *aperçus* are remembered.

While this remark was made about philosophy, Holmes seems to have applied it to rhetoric as well. It is the *aperçus* in the Justice's speeches that one remembers. He does not impress us with his use of conventional appeals to the audience nor with the traditional logical or rhetorical structures. Rather in every speech he commands the thought of the audience by the brilliant elaboration of his insights into fundamental human problems. His ideas are, indeed, "imparted by contagion" rather than by deliberate argument or persuasion. He makes us realize that true rhetoric is art.

THE EXPRESSION OF IDEAS

Holmes's use of language made his ideas vivid and intellectually stimulating. Scarcely an article was written about his later years that did not emphasize his skill in making literature out of law. Lerner called Holmes a poet—a better poet than his father, Dr. Holmes—who by piercing the appearances of life and expressing his vision in moving symbols was able to distill into his writings the sense of American democracy.[51]

Holmes's skill in expression was no accident but came, in part, from his understanding that language is a wily instrument, which even the most careful writer or speaker cannot always control. He recognized that "the ambiguities of language constantly led to fallacies in arguments,"[52] that "we live by symbols, and what shall be symbolized by any image . . . depends upon the mind of him who sees it."[53] He thought that ideas were not difficult, "that the trouble is in the words in which they are expressed."[54] He reminded his listeners that a word was not a crystal "transparent and unchanged" but only the skin of living thought,[55] and urged his hearers to think things, not words. Yet he felt that in interpreting decisions and contracts one could not ask what each man's words meant but must ask instead "what those words would mean in the mouth of the normal speaker of English, using them in the circumstances in which they were used."[56]

Holmes worked hard to make his language reflect his ideas accurately. When he was being considered for the Supreme Court he wrote: "It makes one sick when he has broken his heart in trying to make every word living and real to see a lot of duffers . . . talking with the sanctity of print in a way that at once discloses to the knowing eye that literally they don't know anything about it."[57]

Holmes's letters contain frequent comments about the qualities of good writing so that it is easy to determine his stylistic aims. In reply to a question from Wu he said (October 7, 1923): "The best style that a man can hope for is a free unconscious expression of his own spontaneity, not an echo of someone else." He thought that it was comparatively easy to achieve spontaneity when one was "going free" in the language of speech but that it was a heartbreaking task to give an impression of freedom, elegance, and variety when writing opinions. He dreaded dropping into something ready-made that was not the immediate expression of one's thought, organizing every word.[58] Holmes's speeches create this feeling of spontaneity, for nothing seems to impede the swift progress of the thought. No trite transitions, no mechanical summaries, no laborious restatement, no long modifying phrases and clauses delayed the expression of his ideas.

Holmes was skeptical of catch phrases or technical terms.[59] He was bored by the words "denote" and "connote" and he thought "factual" a barbarism.[60] He was irritated by "journalese jargon" and complained to Pollock (April 6, 1924): "I remember once saying: profanity is vitriol, slang is vinegar, but reporter's English is rancid butter. I don't know that you have the thing to which I refer in England—an intrusion into the language of sentiment, as when they call a house a home. It abounds here." His advice to Wu (November 11, 1923) was to avoid as far as possible the technical words since most things could be said in untechnical English, and it was a help to most readers to have them put so. He followed his own advice. Even his speeches to the members of the bar contain few words not immediately intelligible to the lay reader.

The "sound" of the literary work was also important to Holmes. After rereading Bacon's essays he wrote to Cohen: "They led me to repeat that the first cause of the survival of a great work is its sound—Without the song of his words Shakespeare would not be read as he is—Bacon's Essays with necessary dross have many shrewd remarks—but they are A B C to us and we shouldn't read them if they didn't sound so well—we should get more mental stimulus from a number of the New Republic."[61] Though beauty of sound is not the outstanding quality of Holmes's speeches, some combination of structure, rhythm, and alliteration heightens their effectiveness. In a thoughtful appraisal of his own work he said to the Bar Association of Boston in 1900:

> I look into my book in which I keep a docket of the decisions of the full court which fall to me to write, and find about a thousand cases. A thousand cases, many of them upon trifling or transitory matters, to represent nearly half a lifetime! A thousand cases, when one would have liked to study to the bottom and to say his say on every question which the law ever presented, and then to go on and invent new problems which should be the test of doctrine, and then to generalize it all and write it in continuous, logical, philosophic exposition, setting forth the whole corpus with its roots in history and its justifications of expedience real or supposed![62]

All of Holmes's speeches are rich with metaphorical expressions. He was quick to disapprove of writing in which the theme was "lost in the variations and arabesques,"[63] in which the words trailed rainbows but disguised the meaning.[64] On the other hand he objected to the flatness of unadorned simplicity: "How little pungent, how flat, are the great authors of the past before the time when men saw themselves seeing. How odious a virtue the much praised simplicity. The only simplicity for which I would give a straw is that which is on the other side of the complex—not that which has never divined it."[65] Holmes's speeches are filled with incisive metaphors and similes. Expressions like these help us to visualize his ideas: lonely women "around whom the wand of sorrow has traced its excluding circle"; "glittering generalities, like a swarm of little bodiless cherubs fluttering at the top of one of Correggio's pictures"; science has so pursued analysis that "at last this thrilling world of colors and sounds and passions has seemed fatally to resolve itself into one vast network of vibrations endlessly weaving an aimless web"; "The electric current of large affairs turns even common mould to diamond."[66]

But the literary characteristic for which Holmes is best known and which is revealed in his speeches as well as in his opinions is his "pungent brevity." This quality has produced an abundance of quotable epigrams. The Justice saw no reason for taking half a page to say what could be said in a sentence. He considered a masterly incisive statement necessary to the retention of an idea. Consider the following: "Every calling is great when greatly pursued."[67] "The main part of intellectual education is not the acquisition of facts, but learning to make facts live."[68] "The man of action has the present, but the thinker controls the future."[69] "Man is born a predestined idealist, for he is born to act. To act is to affirm the worth of an end, and to persist in affirming the worth of an end is to make an ideal."[70] "Life is an end in itself, and the only question as to whether it is worth living is whether you have enough of it."[71] "Historic continuity with the past is not a duty, it is only a necessity."[72] "Certainty generally is illusion and repose is not the destiny of man."[73] "It is revolting to have no better reason for a rule of law than so it was laid down in the time of Henry IV."[74]

More could be said of Holmes's style and more could be quoted from others to show the effect the style produced. But a careful reading of any of his occasional addresses will show that he achieved what he was striving for: spontaneity, impelling sound, pungent brevity, simpleness without flatness, and originality without obscurity.

CONCLUSION

Holmes's greatest service to his listeners was to release them from the restraint of details by placing the details in an infinite perspective. He did not care to impose a ready-made philosophical system on his hearers, but he placed before them a pattern of insights which they might use to develop their own views of life.

Holmes seldom presented a speech without talking about his major beliefs: the unimaginable whole, the bettable premises, the life of vigor and meaning. When he spoke, his every concern was to make his ideas clear. He tried to show that man's power, honor, and happiness were by-products of intellectual effort and self-expression. He emphasized constantly the idea which controlled his own life: that to live was to act according to your "can't helps" even though the "can't helps" might not be cosmic or ultimate truth. On the occasion of his ninetieth birthday in 1931, he gave his first radio address and last public speech. In it he affirmed what he had so often said before: "For to live is to function. That is all there is in living."[75]

The impact of his insight was heightened by his incisive statement of it. His concise reasoning, his compact composition, and his apt and lively examples and analogies refresh our thinking. His spontaneous expression, his striking metaphors, and his pungent brevity sharpen our memories. Reading the Justice's speeches brings to mind one of his own paradoxes: "It is not necessary to be heavy to have weight."[6]

Holmes's "chance utterances of faith and doubt" have weight enough to insure his continuous influence in the role which he so greatly admired, the thinker who controls the future.

Footnotes

1. Harry C. Shriver, ed., *Justice Oliver Wendell Holmes, His Book Notices and Uncollected Letters and Papers* (New York, 1936), p. 167.
2. Felix Frankfurter, *Of Law and Men* (New York, 1956), p. 182.
3. Edited by Harold Laski (London, 1920). The book reprints eight of the public addresses found in *Speeches* and adds "Speech at Brown University," "The Path of the Law," "Law in Science and Science in Law," and "Address at Northwestern University Law School." Many of the speeches in both volumes may be found in published form elsewhere, for they were reprinted from law journals, from Harvard publications or from the reports of the Supreme Court of Massachusetts.
4. Oliver Wendell Holmes, *Speeches* (Boston, 1913), p. 96.
5. One speech to the Chicago Bar Association was printed in the *Chicago Law Review*, XVII (1902), 733, and was reported fully in the *Chicago Tribune* for October 22, 1902. A speech at the Middlesex Bar Association dinner in December 1902 was reported in the *Boston Advertiser* for December 4 and is quoted at length in Fiechter's "Preparation of an American Aristocrat," *New England Quarterly*, VI (1933), 27-28. A response to the resolutions honoring William Crowinshield Endicott is published in the Massachusetts *Reports*, CLXXVII (1900), 612-613, and in Shriver, pp. 128-230. Only the conclusion of the speech on the "Profession of the Law" is printed in the collections, but a report of the entire lecture is carried in the *Weekly Law Bulletin*, XVI (1886), 182-185. Several short speeches are printed in M. A. De Wolfe Howe's *History of the Tavern Club* (Cambridge, 1934). Of course, *The Common Law*, published in 1881, was an elaboration of a series of lectures delivered at the Lowell Institute during the winter of 1880-1881, but little reference will be made to them because this paper is limited to Holmes's occasional addresses.
6. *The Chicago Tribune*, October 11, 1902, p. 19.
7. Max Lerner, ed., *The Mind and Faith of Justice Holmes* (Boston, 1943), pp. xlix-1.
8. *Collected Legal Papers*, p. 305.
9. Ralph Barton Perry, *The Thought and Character of William James* (Boston, 1935), I, 504.
10. In addition to the classical philosophers and the Pragmatists, Holmes's notebooks and letters show that he read widely in the works of the Rationalists, the British Empiricists, the Scottish Realists, the French Positivists, the German and British Idealists. See Eleanor N. Little, "The Early Reading of Justice Oliver Wendell Holmes," *Harvard Library Bulletin*, VIII (Spring, 1954) and Mark De Wolfe Howe, *Justice Oliver Wendell Holmes, The Shaping Years* (Cambridge, 1957).

11. Herbert W. Schneider says that when applied to legal judgment this individualism began the movement known as legal pragmatism. *A History of American Philosophy* (New York, 1946), p. 562.

12. Scholars who try to spin out Holmes's principles arrive at surprising conclusions. See B. W. Palmer, "Hobbes, Holmes and Hitler," *American Bar Association Journal,* XXXI (November, 1945), 569-573 and Daniel J. Boorstin, "The Elusiveness of Mr. Justice Holmes," *New England Quarterly,* XIV (September, 1941), 478-487.

13. Mark De Wolfe Howe, ed., *Holmes-Laski Letters* (Cambridge, 1953), p. 1124.

14. Felix S. Cohen, ed., "The Holmes-Cohen Correspondence," *Journal of the History of Ideas,* IX (January, 1948), 24.

15. *Collected Legal Papers,* p. 166.

16. *Speeches,* p. 97.

17. *Ibid.,* p. 24.

18. *Ibid.,* p. 50.

19. *Holmes-Laski Letters,* p. 1208.

20. *Speeches,* p. 23. See also pp. 16-17, 54, 43.

21. Mark De Wolfe Howe, ed., *Holmes-Pollock Letters* (Cambridge, 1941), II, 255-256. See also Holmes, *Speeches,* p. 98.

22. *Collected Legal Papers,* pp. 310-311.

23. *Holmes-Laski Letters,* p. 1165. See also p. 704.

24. Oliver Wendell Holmes, Jr., *The Common Law* (Boston, 1881).

25. *Collected Legal Papers,* p. 181.

26. *Speeches,* pp. 81, 97.

27. Wendell P. Garrison, "Sentimental Jingoism," *Nation,* LXI (1895), 440-441.

28. *Speeches,* p. 17. See also pp. 23, 85.

29. *Ibid.,* pp. 26-27. See also p. 73.

30. *Ibid.,* pp. 14, 39.

31. *Holmes-Laski Letters,* p. 385; Holmes, *Speeches,* p. 97.

32. *Collected Legal Papers,* pp. 272-273.

33. *Ibid.,* p. 202.

34. *Speeches,* p. 54.

35. *Ibid.,* pp. 47-48. See also pp. 43-44.

36. *Ibid.,* pp. 30, 54. See also pp. 26-27, 14, 50-51.

37. *Collected Legal Papers,* pp. 200-201.

38. Francis Biddle, *Mr. Justice Holmes* (New York, 1942), p. 99.

39. Shriver, pp. 156-157.

40. *The Chicago Tribune,* October 21, 1902.

41. *Collected Legal Papers,* p. 165; *Speeches,* pp. 76, 38, 83, 84-85.

42. *Speeches,* pp. 3-4.

43. *Ibid.,* p. 85.

44. *Ibid.,* p. 21. See also pp. 73, 60, 34, 67. *Collected Legal Papers,* pp. 165, 202.

45. *Collected Legal Papers,* p. 273.

46. *Speeches,* p. 47.

47. *Collected Legal Papers,* p. 209.

48. *Speeches,* p. 56.

49. *Ibid.,* p. 49.

50. Shriver, p. 167.

51. Lerner, p. xlviii.

52. Shriver, p. 204.
53. *Speeches*, p. 90.
54. Shriver, p. 163.
55. Alfred Lief, ed., *The Dissenting Opinions of Mr. Justice Holmes* (New York, 1929), p. 307.
56. *Collected Legal Papers*, pp. 203-209.
57. *Holmes-Pollock Letters*, I, 106.
58. *Ibid.*, pp. 131, 271.
59. *Collected Legal Papers*, pp. 238, 230-232.
60. Shriver, p. 203.
61. "Holmes-Cohen Correspondence," p. 46.
62. *Speeches*, p. 83.
63. Shriver, p. 175.
64. "Holmes-Cohen Correspondence," p. 41.
65. *Holmes-Pollock Letters*, I, 109.
66. *Speeches*, pp. 9, 34, 57, 54.
67. *Ibid.*, p. 17.
68. *Ibid.*, p. 29.
69. *Ibid.*, p. 43.
70. *Ibid.*, pp. 96-97.
71. *Ibid.*, p. 86.
72. *Ibid.*, p. 68.
73. *Collected Legal Papers*, p. 181.
74. *Ibid.*, p. 187.
75. Lerner, p. 451.
76. *The Chicago Tribune*, October 21, 1902.

The Speaking of Clarence Darrow

CLARENCE SEWARD DARROW (*April 18, 1857–March 13, 1938*). *Born Kinsman, Ohio; son of Amirus and Emily Darrow; attended elementary school and academy at Kinsman; participated in speeches and debates of the local literary society; attended Allegheny College one year; taught country school three years and began to read law; attended University of Michigan Law School; completed his study in an office in Youngstown, Ohio; admitted to the bar 1878; practiced at Andover and Ashtabula; moved to Chicago 1888; active in the life of the city; held office briefly as acting corporation counsel; became attorney for the Chicago and Northwestern Railway; resumed private practice in 1894. His best known defense pleas—Woodworkers' Conspiracy Case, Oshkosh, Wisconsin, 1898; hearings before the Anthracite Coal Commission, Philadelphia, 1903; Haywood Murder Trial, Boise, Idaho, 1907; pleas in Self-defense, Los Angeles, 1912, 1913; the Case of the Communist Labor Party, Chicago, 1920; defense of Richard Loeb and Nathan Leopold, Jr., 1924; Tennessee Evolution Case, 1925; defense of Henry Sweet, Detroit, 1927. Campaigned for Al Smith and the Democratic party in 1928; chairman National Recovery Review Board, 1934. Author of* A PERSIAN PEARL AND OTHER ESSAYS, *1899;* RESIST NOT EVIL, *1903;* FARMINGTON, *a biographical novel, 1904;* AN EYE FOR AN EYE, *1905;* CRIME: ITS CAUSE AND TREATMENT, *1922;* THE PROHIBITION MANIA, *with Victor S. Yarros, 1927;* INFIDELS AND HERETICS, *1929;* THE STORY OF MY LIFE, *1932 and 1934. Many of Darrow's important lectures, court room arguments, and essays were published and widely distributed in pamphlet form.*

The Speaking of Clarence Darrow

Horace G. Rahskopf*

Students of public address are interested in "the American gadfly," as T. V. Smith dubbed Clarence Darrow, because speech was the principal medium by which he carried on his work. Darrow was not only a successful court room pleader; he was also a brilliant conversationalist and popular lecturer and debater, with a wide following drawn by his striking non-conformist views and his forthright, yet charming and human, manner of utterance. Though he aspired to be a writer and actually produced a considerable body of essay and narrative material, his success and reputation as speaker greatly overmatched his standing as author. He loved to talk; speech was the life-blood of his intellectual and social life.

The Career and Its Setting

Darrow's career spanned the transition from the individualistic, agrarian, frontier America of the nineteenth century to the capitalistic, industrial, urban America of the twentieth century. The industrial revolution which shook the nation in the decades after the Civil War led to concentration of economic power and severe labor-management conflicts which continued well into the new century. Back of the economic struggles lay fundamental intellectual differences between the new and dominant philosophy of pragmatism and the older idealism, between the new materialistic science and the more traditional religious fundamentalism. Liberal religion attempted to incorporate the new scientific attitudes into Christian belief, but the masses of people, especially in the South, adhered to fundamentalism. By the time Darrow appeared on the scene the

* Horace G. Rahskopf (A. B. Willamette University, 1920, M. A. 1927, Ph. D. 1935, State University of Iowa) is professor and executive officer of the Department of Speech at the University of Washington, Seattle.

battle lines were drawn not only in economics and industry but in social and religious life as well.

In the waning years of the nineteenth century, Chicago was probably the dominant center of the rising swirl of conflict in the nation. The city was a lusty, booming, young giant which had the economic growth, racial complexity, industrial strife, political corruption, social reform, and cultural and artistic progress to make a complete cross-section of Middle America. The place "offered a study in contrasts: squalor matching splendor, municipal boodle contending with civic spirit; the very air now reeking with the foul stench of the stockyards, now fresh-blown from prairie or lake."[1] A series of violent industrial disputes reached their climax in the horror of the Haymarket affair (1886).[2]

Into this maelstrom of activity came the young man from Kinsman via Ashtabula and rented desk room in an office for the practice of law. The city ignored him, but he did two things which broke the barriers and set him on his way: he sought out judge, later governor, John P. Altgeld; and he began to make speeches. The friendship with Altgeld became strong and abiding and motivated the younger man deeply.[3] The opportunities for speaking were numerous, and Darrow took them as they came—at study clubs, before civic organizations, and in political rallies. He joined the select Sunset Club as well as the Henry George Single Tax Club, and campaigned for the Democratic party.[4] As a result he was invited to speak at a Democratic free trade convention in February, 1889. His address, "The Workingmen and the Tariff," captivated the assembly.[5] In that event a career was born. The newcomer was appointed to civic office and advanced rapidly.[6] When Eugene Debs was arrested for leading his American Railway Union to strike in sympathy with employees of the Pullman Palace Car Company in 1894, Darrow felt obliged to resign his position as railroad attorney to defend the despised radical. The criminal trial was dismissed, but Debs was sentenced to prison for contempt of court.[7] The event sealed the destiny of Clarence Darrow. He returned to private practice and found that "more and more of the distressed and harassed and pursued came fleeing to my office door."[8]

During the years that followed the Pullman strike Darrow became known primarily as a labor attorney. By the time World War I broke out, however, labor had won substantial improvements in wages and conditions of work and the vengeful attitude of the public towards unions had declined.[9] The war period and years immediately following, moreover, brought forward new problems to which Darrow turned his attention. Temporarily and with misgivings he abandoned his pacifism and his belief in non-resistance to support the struggle against German militarism.[10] During this time there was a wave of "anti-red" hysteria, national prohibition was enacted, racial tensions increased, a new criminology was developed, and the nineteenth century conflict between naturalism in science and fundamentalism in religion continued. In the courtroom and on the public platform Darrow fought for civil and constitutional rights, racial tolerance, humane attitudes toward crime and criminals, and freedom of thought and education.

The total number of his public speeches is impossible to count. A contemporary estimated that he appeared in 2000 trials.[11] The number of lectures, debates, and platform speeches must be estimated in even larger thousands. In cities where he tried cases he was usually invited to lecture on some of the literary or social topics in which he was interested. As early as 1908 he was speaking against prohibition. In 1912 he made a tour of the Pacific Northwest.[12] In 1928 and in 1930-1931 after returning from Europe he made extended tours under management of George G. Whitehead of the Redpath Lyceum Bureau.[13] Many of the engagements of these tours were symposia on religion which pitted the great agnostic against representatives of Protestant, Catholic, and Jewish faiths from the local communities.[14] Darrow once remarked that there was scarcely a city of any size in the United States in which he had not spoken at least once and in all the larger cities many times, and that "probably few men in America have ever spoken to so many people or over so long a stretch of time."[15]

Darrow's Philosophy—His Message

Contradictory though it may seem, Darrow the iconoclast and debunker was largely a product of his time. The experiences of childhood burned into his soul a sensitivity to the struggles of the common people.[16] As he grew into manhood his mind was shaped by the philosophy of his era. He took from pragmatism something of its faith in science and in human endeavor as well as its plain down-to-earth approach to problems. He believed that the universe operated according to a rigid cause-and-effect determinism; and that man, as part of the natural order, had neither free will nor moral responsibility.[17]

Over against this philosophy of determinism was a practical commitment to complete intellectual freedom. Clarence Darrow "determined" to hold his mind unfettered and to fight for freedom for everyone else. His realism was of the type which took a critical look at everything. Darrow once remarked to a fellow attorney, "I can say with perfect honesty that I have never knowingly catered to anyone's ideas, and I have expressed what was within me, regardless of consequences."[18] Though he lectured on socialism and sometimes worked for the Socialist program, he never could convince himself it was consistent with individual liberty.[19] The standard assumptions and codes of his day gained no favor in his view just because they were traditional.

The conflict between determinism and freedom was only one, although probably the most fundamental, of the paradoxes in Darrow's life. Like many another great personality, he was a bundle of inconsistencies. He regarded the human being as a machine, yet he was a deep and friendly humanitarian. He professed to despise reformers and reform organizations,[20] yet in his own legalistic way he was a zealot for human welfare. He was a realist and pragmatist, yet idealist enough to defy the dominant wealth and power of his time in the interests of the working class. He was a Tolstoyan pacifist who did not believe in force or violence;[21] yet he had learned that sometimes conflict was inevitable, and when it arose for a cause in which he believed, was ready to take his part. He denied the criminal's responsibility for crime, but held all other men responsible. He denied the validity of moral judgments, yet passed judgment on society. He urged justice for the criminal in spite of his conviction that the inexorable operation of heredity and environment made attainment of justice beyond the power of individual will or purpose. As his biographer has said, Clarence Darrow "was a sentimental cynic. He was a gullible skeptic. He was an organized anarchist. He was a happy pessimist. He was a modest egocentric.

He was a hopeful defeatist. . . . He didn't like life; it was all a silly mess, yet he squeezed the last drop of juice out of it."[22]

In spite of these inconsistencies there were deep and abiding elements of stability in Darrow's life and career. He was constant in his efforts for freedom of thought, personal liberty, and human welfare. His typical role was that of opposition speaker. In public debate he usually took the negative. In court he was never a prosecutor. This feature of his speaking seems to follow inevitably from both sides of the conflict between freedom and determinism. On one side the commitment to freedom of thought prevented him from attaching himself permanently to any specific cause. He was, therefore, free to move quickly from opposition to opposition. His negative role seemed to follow also from his deterministic concept of life. The forces which "determined" his "peculiar organism" had put him in the stance of defender. Many of his greatest cases were undertaken because of a compelling inner sense of obligation. He defended strikers, radicals, communists, and members of racial minorities in face of bitter social condemnation. For Darrow this was not merely the lawyer's customary professional obligation to give every man his defense before the law, but the result of passionate conviction that the social order created injustices for the poor and weak. "When the cry is loudest," he said, "the defendant needs the lawyer most."[23] In all his speaking Darrow was dissenter, champion of the underdog, and critic of the social order.

So strong was this feeling of social protest in him that at times he skirted the borders of anarchism. He restrained no censure of laws or Constitution or anything in the established order if it seemed to him a threat to welfare of the masses of people.[24] In his times of greatest bitterness he condemned all government as arbitrary power exercised by a dominant ruler or ruling class to keep the mass of men in subjection and exploit them. In his prime at the age of forty-six he wrote: ". . . nature, unaided by man's laws can evolve social order . . . in new countries amongst unexploited people, suggestions of order and symmetry regulated by natural instincts and common social needs are ample to show the possibility at least of order or a considerable measure of justice without penal law. It is only when the arrogance and avarice of rulers and chiefs make it necessary to exploit men that these rulers must lay down laws and regulations to control the actions of their fellows."[25]

Back of this lay his reading of Paine, Voltaire, and Tolstoy. Back of this lay the Haymarket riots, the Pullman strike, and the defense of the Woodworkers at Oshkosh. The next year (1904) he spoke to the prisoners in the Cook County jail, telling them that "if every man and woman and child in the world had a chance to make a decent, fair, honest living, there would be no jails and no lawyers and no courts."[26] He opposed the open shop because he considered it a means of exploiting workers.[27] His opposition to prohibition was a dissent against legislative restriction of the liberty of the individual. His efforts to secure equal rights for racial minorities, especially the Negroes, was a challenge to hatred, prejudice, and discrimination. The era was a time of social protest. Clarence Darrow, idealist grown acrid, though not its chief promulgator, was one of its chief heralds.

At no point, however, did the social protest appear more strongly than in his views on crime. He was a passionate exponent of the new criminology that advocated reformation instead of punishment. The sources of this conviction were in part the influences of his childhood, in part the example of Altgeld, in part Darrow's own mechanistic philosophy.[28] The criminal, he thought, was a victim of circumstance, usually inferior by heredity, deprived of normal opportunities in life, frustrated and desperate, punished hatefully by society, and therefore often hating society. Continued violation of the legal code followed inevitably. The act, the so-called crime, "had an all-sufficient cause for which the individual was in no way responsible." The definition of crime in Darrow's view, "can never mean anything except the violation of law when the violator is convicted, [and] . . . has no necessary reference to the general moral condition of man."[29] He pleaded that society should treat the criminal with the same compassion it showed for the sick and maimed.[30]

Opposition to capital punishment, of course, was central in the attitude toward crime. This opposition was reinforced by his abhorrence of death, his memories of the executions following the Haymarket riots, and many tense moments of waiting for verdicts in courtrooms with knowledge that the word "guilty" probably would mean death to his client. His logical reasons for opposing the death penalty were that it did nothing to remedy the causes of crime and tended to brutalize society. As a practical policy, he argued, crime "can be diminished . . . only by finding the causes and intelligently treating these causes rather than rending and destroying in anger and hate."[31]

Through all of Darrow's philosophy ran a deep current of pessimism. A pessimist he defined as one "who looks at life as it is . . . [who] doesn't necessarily think that everything is bad, but . . . looks for the worst."[32] He argued that civilization is a failure, that the human race is not getting anywhere, that life is not worth living.[33] Darrow's pessimism was also founded on the conviction that man is fundamentally dishonest. Honest men "find themselves doubted, distrusted, and outcast. . . . They are obliged to conform or die."[34] And again he wrote, "The number of homeless men and women, ruined fortunes, idle workmen . . . is evidence of the ease with which adroit men can defraud and cheat and transfer the property of the world into the hands of the few."[35] His final and conclusive basis for pessimism, however, was the frustration of death. "All roads lead to futility and oblivion," he said. "The constant cries and pleadings of the ages have brought back no answering sound to prove that death is anything but death"; and he added, "while this makes less of man, it . . . covers his deeds with the cloak of charity which is the ultimate garment of the great Unknown."[36]

This doubt about getting answers to life's basic questions was the key to Darrow's religious attitudes. He was considered by many to be the greatest agnostic of his day, and proudly took the designation literally—one who "doubts the verity of accepted religious creeds or faiths."[37] He did not quite deny the reality of God. He simply found the evidence for God's existence insufficient to convince him, and claimed the right to say so while leaving others free to draw their own conclusions. He found no evidence of purpose or design in the world; and asked, "Isn't it a bit more modest and less foolish to answer, as I do, that I know nothing about it . . .?"[38]

On some other articles of religious faith, however, Darrow was adamant. He could not reconcile the cruelty and violence he saw everywhere in nature with the belief that a merciful and kind Supreme Being was ruler of the universe.[39] He refused to accept the literal interpretation of the Bible as a supernatural book, because such authoritarian reverence for the Scriptures seemed to him a narrow and bigoted denial of intellectual freedom and a contradiction of the facts of science. He went to Dayton, Tennessee, not primarily to defend John Thomas Scopes, but to wage war on this denial.

Belief in immortality also seemed to him utterly impossible.[40] He found no evidence that memory of this life persists after death, nor could he believe that mind and personality exist outside the physical body, which after death completely disintegrates and is mingled with other elements and absorbed into other life forms. This denial of spirit, he admitted, took some of the glamor and illusion from life and some of man's egotism, but added that "peace and comfort, when gained at the sacrifice of courage and integrity, are purchased at too high a price."[41] He believed in facing life fearlessly, even though it seemed futile and meaningless.

Actually, however, Darrow was not entirely devoid of religious faith. He was, as Charles Edward Russell once remarked, too sensitive to keep out all faith.[42] In spite of his refusal to believe in a God who permits men to suffer pain and misfortune, he was not able to follow completely his postulate of impersonal, cause-and-effect materialism. In grief at the passing of his friend he could say: "If there shall be a great, wise, humane judge, before whom the sons of men shall come, we can hope for nothing better for ourselves than to pass into that infinite presence as the comrades and friends of John Pardon Altgeld."[43] He wrote of "infinite bubbles poured out by the great creative power."[44] In some of his noblest moments as speaker he proclaimed a law of love and human brotherhood. This was the religion he practiced, but he did not call it Christian. For him Christianity was still synonymous with the fundamentalist beliefs he could not accept.[45] In their stead he lived a creed of benevolence, which he professed to derive, not from any sentiment or religious faith, but from his belief in a universe of law. "People who believe in a universe of law," he said, "never condemn or hate individuals."[46] His humanitarian life was also derived in part from rejection of belief in immortality. "When we abandon the thought of immortality," he said, "we cast out fear and gain a certain dignity and self-respect. We regard our fellow-travelers as companions . . . traveling the same route to a common doom. No one can feel this universal relationship without being gentler, kindlier, and more humane toward all the infinite forms of beings that live with us, and must die with us."[47] Here appears the crowning contradiction of Darrow's career: the mechanist and determinist who believed man to be utterly irresponsible, nevertheless lived a responsible life of kindness and tolerance and service to humanity.

In the words of his poetic contemporary and associate,

> This is Darrow,
> Inadequately scrawled, with his young, old heart,
> And his drawl, and his infinite paradox,
> And his sadness, and kindness,
> And his artist sense that drives him to shape his life
> To something harmonious, even against the schemes of God.[48]

SPEAKING METHODS

Throughout most of his life Clarence Darrow strove for a direct and thoughtful kind of discourse; and though he once remarked that oratory is a disease of youth,[49] his career exemplified that better meaning of the word suggested in John P. Altgeld's comment that "The orator must be absolutely independent. . . . Great manhood must go with great oratory."[50]

Because of his abhorrence of artificiality, Darrow never submitted himself, at least so far as any records show, to rigorous training in the use of voice and action. He professed to believe that when he really had something to say he could make himself understood.[51] Here was a mechanist in philosophy declaring a think-the-thought method of training. His disgust with early school exercises in declamation blinded him to Altgeld's advice that delivery requires as much attention to voice and action as is given by a singer.[52] Darrow's manner of speaking was indeed effective in its own peculiar way, but there is little evidence that this effectiveness came out of any deep understanding of the processes involved or was anything more than the fortunate result of years of trial and error experience on the platform.

Likewise in preparation of thought Darrow did not subject himself to intensive discipline.[53] His was a free-wheeling and independent genius which followed its own methods. Although the speeches on favorite themes had the advantage of continued study and frequent repetition as the years passed,[54] the popular lecturer depended primarily on his general fund of knowledge and almost never made specific and intensive preparation for any speech.[55] In the court-room the prolonged activity of examining witnesses and gathering evidence served in part as substitute for study and writing, and Darrow's prodigious memory enabled him to recall and use readily without written notes all the detailed facts of a case in a plea of several hours' length.

This attorney held legal technicalities in contempt and studied philosophy, psychology, biology, and history more than he studied law.[56] He usually emphasized, therefore, those broader issues of a case which lay beyond the immediate guilt or innocence of the particular defendant. This method first appeared significantly in the defense of Eugene Debs when Darrow accused the General Man-agers' Association of conspiracy to use the government as a cloak to conceal its infamous treatment of labor and argued that the injunc-tion had been used illegally by a court of equity to deny the right of trial by jury.[57] In like manner many of Darrow's greatest cases were but "episodes in the great battle for human liberty."[58] The crimes charged against his clients he presented as inevitable social consequences of the long struggle for justice.[59] At Dayton, Ten-nessee, Darrow and his colleagues looked upon the entire proceeding as part of the battle for intellectual freedom; Scopes' guilt or inno-cence was all but lost sight of in the struggle over admissibility of expert testimony on the relation between evolution and Christian-ity.[60] Again, the trials of Loeb and Leopold in Chicago and of the Sweets in Detroit were not simply murder cases. At Darrow's hands the former became part of the campaign against capital punishment and an extended statement of the philosophy of humanitarianism, and the latter a test of a man's right to defend his home and person.

Darrow, however, was also a master of courtroom strategy. He could doodle over cross-word puzzles at the counsel table to create an impression of casual indifference. Although noted for careless dress, he knew how to change from the shirt-sleeve and suspender aura of Dayton, Tennessee, to a correct and sophisticated appear-ance in metropolitan Detroit.[61] He could bait a prosecuting attorney to distraction and confuse witnesses by repeated heckling. He knew that delay in starting a trial often gave passions time to cool, that prolonging a case gave the jury opportunity to develop a friendly feeling for the defendant, that a light touch of humor could sway a jury more than argument. On one occasion he brought a defendant's infant daughter into court.[62] On a higher plane of strategy he met the perfect hanging case in the Loeb-Leopold trial by combining a plea of guilty with extended testimony of alienists.[63]

Out of his experience Darrow developed definite opinions about the kind of jurors advantageous to a defense. He preferred men (no women wanted) who were imaginative, idealistic, able to laugh and to put themselves in another man's place. Whenever possible he avoided prohibitionists and religious people because, he said, they believed in sin and punishment and might be vindictive; but if he had to accept them on a jury he much preferred Roman Catholics, with Methodists second choice. The wealthy and ultra-respectable he also avoided because they were inclined to regard themselves as guardians of the law. Germans he thought too bullheaded, Swedes too stubborn, Scotsmen too inhuman in feeling. Irishmen and Jews he found most sympathetic and susceptible to emotional appeals. He always sought to find jurors who were the same sort of men as his client or who themselves had been in trouble, and old men instead of young because the experiences of life tended to make them more charitable.[64]

In keeping with these viewpoints Darrow's methods of persuasion and proof were based on his belief that man is not primarily rational, but imaginative and emotional. "If a jury wants to save the client," he said, "they can find a good reason why they should, and will. The problem is to bring about a situation where court and jury want a lawyer's client to win."[65] His basic means of proof, therefore, were more largely motivational than logical.

The most frequent appeal was to the common humanity of all men. Even after the bitterness of the anthracite coal strike in Pennsylvania he could say of the operators: "If they will learn to come to us as brothers, . . . they will find that we will extend the right hand of fellowship. . . . I wish they could understand that back of the black hands of these, their servants, . . . are consciences, intellects, hearts and minds as true as in any man who ever lived."[66] In most of his labor cases he pleaded for sympathy for "thousands of men, and of women and children . . . weary with care and toil."[67] To a jury of white men called upon to judge the motives of Negroes defending their home he said, "Put yourselves in their place. Make yourselves colored for a little while . . . before any of you would want to be judged, you would want your juror to put himself in your place."[68] Most of the argument in defense of Loeb and Leopold was a plea for "every other boy who in ignorance and darkness must grope his way through the mazes which only childhood knows," for "understanding, charity, kindness, and . . . for a time when hatred and cruelty will not control the hearts of men."[69]

Closely related to this appeal for human brotherhood, in fact often mingled with it, was reference to man's love of liberty. Clarence Darrow regarded labor organizers as leaders in the struggle to free men from economic slavery. By subtle analogy Thomas I. Kidd was one with such men as Garrison, Kelley, Foster, and Pillsbury of an earlier generation who worked for freedom of slaves in the underground railroad.[70] In his first self-defense Darrow spoke to the members of the jury as men who valued their own liberty;[71] and he argued the case of Arthur Person as "one that reaches down to the foundation of your freedom and mine."[72] The champion of justice defended others who, like Person, were arrested in the post-war raids against subversive organizations, not to defend their views as such, but because they had "the same right to their belief under the laws of this country as you have to yours," and because "you can only be free if I am free." He excoriated fiercely those prosecutors who had broken into houses and made arrests without warrants and urged the jury to stand for "the right of men to think; . . . to speak boldly and unafraid; . . . to be master of their souls; . . . to live free and to die free."[73]

The great agnostic occasionally used appeals to religious sentiment. This practice raises a challenging question: What should we think of an agnostic who in impassioned defense argument referred to the "infinite God of the infinite universe,"[74] pleaded for recognition of the God in men, made extended analogy from the Sermon on the Mount, quoted Scripture to support argument, declared he did not believe in "tinkering with the work of God," and spoke of the Infinite Being who gave him light to see his duty?[75] Were such appeals to religion merely devices of rhetoric? Possibly! Darrow must have used them with some awareness of their potential effect on audiences. In view of the man's lifelong idealism, however, any critic should hesitate to impugn his sincerity. At least one other interpretation of this religious material is possible. Darrow's agnosticism and his pessimism were intellectual convictions based on such facts of life as he could observe directly. He freely acknowledged, however, that instincts and emotions more fundamental than intellect keep man alive.[76] Perhaps his uses of religious material came out of these deeper instincts and emotions of his life, broke through the surface crust of cynicism, and like his humanitarianism were evidences of a submerged religious belief which he scoffed at intellectually but which he could not entirely obliterate? In his moments of most impassioned pleading when issues of human welfare were at stake, these hidden springs inevitably overflowed. The religion of the heart which this man lived may well be regarded as one of the sources of his emotional power with audiences.

In fact Darrow's character and personality were generally his most powerful persuaders, and the strength of his beliefs was a major source of that power. He gave his clients a deep personal and emotional commitment.[77] The great courtroom pleas were great primarily because motivated by depth of conviction.

The influence of a personality on audiences is difficult to assess, but we should at least notice some of the ways Darrow used to enhance his credibility with listeners. He was well aware that an attorney's every look and gesture could influence a jury; and he, therefore, made it a rule seldom to quarrel with judge or opposing lawyers or witnesses.[78] Though he could be ruthless in challenge and intense in question, as he was in the Haywood and Scopes trials,[79] his methods of cross-examination were typically casual and easygoing, "in the spirit of browsing along the way."[80] Juries he complimented, defied, or challenged as subject and occasion required. Frequently he expressed confidence in them. His most significant personal approach was to put responsibility directly on them:

> I will submit this case squarely to this jury to see what you are going to do in the cause of freedom of speech. . . .
>
> You can only convict yourselves in the face of the civilized world . . . ; you are trying the jury system.
>
> There is no power on earth can relieve you of your obligation. This jury alone stands between this boy and the gallows.

Bill Haywood can't die unless you kill him. You must tie the rope. You twelve men of Idaho, the burden will be on you.[81]

The most dramatic of all this attorney's personal proofs were his attacks on opponents. Although he was often blunt and forthright on the public platform, he could also be courteous and friendly. Indeed some of his strongest opponents, even on issues like prohibition and capital punishment about which he felt deeply, came to be his close friends.[82] In court, however, he gave no quarter and asked none. His exposures of false or distorted testimony were merciless, as when he showed that George Baer had misrepresented wages paid the miners, that George Paine had lied about child labor in his mills, and that the prosecution had coached some of the seventy witnesses who testified that no mob was at Doctor Sweet's house, although all seventy admitted being there. Prosecutors he frequently branded as the tools of vested interests or of the mob, and some prosecution arguments as disgraceful even among savage tribes.[83] Of prosecutor Gray in the bribery trial in Los Angeles, 1913, he said, "I will guarantee that Chandler has visited Gray's pen a great many times and poured many a pail of swill down his trough."[84]

When issues were tensely drawn, Darrow's power of invective, ridicule, and sarcasm could be terrible to encounter. Who would have wanted to be Mill Owner Paine or District Attorney Quartermass, or Special Counsel Houghton on that autumn afternoon, 1898, in Oshkosh, Wisconsin, when the defender of labor stood up to speak in behalf of Thomas I. Kidd charged with conspiracy to injure the business of the Paine Lumber Company because he directed a strike of woodworkers for abolition of woman and child labor, recognition of the Union, better wages and a weekly pay day? On that day, especially, Clarence Darrow was one of God's angry men, and his anger overflowed in bitter and scathing denunciation:

> Fie on you for hypocrites and cowards, who would combine every manufacturer in the city of Oshkosh, not into a "union," but into an "association." A body of employers living from the unpaid labor of the poor is an "association." A body of their slaves is a "labor union." George M. Paine says, "I will not meet your union; I will not meet your committee. If one of you have anything to say, come to me alone and talk." And they did go alone, and what did they get? . . .

Herman Daus went to his employer. . . . Eight or ten years'
experience, and getting a dollar and a quarter a day; . . . only
about a dollar a day for the number of days that a man must
live, for he must live Sundays as well as other days, unless
perhaps he is so religious that he can go to Brother Houghton's
Sunday School and needs no food except his teachings. Seven
dollars and a half a week for a man who had worked at
dangerous machinery for ten years, and they had promised
him a raise; and he went singly, singly the way this great
corporation desired to have a man meet them; singly—the
cowards. I do not know whether he carried his cap in his
hand; . . . I do not know whether he said "Your lordship."
. . . But he did decently ask for a raise. And what did they
say? They said, "Go to hell, God damn you. . . ." These high-
toned gentlemen, who come into this court of justice with
kid gloves and well-brushed clothes, who can study manners
at foreign courts, and send their children to foreign lands to
be educated; and yet, when a poor laborer asks them for something more than seven dollars and a half a week, they tell him
to go to hell. Well, he would not have far to go, Mr. Paine. . . .

And this is the man, Mr. District Attorney, for whom you
prostituted the great State of Wisconsin, for whom you prostitute the office that you hold, to whom you have turned over
this State to do the work of a bloodhound to track innocent
men to jail.[85]

For such a vitriolic pleader, logical reasoning served more as a
framework and foundation for his proof than as a primary means of
its development. The basis of his logic lay in his philosophy of life.
He believed, as we have seen, that the universe operated as a rigid
cause and effect determinism; his basic method of reasoning, therefore, was causal. The most pervasive of these causal arguments, both
in court and on the lecture platform, was that actions of men are not
the result of their own will and intention but arise from forces of
heredity and environment. On this principle Loeb and Leopold
were victims of their backgrounds, the McNamara brothers were
but performing the inevitable consequences of generations of mis-
treatment of labor, the inhumanity of employers was the primary
cause of all labor conflicts, and the Sweets were compelled to shoot
in self-defense by fear ingrained in their race through generations of
mobbing and lynching.

These broad outlines of causal reasoning were developed and

amplified not only by more detailed casual inferences, but also by inductive forms of argument. Sometimes Darrow would use analogy with brilliant effect, but the more frequent form of his inductive inferences was broad generalization based on a body of detailed facts. In the courtroom Darrow's marshalling of evidence was typically exhaustive and precise. Anyone who reads the analysis of wages and conditions in the mines before the Anthracite Coal Commission, or the extended accounts of labor history in the Haywood trial and in the self-defense pleas of 1912 and 1913, or the assembling of testimony to show the abnormal mental condition of Loeb and Leopold, must inevitably come away with renewed respect for the intellect which could marshal and reduce to order so vast an array of detail and argue issues so broadly against a backdrop of history and social conditions.

By contrast, Darrow the platform lecturer and debater was often negligent, inexact, and even flippant in his use of facts and inferences. He derided statistics, but sometimes resorted instead to unsupported assertion and sweeping generalization. Occasionally his only source was personal experience, which though wide and challenging could hardly be conclusive. For want of citations he could dispose of a point with a terse, "Every intelligent man knows," or "Is there anyone who doesn't know?" In a debate with Will Durant on the mechanistic nature of man Darrow begged the entire question by defining "mechanism" so as to include both purpose and growth, two of the main characteristics of organisms; and then used glaring examples of *non sequitur* by arguing that man is a machine because (1) the human body is imperfect and because (2) we do not know where or how the first form of life began.[86] In some of the debates on prohibition the defender of personal liberty implied that drinking alcoholic beverages was responsible for "all the poetry and literature and practically all the works of genius that the world has produced," clinched the argument by asking what kind of a poem you would get out of a glass of ice water, and in reply to the dangers of drunken driving quipped, "Then let's get rid of automobiles."[87] Audiences laughed with such flippancy and even applauded the statement that "in civilization men read more books and get less out of them than they do in savagery."[88] No wonder Darrow asserted that men are not motivated primarily by reason, although in fairness we should add that he often admitted lack of knowledge and conceded points made by opponents.

In style of discourse his striking qualities were amplification and cumulation, mingled with humor, sometimes subtle and again caustic, and with frequent sprinklings of sarcasm and irony. There was a Ciceronian echo in his use of amplification. He would hold an idea up, turn it over and around by restatement, repetition, rhetorical questions, and accumulation of vivid details, until it was expanded to full-bodied significance.

During some of his earlier years Darrow affected an ornate style, which arose from his admiration for the great Robert Ingersoll.[89] A typical example was the opening of the address at the Free Trade Convention:

> When the untutored savage—nature's eldest child—first occupied the earth and freely roamed where he would, and took as he wished, his wages were the full amount that his strength and cunning enabled him to gather from the elements of nature —the earth, the sea, the air—from which all productions are originally drawn. In those primitive days, ere yet the soil had been parcelled out to individual owners, and before the accumulated earnings of by-gone days had ripened into capital, each was his own employer and his wages, fixed by nature, were the full product of his toil. . . .[90]

By 1905, however, Darrow was setting the stylistic tone of his mature career: "As the man possessed of vital truth will not waste a moment of his precious time on vacant forms, so, too, when he tells his truth to the listening world, he will waste no time in the effort for effect."[91] The application of this philosophy is evident in the preponderance of one-syllable words and short, simple sentences in the discourses of his middle and later years.[92] Sometimes in the more impassioned pleas he would build a series of clauses through mounting sequence to strong climax. The choice and management of words, however, were always clear, usually plain and simple, seldom ornate. His diction at its best had the same rich and noble music that Hamlin Garland noted in *Farmington*.[93] Most of Darrow's illustrations were from the common experiences of daily life. Such embellishment as occurred consisted primarily of references to literature. In almost all of his defense pleas he quoted poetry, and sprinkled them generously, too, with references to prose writers, philosophers, and dramatists. He carried his love of literature even into the intense struggles of the courtroom.

Let us look at Darrow, the speaker, in action.[94] He sits slumped down on the end of his spine, sometimes preoccupied, often motionless. When the time comes to speak, he rises and ambles slowly and deliberately to the speakers' stand or close to the jury rail, his broad shoulders slightly rounded, massive head thrust forward, hair disarrayed with one unruly lock hanging down over the right side of the broad forehead, the homely, deeply-lined, Lincolnesque face stern, and the cavernous, blue-grey eyes kindly.

He begins quietly in a pleasant, drawling baritone, without fanfare. The voice is often too low to hear easily beyond the front rows, but can change from barely audible whisper to resounding power. For the most part he speaks slowly and thoughtfully with restrained modulation and conversational quality, giving the impression of utter simplicity and sincerity combined with a kind of whimsey. His greatest defense pleas, nevertheless, reveal him as a man of deep emotion, the voice often fading away at the end into silence so intense and throbbing that one can scarcely tell where the sound ceases and stillness begins.

Darrow's bodily action is a little ungainly; he may lean on the desk and at times shuffle awkwardly. Perhaps he will point a long finger to emphasize a remark, or make a sweeping backhand motion across the body with his right hand, or thrust his left hand deep in his trousers' pocket, or even hook his thumbs in the galluses and snap them. As the fires of conviction warm up, he may pound one fist in the other hand, or use some windmill gestures of the arms, or wrap them around his body and glare at the listeners. His whole frame may reverberate with the intensity of his emotion. The face is an expressive map of varied feelings. The more eloquent gestures, however, are with the shoulders. They "can express more hatred and contempt, or sympathy and understanding, or cynicism and despair in one hunch . . . than one could ever imagine possible if he did not see it." ". . . the shoulders . . . dominate the room, . . . insult the prosecutor, snub the judge, flatter the jury, comfort the defendants, joke with the newspaper men and clown for the crowd. . . ."[95]

The whole effect was more than sincerity or directness or what teachers of speech call "audience contact." Though one man might consider Darrow's bitterness and cynicism repellent, and another call him a "gaunt, loose-skinned, fiery-eyed rebel," or describe him as "gloomy, blunt and sardonic," or refer sarcastically to his acting ability,[96] his infinite capacity for friendship nevertheless shone through his rough exterior and broke down whatever hostility might be in the listeners. Whether reading to a few friends at his fireside, or talking to twelve men in a jury box, or lecturing in a great auditorium, he created a sense of intimacy which took the listeners into a friendly circle.[97] There was a nameless charm about the man which enchanted the souls of listeners and carried them away captive. Therein lay the heart of Clarence Darrow's power as a speaker.

SUMMARY AND EVALUATION

What then shall we think of him? Obviously no simple answer is possible, nor even any single answer. He was many-sided and contradictory, a rebel and an eccentric, who by his speaking shattered the intellectual patterns of his time. It is difficult if not impossible to steer a middle course of judgment between, on the one hand, those caustic critics who condemned his convictions and purposes, and on the other hand, the hero-worshippers who spoke only fulsome praise.

Darrow's immediate effectiveness as a speaker was demonstrated repeatedly—in the courtroom by number of verdicts won, on the lecture platform by wide popularity and return engagements. At his great defense pleas crowds milled outside the doors, listeners often wept. At his lectures and debates large audiences listened intently and applauded, and returned to listen and applaud again.

His speaking had limitations, however. Here was a man whose neglect of disciplined study of speech method robbed him of his highest development as a speaker; whose power in logical proof was sometimes dissipated by carelessness in preparation and in use of evidence and inference; and whose greatest skills were emotional appeal and vituperation of opponents. Here, too, was a man whose idealism was weakened by pessimism and sense of futility. In its way the materialistic determinism to which he adhered was as much out of balance as was religious fundamentalism. If Bryan was a bigot,

Darrow was a cynic, and there may be some question which presents the greater liabilities to society. If one violates freedom of thought, the other lacks constructive purpose.

When we have said all this, however, we have not plumbed the basic values of the Darrow career. Here was a man who by personal charm and wit could captivate an audience; who could analyze evidence with devastating effect, and reason with broad, philosophic insight; whose speech was so thoughtful, direct, and honest, and so powerful in its conviction and in blazing appeals to imagination and emotion that many who listened were moved profoundly. Here, also, was a man of ideals carried into action, a fearless man and magnificent humanitarian, who spoke out against the dominant powers of his day. He was the type of intellectual radical every country needs for its own good. He stood for fundamental rights when they were unpopular. Under his leadership education and science took the initiative against militant ignorance. As one of Darrow's younger contemporaries said in honor of his seventieth birthday:

> To a smug generation he has been a dash of vinegar. Upon an age satisfied with its superiority, he has played the hose of his skepticism. In an era when wealth and position are unduly exalted, he has made himself the champion of the outcast and disinherited of the earth. Among a people prone to swallow what is handed to them, he has exercised his corrosive common sense. In a time when liberty languishes, he carries on the good fight.[98]

Footnotes

1. Arthur M. Schlesinger, *The American as Reformer* (Cambridge, 1950), p. 86. See also Edgar Lee Masters, *The Tale of Chicago* (New York, 1933) and *Across Spoon River* (New York, 1936).
2. Henry David, *The History of the Haymarket Affair* (New York, 1936).
3. *The Story of My Life* (New York, 1932 and 1934), pp. 89-90, 96-97, 101, 110-111. See also Darrow's address at Altgeld's funeral, March 14, 1902, *ibid.*, Appendix. For brevity all later references to this work will be listed as *Story*.
4. *Ibid.*, pp. 41-45; and Sunset Club *Yearbooks*, 1891-1892 to 1894-1895.
5. Full text of the speech is in *The Chicago Herald*, Feb. 21, 1889, p. 2. Copy is in the Chicago Historical Society.
6. *Story*, pp. 49-51, 57. Mayor De Witt C. Cregier himself told Darrow he was appointed because of his address at the Free Trade Convention.
7. Clarence Darrow, *Argument for Petitioners*, Ex parte Eugene V. Debs, *et al.*, in the Supreme Court of the United States, October term 1894, 97 pp. See also

"United States v. Debs *et al.*" (Circuit Court, N. D. Illinois, Dec. 14, 1894), *The Federal Reporter* (St. Paul, 1895), Vol. 64, 724-766; and "In re Debs *et al.*," *The Supreme Court Reporter* (St. Paul, 1895), Vol. 15, October term 1894, pp. 900-912.

8. *Story*, pp. 61-62, 66, 75.

9. John R. Commons *et al.*, *History of Labor in the United States* (New York, 1918), II, 521-530, and IV, 289-317.

10. *The War*, delivered under auspices of the National Security League, Nov. 1, 1917 (New York, 1917); "Clarence Darrow on the War," Chicago, October 8, 1917, *Everyman* (October-November 1914); *The War in Europe*, lecture before the Chicago Society of Rationalism (Chicago, [n. d.]); and *War Prisoners*, November 9, 1919 (Chicago, 1919).

11. "Darrow: Tender-hearted Cynic and Fixture of American Law," *Newsweek*, III (May 19, 1934), 14.

12. *Portland Oregon Journal* and *Oregonian*, Sept. 11, 1912; *Seattle Post-Intelligencer*, *Star*, and *Union Record*, Sept. 7, 13, 14, 1912.

13. George G. Whitehead, *Clarence Darrow: Evangelist of Sane Thinking* (Girard, Kansas, 1931), and "Clarence Darrow—the Big Minority Man," *The Debunker*, IX (May 1927), 6. Among Mrs. Darrow's papers was an undated fragment of a letter which obviously had been addressed to her husband and was signed "George." It summarized the success of one of these seasons. For eighteen lectures from October to May, Darrow received a total of $13,921.50. The letter added that "the forum clicks better than the other events," probably referring to the symposia on religion. Much of the lecturing Darrow did during his lifetime was without compensation and for the support of humanitarian organizations and causes. In some instances he even paid his own expenses. *Story*, pp. 379-380, 383.

14. See, for example, John A. Lapp, Charles W. Gilkey, Darrow, and Solomon Goldman, *Why I am a Catholic . . . Protestant . . . Agnostic . . . Jew* (Chicago, 1932).

15. *Story*, pp. 209, 382.

16. *Story*, Chap. 2, and *Farmington* (Chicago, 1904), Chaps. 2, 3, and 4. Martin Maloney has analyzed the influence of Darrow's father. See "Clarence Darrow," in *A History and Criticism of American Public Address*, ed. Marie Hochmuth (New York, 1955), III, 262-313.

17. "The Human Being's World," *A Preface to the Universe*, ed. Baker Brownell (New York, 1929), p. 74. See also *Crime: Its Cause and Treatment* (New York, 1922), pp. 274-275, and *Story*, p. 425.

18. Quoted by Irving Stone, *Clarence Darrow for the Defense* (New York, 1941), p. 171.

19. *Story*, pp. 52-53.

20. *Story*, p. 123.

21. *Resist Not Evil* (Chicago, 1903).

22. Stone, p. 172.

23. *Argument . . . in the Case of the Communist Labor Party* (Chicago, 1920), p. 12.

24. "Personal Liberty," *Freedom in the Modern World*, ed. H. M. Kallen (New York, 1928), pp. 115-137.

25. *Resist Not Evil*, Chap. 4.

26. *Crime and Criminals* (Chicago, 1919), p. 19.

27. *The Open Shop* (Chicago, 1904).

28. *Story*, pp. 41, 96, 121-122, 337-349, 361, 455-457; and *Resist Not Evil*, Chap. 7.

29. *Crime: Its Cause and Treatment*, pp. 36, 135.

30. *Story*, pp. 332, 357-358.

31. "Crime and Punishment," *Century*, CIX (March, 1925), 625.

32. *Facing Life Fearlessly* (Girard, Kansas, [n.d.]), pp. 30-31; and *Pessimism* (Chicago, 1920).

33. John C. Kennedy and Darrow, *Is the Human Race Permanently Progressing Toward a Better Civilization?* (Chicago, 1919); Frederick Starr and Darrow, *Is the Human Race Getting Anywhere?* (Chicago, 1920); George Burman Foster and Darrow, *Is Life Worth Living?* (Chicago, 1917).

34. "Is Man Fundamentally Dishonest?" *The Forum*, LXXVIII (December, 1927), 887.

35. *Story*, p. 344.

36. *Ibid.*, p. 444, and "The Human Being's World," pp. 69-70, 86.

37. Edwin Holt Hughes, John P. McGoorty, Jacob Tarshish, and Darrow, *Why I am an Agnostic, Including Expressions of Faith from a Protestant, a Catholic, and a Jew* (Girard, Kansas, [n.d.]), p. 27.

38. *Story*, pp. 389, 412. See also "Darrow's Speech in the Haywood Case," *Wayland's Monthly*, No. 90 (October, 1907), 23-25.

39. Rev. Robert MacGowan and Darrow, *Is Religion Necessary?* (Girard, Kansas, 1931), p. 8.

40. M. A. Musmanno and Darrow, *Does Man Live Again?* (Girard, Kansas, 1936).

41. "Human Being's World," p. 87.

42. Quoted by Irving Stone, p. 171, from an unpublished letter.

43. *Story*, p. 457.

44. "The Human Being's World," p. 98.

45. John Haynes Holmes remarked that Darrow's religious thought moved in the realm of early nineteenth century agnosticism, and that both he and Bryan were behind the times in the Scopes trial. See "Clarence Darrow, Lovable Pessimist," *Unity*, CXXI (May 16, 1938), 89.

46. *Facing Life Fearlessly*, p. 15.

47. *Story*, p. 411.

48. Edgar Lee Masters, "The Man With an Old Face," *Rockford Republic*, October 11, 1922.

49. Quoted by John B. Roberts in "Speech Philosophy of Clarence Darrow" (unpublished Master's thesis, State University of Iowa), p. 172.

50. *Oratory* (Chicago, 1901), p. 48.

51. *Farmington*, p. 54.

52. *Ibid.*, pp. 81-82, and *Oratory*, p. 8.

53. Hamlin Garland remarked when he visited Darrow in 1907 that his mind was "uncultivated and undisciplined." *Companions on the Trail* (New York, 1931), p. 322.

54. The Darrow papers in the Library of Congress, for example, include four manuscripts on Tolstoy, which indicate considerable reworking of both content and style. Similar variable manuscripts on Voltaire and ethics are also in the collection.

55. See *Across Spoon River*, p. 291; Roberts' thesis, pp. 149, 155, 161, 172, 174; "Biography in Sound—Clarence Darrow," National Broadcasting Co., Dec. 18, 1955; and Victor S. Yarros, *My Eleven Years with Clarence Darrow* (Girard, Kansas, 1950), p. 6.

56. Arthur Garfield Hays, *City Lawyer* (New York, 1942), pp. 215-216.

57. *Debs: His Life, Writings, and Speeches*, ed. Bruce Rogers (Girard, Kansas, 1908), pp. 23-24.

58. *Argument . . . in the Case of the State of Wisconsin vs. Thomas I. Kidd et al.* (Chicago, 1900), p. 5.

59. Darrow, "If Men Had Opportunity," *Everyman*, X (Jan.-Feb. 1915), 22; and "Second Plea of Clarence Darrow in His Own Defense," *Everyman*, IX (May 1913), 8-10.

60. *The World's Most Famous Court Trial: Tennessee Evolution Case* (Cincinnati, 1925). See also Richard M. Weaver, *The Ethics of Rhetoric* (Chicago, 1953), pp. 27-54.

61. Arthur Garfield Hays, *Let Freedom Ring* (New York, 1937), pp. 208-209, 214, 229; Marcet Haldeman-Julius, "Famous and Interesting Guests at a Kansas Farm," *Reviewer's Library*, No. 8 (1936), 19. Darrow resented the reputation for carelessness in dress which the newspapers had given him. See George Jean Nathan, *The Intimate Notebooks* (New York, 1933), p. 85; and "Clarence Darrow—The Big Minority Man," p. 4.

62. Edwin C. Hill, "Darrow, Colossal Court Rebel," *New York Sun*, Dec. 23, 1927, p. 15; and T. V. Smith in "Biography in Sound—Clarence Darrow."

63. According to Illinois law a defendant who admitted guilt could not plead insanity. Darrow avoided this dilemma by throwing the defense on the mercy of the court and introducing testimony of alienists in mitigation of punishment.

64. Darrow, "Attorney for the Defense," *Esquire*, V (May, 1936), 36-37, 211, 213; and T. V. Smith and Darrow, *Can the Individual Control His Conduct?* (Girard, Kansas, [n.d.]), pp. 28, 33.

65. *Story*, pp. 427-428.

66. "Argument Before the Anthracite Coal Commission," *North American* (Philadelphia), Feb. 13, 14, 15, 16, 1903. See Feb. 16, p. 6.

67. "Darrow's Speech in the Haywood Case," p. 111.

68. *Argument in the Case of Henry Sweet* (New York, 1927), p. 27.

69. *The Plea . . . in Defense of Richard Loeb and Nathan Leopold, Jr., on Trial for Murder* (Chicago, 1924), pp. 120-121.

70. *Wisconsin vs. Thomas I. Kidd et al.*, pp. 77-78.

71. *Plea of Clarence Darrow in His Own Defense* (Los Angeles, 1912), p. 10. For background of the two self-defense cases and their relation to defense of the McNamara brothers in the Los Angeles *Times* dynamiting case see Alexander Irvine, *Revolution in Los Angeles* (Los Angeles, 1911) and Lincoln Steffens, *The Autobiography of Lincoln Steffens* (New York, 1931), p. 658 ff.

72. *Address in the Trial of Arthur Person*, Defense Committee, Communist Labor Party of Illinois (1920), p. 26.

73. *Argument . . . in the Case of the Communist Labor Party*, pp. 20, 38-39, 116.

74. See "Mr. Darrow's Closing Argument, Defense of Patrick Eugene Prendergast," Oct. 28, 1893, MS, Library of Congress. Many features of Darrow's argument in this early case predicted his method in the Loeb-Leopold plea 31 years later.

75. "Argument Before the Anthracite Coal Commission;" *Wisconsin vs. Thomas I. Kidd et al.*, pp. 65-66; *Argument . . . Communist Labor Party*, p. 61; "Speech in the Haywood Case," p. 24; and "Second Plea . . . in His Own Defense," p. 23.

76. "Clarence Darrow on the War," p. 23.

77. Darrow once said, "When one has worked with a client through a trial one gets so wrapped up in him that he becomes a part of one's self." Quoted from personal interview by Raymond H. Myers, "Persuasive Methods of Clarence Darrow" (unpublished Master's thesis, University of Wisconsin, 1935), p. 26.

78. *Story*, p. 427.

79. Haywood, William D., *Bill Haywood's Book* (New York, 1929), p. 209; and *The World's Most Famous Court Trial . . .* pp. 284-304.

80. Lowell B. Mason, interview, Jan. 15, 1957.

81. *Argument . . . Communist Labor Party*, p. 11; *Wisconsin vs. Thomas I. Kidd et al.*, pp. 13, 32; "Defense of Patrick Eugene Prendergast"; "Speech in the Haywood Case," p. 29.

82. See the memorials to Darrow in *Unity*, CXXI (May 16, 1938); and Clarence True Wilson, "Darrow, Friendly Enemy," *The Forum and Century*, C (July, 1938), 12-16. Wilson's letter to Mrs. Darrow on the death of his great opponent said that he "came to love him as a brother." MS, Library of Congress.

83. See, for example, his *Argument . . . Communist Labor Party*, p. 9; and *Defense of Richard Loeb and Nathan Leopold, Jr.*, p. 6.

84. "Second Plea . . . in His Own Defense," p. 6. Chandler was son-in-law of Harrison Gray Otis, owner of the dynamited *Times*.

85. *Wisconsin vs. Thomas I. Kidd et al.*, pp. 16, 22-23, 30-31, 49.

86. *Are We Machines?* (Girard, Kansas, [n.d.]), pp. 34, 41, 43-44.

87. John Haynes Holmes and Darrow, *Resolved: That the United States should Continue the Policy of Prohibition as Defined in the Eighteenth Amendment* (New York, 1924), pp. 36-37, 51; Clarence True Wilson and Darrow, *Should the Eighteenth Amendment be Repealed?* (Girard, Kansas, 1931), p. 8.

88. Frederick Starr and Darrow, *Is Civilization a Failure?* (Chicago, 1924), p. 12.

89. *Story*, pp. 42, 381.

90. "The Workingmen and the Tariff." See also *Story*, pp. 46-47.

91. "Literary Style," *Tomorrow: A Monthly Handbook of the Changing Order*, I (January, 1905), 28.

92. Tabulations of word length and sentence length are given in the theses by Raymond H. Myers and John B. Roberts.

93. *Companions on the Trail*, p. 321.

94. This description of Darrow's voice and action is based on observers' reports: Quin Ryan, "Biography in Sound—Clarence Darrow"; Allen Crandall, *The Man From Kinsman* (Sterling, Colorado, 1933), pp. 10-11, 15, 18; Marcet Haldeman-Julius, *Clarence Darrow's Two Great Trials* (Girard, Kansas, 1927), p. 7, and "Famous and Interesting Guests at a Kansas Farm," p. 14; M. L. Edgar, "Clarence S. Darrow," *The Mirror*, XVII (May 16, 1907), 13; James Weldon Johnson, "Clarence Darrow as I Knew Him," *Unity*, CXXI (May 16, 1938), 88; George Burman Foster, "The Echo—Sixty-first Birthday Celebration," transcription by Ethel McClaskey, MS, Library of Congress; Francis X. Busch, *Prisoners at the Bar* (Indianapolis, 1952), p. 193; Alfred Cohn and Joe Chisholm, *Take the Witness* (New York, 1934), p. 223; Edward Albert Wiggam and Darrow, *Environment and Heredity* (Girard, Kansas [n.d.]), p. 5; *New York World*,

Dec. 23, 1927, 13; Arturo Giovannitti, "Communism on Trial," *The Liberator,* III (March, 1920), 8; Edwin C. Hill, "Darrow, Colossal Court Rebel"; Lincoln Steffens, *Autobiography,* pp. 465-466, 666; and others summarized by John B. Roberts, pp. 147, 153, 159, 165, 170, 172, 173.

95. Allen Crandall, p. 16. See also Heywood Broun, "It Seems To Me," *New York Telegram,* Feb. 18, 1927, 2d sec., 1; and Edwin C. Hill.

96. Hamlin Garland, p. 322; William Allen White, *Autobiography* (New York, 1946), p. 289; Paul Y. Anderson, "Clarence Darrow, Humanitarian," *St. Louis Post-Dispatch,* July 3, 1927, 1C, 3C; Masters, *Across Spoon River,* p. 273.

97. Clarence True Wilson, "Clarence Darrow as a Friend," *Unity,* CXXI (May 16, 1938), 12; James H. Griffes (alias Luke North), "A Man of the People," *The Golden Elk,* VI (May, 1907), 19; Mary Bell Decker, "The Man Clarence Darrow," *The University Review,* IV (Summer 1938), 239; James Weldon Johnson, *Along This Way* (New York, 1933), p. 379.

98. Paul Y. Anderson, p. 3C.

THE MINISTRY

Harry Emerson Fosdick
A Study in Sources of Effectiveness

HARRY EMERSON FOSDICK *(May 24, 1878—   ). Born at Buffalo, New York; attended Buffalo public schools, where his father was principal of the high school; A.B. Colgate University, 1900; B.D. Union Theological Seminary, 1904; D.D. Colgate University, 1914; numerous honorary degrees from leading American universities; ordained Baptist ministry, 1903; pastor of Baptist Church, Montclair, New Jersey, 1904-1915; minister of Fifth Avenue Presbyterian Church, New York City, as an experiment in inter-denominational preaching, 1915-1924; minister of Riverside Church, New York City, until retirement; instructor in homiletics, Union Theological Seminary, 1908-1915, and of practical theology, 1915-1946; Phi Beta Kappa; author of numerous collections of sermons and books on religion; popular lecturer on subjects related to moral and spiritual values.*

Harry Emerson Fosdick
A Study in Sources of Effectiveness

ROY C. MCCALL*

FOR more than two decades Harry Emerson Fosdick was "the most important popular figure in the Protestant pulpit." He combined "in his person the rare art of the preacher with the spirit of the earnest student if not of the academic scholar."[1] Although a dissident minority once held that he "is no authentic representative of the Christian religion,"[2] certainly he was during his active ministry "a conspicuously successful preacher . . . whose good report . . . filled the whole city";[3] "one of the most popular and distinguished clergymen of America."[4]

In England he was regarded as "the true successor of Phillips Brooks," one who made the English "prouder than ever" of their "communion in language with the United States." His was "real eloquence," the kind which for three days kept "Scotland . . . sitting at his feet."[5]

His radio broadcasts, begun with one station in 1926, became soon the major attraction of National Vespers, which opened in 1927 and eventually was carried nationwide every Sunday over NBC. In 1936 was initiated the mimeographed service which made his vesper sermons available by mail to all who requested them; and until necessity forced retrenchment during the war, his broadcasts were carried by short wave to England, Africa, New Zealand, and Australia.[6] Sermons, lectures, and essays, bound into books, sold in excess of a million copies during the twenties.[7]

Dean Karl Onthank of the University of Oregon tells of going two hours early to get a good seat in an assembly hall at Columbia

* Roy C. McCall (A.B. University of Redlands 1930, M.A. 1931, Ph.D. 1936, University of Iowa) is president, College of the Desert.

University where Fosdick was scheduled to speak, only to find the place packed and people standing outside. Everett L. Waid, long time president of the Art Students League of New York City, reports that when he was an usher at the First Presbyterian Church of New York, the staff was forced to close the doors against hundreds nearly every Sunday. It was during this period that Fosdick preached the sermon "Shall the Fundamentalists Win?" which caused the storm that eventually drove him from that pulpit and built "a sounding board behind" him so that his "message reached farther than [he] ever dreamed it could."[8]

Dr. Loren Reid, professor of speech at the University of Missouri, writes: "I remember vividly a series of lectures that Fosdick gave at Grinnell College, about 1926 or 1927. Every morning one week he gave a chapel lecture; the chapel period was lengthened from its usual 20 minutes to an hour in order to feature his talk. Morning classes were correspondingly shortened. I recall that many, many of us actually ran to chapel in order to be sure of a seat."

"He received 125,000 letters a year from his radio talks alone."[9] One contemporary said of him: "The most pre-eminent pulpit of the Christian faith in America, if not in the world, is that of Dr. Harry Emerson Fosdick in Riverside Church."[10]

When in 1924, ninety thousand ministers of the United States were asked to select the twenty-five outstanding preachers of the land, Fosdick was named among the twenty-five.[11]

Whether such a man stood highest in popularity and influence among Protestant preachers of his age, there is little doubt that his eminence justifies examination of the causes that have rendered him outstanding in the art of preaching. To what extent were his achievements attributable to intellect, to training, to conviction, to empathy with the dominant needs of mankind?

CHARACTER, CONSCIENCE, AND CONVICTION

In the theological controversy which developed among the Presbyterians following Fosdick's sermon "Shall the Fundamentalists Win?" his "sanity and poise" were judged remarkable.[12] When a committee invited him in the interests of peace to subscribe to the creed of the Presbyterian Church, Fosdick replied: "After two years of vehement personal attack from a powerful section of the Presbyterian Church, I face now an official proposal which calls on me either to make a theological subscription or else leave an influential pulpit. Any subscription made under such circumstances would be generally, and, I think, truly interpreted as moral surrender. I am entirely willing that my theology should be questioned; I am entirely unwilling to give any occasion for the questioning of my ethics."[13]

In an appraisal of what was wrong with the preaching of his time Fosdick wrote: "There is no process by which wise and useful discourses can be distilled from unwise and useless personalities, and the ultimate necessity in the ministry, as everywhere else, is sound and intelligent character."[14]

Whether hearing Fosdick's voice unexpectedly from a neighbor's radio on a Sunday during the twenties and thirties, or reading one of his sermons in any later decade, the recipients of Fosdick's preaching all testify to a sense of his strong conviction. His sermons seemed to be tearing "off the grave-clothes of Christianity, accumulated through the ages by musty theologians . . . to reveal the religion of Jesus in all its imperishable freshness and pertinency . . . dissolving the incrustations of Christianity and . . . challenging the local parsons of thousands of communities to shake themselves out of their lethargy."[15]

The boy who as a returning junior at Colgate wrote his mother, "I'm throwing over my old idea of the universe! I'm building another—and leaving God out!" later considered his ideas too radical to allow him to attempt the career of minister.[16] At the height of his preaching career he wrote:

> Every problem that the preacher faces thus leads back to one basic question: how well does he understand the thoughts and lives of his people? That he should know his Gospel goes without saying, but he may know it ever so well and yet fail to get it within reaching distance of anybody unless he intimately understands people and cares more than he cares for anything else what is happening inside of them. Preaching is wrestling with individuals over questions of life and death, and until that idea of it commands a preacher's mind and method, eloquence will avail him little and theology not at all.[17]

Likewise in his farewell sermon to his congregation at the First Presbyterian Church, where he chose to be ousted rather than yield his principles, he boldly set forth his declaration of independence and devotion, as well as the major premises on which his preaching career was built:

> These are the things we have stood for: tolerance, an inclusive Church, the right to think religion through in modern terms, the social application of the principles of Jesus, the abiding verities and experiences of the Gospel. And these are right. I am not sorry we tried this experiment. It was worth trying. We have listed a standard that no one will pull down. We have stated an issue that no man or denomination is strong enough to brush aside.
>
> The future belongs to the things we have been standing for. Some day the whole Church will swing around to them, take them for granted, wonder why they ever seemed new or strange, and what is the heresy of one generation will become the orthodoxy of the next. We say farewell to each other, but let no man say farewell to the things we have been standing for![18]

Such was the man who rode "rough-shod over ecclesiastical decrees and won a hearing which no decree could suppress"[19] because he "wouldn't live in a generation like this and be anything but a heretic."[20]

A Prodigious and Meticulous Worker

In 1933, Edgar DeWitt Jones wrote of Fosdick: "For thirty years . . . he has spent the mornings of five days a week in his study. No message can get to him there, no telephone calls can reach him, no visitors are admitted. In such seclusion, he 'toils terribly' over his sermons."[21] He "used to burn up the logwood in the morning and the chips at night, and the first sometimes made a slow blaze and the latter a thin one."[22] In his view, "nothing can make preaching easy. At best it means drenching a congregation with one's lifeblood."[23] Consequently, the general process of sermon preparation caused him "to read every first-rate book that comes out in almost every field." He wrote:

> Early in my ministry I made it my practice to take some special subject, . . . and then to read every worthwhile thing that has been written in the last fifty years about it, . . . Without such consecutive, continuous, well organized study I do not see how any man can grow in his ministry in general or in his

preaching in particular. . . . I read all the time, and read omnivorously.[24]

Wanting to know what I really thought about immortality, I broke my question into as orderly an arrangement as I could manage, and announced a series of Sunday evening sermons on the subject. Then I was in for it. I read everything pro and con I could lay my hands on and, under the coercion of teaching others, taught myself everything I could learn from books, and searched my mind for what I thought.[25]

The more specific process of composition required that he write out "every word of every sermon. . . . I do not see how anyone can keep strength of thought and variety and facility of language and illustration, if he does not discipline himself to the severe task of writing everything he says."[26] "I write with meticulous care and make many corrections."[27]

INDIVIDUALIST

The following characteristics of Fosdick's spoken and written works had caused the writer to assume that the great preacher was schooled in classical rhetoric: (1) the admirable symmetry of Fosdick's sermons, lectures, and essays; (2) his consistent conformity with the classical pattern of organization; (3) his clear and forceful style, rich in imagery and abundant with antithesis, alliteration, and climax; (4) an obvious pattern of decreasing intellectual appeal, increasing emotional charge, and decreasing length in the progression through the sections of the body of the sermon. In addition, Fosdick's father, principal of a Buffalo high school, was a professor of Greek and Latin, which subjects his son mastered early and read in the original with facility.

A startling discovery, therefore, was learning that Fosdick had "read no textbooks on rhetoric since Genung's *Rhetoric*," except to note some passages in Phillips' *Effective Speaking*, which "seemed to make sense" and were therefore suggested reading for his students in homiletics at Union. Richard Whately's inductive arrangement and Alan H. Monroe's motivated sequence sounded "awfully academic" to him. He further mused: "While books have profoundly influenced me, the influence of two kinds of books has been minor, books about preaching, and sermons." His speech training in high school and college, while intensive, was nonetheless almost exclusively in the mechanics of delivery. Brought up in the tradition of elocution, he "mowed 'em down," as he expressed it, with recitation during his grammar school days—though in his second experience he forgot his "piece" and gave up—was elected president of his debating society in high school but was too overcome with fear and embarrassment to express his thanks for the honor, and in college, where "old fashioned oratory still held sway," he was "drilled for four years on gesture and inflection," practiced "breathing for power," and "won every first" in his course. In later years he "completely abandoned the theory of elocution, never studied effects of oral delivery in advance," and held to the ideal of "animated conversation" as the best mode of delivery. Although early in his preaching career he sought help from the husband of his church organist at his office in Carnegie Hall, and, through singing exercises, gradually worked some huskiness out of his voice, he never "wished to put on a show," hated tricks, "always wanted to talk sense in the pulpit," and looked upon preaching "not as just a speech on Sunday, not just a topical address, but a message to people who needed it."[28]

INFLUENCE OF THE AUDIENCE

Undoubtedly the most significant element in Fosdick's theory and practice of public address is his emphasis on the audience, not only as the focal point of all preaching but also as influencing method in both composition and delivery. He reports that in his early experiences at Montclair, New Jersey, he had great difficulty with himself. "I can recall many hours of complete despair about myself. I didn't know a thing about preaching when I went to Montclair. I really don't know how I got away with it."[29]

> My greater difficulty during my years at Montclair was not with others, but with myself. I did not know how to preach. Doubtless part of the trouble was due to my still unsteady nerves, but much of it was still downright ignorance of how to tackle the preparation of a sermon. What saved me, I suspect, was the fact that I had been trained to stand up and talk in public, so that, however little I had to say, I could at least say it. In those first years I made it a matter of profound pride— which I now deprecate—never to take a scrap of paper into the pulpit, but to preach entirely without notes. While my sermons were therefore immature, often violating the primary

canons of homiletics, they were at least not formal, pedantic, and stereotyped, but direct talks.[30]

During this period two occurrences combined to awaken him to the audience factor in preaching and to strengthen his conviction concerning its relation to rhetorical technique. The first of these was his successful counseling of a man in dire difficulty. At approximately the time a year's intensive work had revealed to him "what could be done with an individual when you sat down with him and brought to bear upon him the resources of the Christian Gospel,"[31] one of his sermons unexpectedly "caught fire." He writes:

> Probably my memory exaggerates the precise occasion when improvement began. One Sunday morning, quite unexpectedly, in the midst of my sermon, the idea I was dealing with caught fire. I had a flaming few minutes when I could feel the congregation's kindling response. I am sure they were as much surprised as I was. I had never preached like that before, and I went home sure that preaching could mean that kind of moving and effective communication of truth.[32]

From this point forward his first concern and constant guide were "clairvoyance as to what is going on in John Doe"; and out of this concept developed his philosophy of "personal counseling on a group scale," or the "project method" of preaching, intended always to "work a miracle on some individual in the congregation." Each sermon from that time on was conceived as a project in counseling the members of his congregation in terms of their personal needs. All his sermons delivered before that conviction struck, he later destroyed. This method, which finds its expression in the introductory portion of every sermon in the determination that all listeners shall say to themselves, "He's bowling down my alley,"[33] remained the strongest guiding force in his preaching to the end of his active ministry.

> Every sermon should have for its main business the solving of some problem—a vital, important problem. . . .
> This endeavor to help people to solve their spiritual problems is a sermon's only justifiable aim. The point of departure and of constant reference, the reason for preaching the sermon in the first place, and the inspiration for its method of approach and the organization of its material should not be something outside the congregation but inside. Within a paragraph or two

after a sermon has started, wide areas of any congregation ought to begin recognizing that the preacher is tackling something of vital concern to them. . . .

Any preacher who even with moderate skill is thus helping folk to solve their real problems is functioning. . . .

What all the great writers of Scripture were interested in was human living, and the modern preacher who honors them should start with that. . . .[34]

He strenuously objects to "topical preachers who turn their pulpits into platforms and their sermons into lectures. . . ." He says: "One who listens to such preaching or reads it knows that the preacher is starting at the wrong end. . . . He is starting with a subject whereas he should start with an object. His one business is with the real problems of these individual people in his congregation."[35]

The Basis for Structure

When asked why nearly all his sermons contained three ideas subordinate to the main theme, Fosdick replied that audiences can not grasp more than three at one sitting; four, perhaps, if the speaker exercises special care in keeping the outline constantly before them. "I preached a sermon at Montclair once with six points," he said. "It came out like a broom, in a multitude of small straws."[36]

When pressed on the question of whether he designed his sermons so that his first point was longest, and strongest in intellectual appeal, whereas his last point was shortest, and strongest in emotional appeal, he professed no consciousness of such method, but said it made sense in terms of the audience's increasing familiarity with the subject as well as their growing fatigue, and the speaker's naturally increasing emotion. The questioner gained the impression, however, that such design was, in Fosdick's mind, possibly too studied to allow the complete genuineness, openness, sincerity, and earnestness compatible with the minister's purpose. He says: "Tell them the truth you want to tell them right off. . . . Climax is achieved by showing them the Matterhorn in the beginning, reshowing it, reshowing it, and each time the Matterhorn gets bigger."[37]

As for his sources of ideas and illustrations, he says: "One gets a theme in his mind and broods over it;[38] his reading contributes to it, his intimate personal experiences in dealing with the problems of other people enrich his thought about it. . . . I get my illustrations from all sorts of places; primarily from personal life, from keeping my eyes open and watching things go, from my reading."[39]

Transitions, which he consistently makes with fine care, arise, he says, "largely from the speaker's sense of audience needs."[40] Figuratively expressed, the members of the audience are carried along ". . . by showing them the Matterhorn in the beginning, reshowing it, reshowing it. . . ."

SOURCES OF STYLE

Fosdick's style is inimitably clear,[41] forceful, easy, unaffected, intimate without being personal, vivid without being florid, full of imagery without straining at figures or even being noticeably figurative. He considers writing "indispensable to preaching if it is going to grow, and not to slump as the years pass,"[42] and credits his wife with being his "best literary critic," who deserves credit for "the absence of numberless words, phrases, sentences, and paragraphs" because "she ruthlessly cut out the excess verbiage"[43] and literally "purged" his style.[44] Although he insists that "the essential nature of a sermon as an intimate, conversational message from soul to soul makes it impossible for printing to reproduce preaching,"[45] both listener and reader gain the impression that his sentences spring from a full heart, unimpeded by consciousness of technique or striving for any effect other than driving home his message. Such spontaneity is consistent with his unwavering integrity and selflessness, lost in his eagerness to reach the audience, but at the same time subconsciously depending on all the best he has read and practiced until it has become an integral part of him in action. He suspects that he was influenced most by Phillips Brooks, whom he greatly admires, by his reading of the classics in the original,[46] and by "a background of great English literature, poetry, history, sociology, etc." without which no one could "be a competent preacher."[47]

Note the consistency and naturalness with which the three phases of the following analogy occur: "The idea I was dealing with caught fire. I had a flaming few minutes when I could feel the congregation's kindling response."

A good example of antithesis: "Who at that far off time could have dreamed that humanity would climb from the Galilee man to the Man of Galilee?"[48]

Again: "It is not Christ's message that needs to be accommodated to this mad scene; it is this mad scene into which our civilization has collapsed that needs to be judged and saved by Christ's message. This is the most significant change distinguishing the beginning of my ministry from now. Then we were trying to accommodate Christ to our civilization; now we face the desperate need of accommodating our scientific civilization to Christ."[49]

For combined metaphor and alliteration, the following is typical: "Here is a home economically imprisoned, no financial elbow-room, the natural desires of family life confronting everywhere the prohibitions of penury."[50]

"The mind always walks as uneasily in new ideas as the feet in new shoes."[51]

Whether his style be judged unconsciously eclectic or consciously skillful, it must finally be declared distinctively Fosdick, the lance with which he became "a preacher who reaches the heart through the intellect."[52]

DISCIPLINED SPONTANEITY

In his early preaching he "memorized his sermons, with no great difficulty," but later "took notes into the pulpit—notes only" and finally the complete manuscript, because he considered "clairvoyance too difficult a matter to be extemporized." The manuscript which he had written "with meticulous care" and "many corrections" had now, without any attempt to memorize it, become so much a part of him that, "I forget that I am reading," hardly more than glancing at the pages now and then, sometimes changing or departing from the manuscript, but always profiting from the discipline of having written it as he would like to say it.[53]

Impatient to meet his audience face to face, he often had to take sedatives on Saturday night in order to get his rest for Sunday's adventure. "Not anxiety, but tension that was a stimulus" caused him to be "aroused." "Any man who isn't tense before he speaks can't speak. Fear is not something to be feared, but something to be sublimated."[54]

In the actual delivery of his sermons, Fosdick, who had been schooled in gesture and posture, inflection and power, cast out consciousness of such physical factors as insincere and artificial, and allowed the welling thoughts within as aroused by the visible audience to dictate the behavior of voice and body. His bearing is best described as restrained and dignified, but expressively consistent with the thought and mood of his message; his voice might well be classed as high and thin, and somewhat monotonous in its cadence, but always suggestive of earnestness and conviction; his articulation was overly precise, and perhaps came nearest to justifying being termed artificial of any of his traits; and yet the sum total of what one heard by radio or in the cathedral was distinctive, a national trademark which, when combined with his written style, enabled listeners always readily to identify him.

His personal magnetism can not be overrated. Whether his radiance was of the spirit, or a happy combination of physical features, good health, and unbounded energy—or both—can not be declared. Only those who have met him face to face know that friendliness encompasses all those near him; only those who have heard him speak know the experience of being arrested and held by an intangible power.

Summary

Thus Fosdick, a consummate artist in public speaking, achieved his art without artifice. A scholar who sought cause and effect in all relations of life and made himself conversant with beginning, end, and middle of every subject he discussed; an evangelist who attempted to reconcile the spiritual and the scientific, history and the present, he disdained help from books on public speaking, forged his own theory of oral communication out of his daily experience, and practiced what the pedagogues have preached but could not produce. Such was the man who "could preach in a theatre or a carbarn and get his audience."[55]

Footnotes

1. *Christian Century*, LII, 20 (November, 1935), 1480.
2. *Catholic World*, CXXXIV, 799 (October, 1931), 100, editorial comment.
3. *Current Opinion*, LXXVII (December, 1924), 756-757.
4. *American Magazine*, XCVII (January, 1924), 32.
5. *Fosdick and the Fundamentalists*, New York, League for Public Discussion, 1925.
6. Mrs. Dorothy Noyes, for 23 years Fosdick's secretary.
7. *Current Biography* (New York, 1940), p. 309.

8. *Farewell Sermon to First Presbyterian Church of New York*, March 1, 1925, published and distributed by Ivy Lee, p. 29.

9. *Time*, XLV (June 18, 1945), 56.

10. Edgar DeWitt Jones, *American Preachers of Today* (Indianapolis, 1933), p. 27.

11. *Literary Digest*, LXXXIV (March 21, 1925), 31-32.

12. *Current Opinion*, LXXVII (December, 1924), 757.

13. Letter to Edgar Whitaker Work, quoted in pamphlet, *The First Presbyterian Church of New York and Doctor Fosdick* (New York, 1924), p. 38.

14. Harry Emerson Fosdick, "What is the Matter with Preaching?" *Harper's Magazine*, CLVII (July, 1928), 133.

15. *Literary Digest*, CVII (November 1, 1930), 20-21.

16. *Current Biography*, p. 309.

17. Fosdick, "What is the Matter with Preaching?" p. 141.

18. *Farewell Sermon* . . . , p. 23.

19. *Literary Digest*, LXXXIV (March 21, 1925), 31.

20. *Farewell Sermon* . . . , p. 28.

21. Jones, p. 29.

22. *Autobiography, a Manuscript,* prepared by Fosdick for his grandchildren, and loaned to the author. Referred to hereafter as *Autobiography*.

23. Fosdick, "What is the Matter with Preaching?" p. 140.

24. Letter of November 23, 1945, to G.E.M. The identity of the recipient is so indicated at Fosdick's request. Referred to hereafter as Letter to G.E.M.

25. *Autobiography*.

26. Letter to G.E.M.

27. Interview.

28. Interview.

29. Interview.

30. *Autobiography*.

31. Interview.

32. *Autobiography*.

33. Interview.

34. Fosdick, "What is the Matter with Preaching?" pp. 134-136.

35. *Ibid*.

36. Interview.

37. Interview.

38. "Brooding" is reminiscent of Henry Ward Beecher's method, but Fosdick's careful writing out of his sermons is quite the opposite. Beecher said: "I brood it and ponder it, and dream over it, . . . I don't dare to . . . put it down on paper. If I once write a thing out, it is almost impossible for me to kindle to it again. I never dare nowadays, to write out a sermon during the week; that is sure to kill it." Lyman Abbott and S. B. Halliday, *Life of Henry Ward Beecher* (Hartford, 1888), p. 211. Fosdick studied both Beecher and Brooks, and feels that he was unconsciously strongly influenced by both. (Interview.)

39. Letter to G.E.M.

40. Interview. The following sentence taken verbatim from "The Deathless Hope that Man Can Not Escape," printed in *A Great Time to Be Alive* (New York, 1944), p. 233, is typical: "From one more major source rises this deathless hope— not alone from the way we ourselves are constituted, nor from our love of other people, but from our personal fellowship with God." Note that the sentence

(1) clearly reiterates the central theme, (2) obviously restates both points already developed, and (3) definitely states the third point which is next to be developed.

41. "His power of clear statement is probably unexcelled in America today." Jones, p. 28.
42. Letter to G.E.M.
43. Harry Emerson Fosdick, *On Being a Real Person* (New York, 1943), p. 14.
44. Interview.
45. Harry Emerson Fosdick, *The Hope of the World* (New York, 1933), p. 7.
46. Interview.
47. Letter to G.E.M.
48. Harry Emerson Fosdick, *A Pilgrimage to Palestine* (New York, 1927), p. 29.
49. *A Great Time to Be Alive*, pp. 20-21.
50. *Ibid.*, p. 134.
51. Harry Emerson Fosdick, *Adventurous Religion* (New York, 1926), p. 244.
52. Wm. G. Shepherd, *Great Preachers as Seen by a Journalist* (London and Edinburgh, New York, and Chicago, 1924), p. 9.
53. Interview.
54. Interview.
55. *Literary Digest*, LXXXI (June 21, 1924), 33.

Ralph Washington Sockman
Twentieth Century Circuit Rider

RALPH WASHINGTON SOCKMAN *(October 1, 1889—   ). Born in Mount Vernon, Ohio; attended district schools; graduated from Fredericktown High School, Ohio, in 1906; Ohio Wesleyan University, B.A., 1911; studied liberal arts curriculum; speech classes under Robert Isaac Fulton; active in extra-class speech activities and Delta Sigma Rho; Columbia University, M.A. 1913, Ph.D. 1917; majored in history of thought and culture and in political science; graduated from Union Theological Seminary, 1916; studied preaching under Harry Emerson Fosdick; holds numerous honorary degrees; minister, Madison Avenue Methodist Episcopal Church (now Christ Church, Park Avenue at Sixtieth Street), since 1917; preacher, National Radio Pulpit, since 1936; Lyman Beecher lecturer at Yale, 1941; visiting professor of homiletics at Yale, 1947-1948; associate professor of practical theology at Union Theological Seminary, since 1950; chaplain of New York University, since 1944; trustee of a number of colleges and universities; extensive lecturer before business, civic, educational, and religious groups; author of numerous volumes of sermons and other religious books.*

Ralph Washington Sockman
Twentieth Century Circuit Rider

FRED J. BARTON*

A UNIQUE PREACHING CAREER

IT WAS an Easter morning, April 1, 1956. More than two thousand people had gathered in the Byzantine-styled Christ Church, at the corner of New York's Park Avenue and Sixtieth Street. Hymns and prayers and liturgy comprised the first half of the nine o'clock worship program, but after the singing of Handel's "Hallelujah Chorus," in which the congregation joined the choir, the preacher arose and moved deliberately to his place. The crowd stirred expectantly as he adjusted a lapel microphone, and then hushed as his eyes met theirs. The preacher began, slowly, and in a deep, well-modulated conversational voice: "According to the gospel the Easter news began in a garden."[1]

The sermon concluded; the service ended. The people were ushered through exits at the side, to make room for the lines awaiting the second service at ten o'clock—and to ponder the preacher's Easter thoughts.

Other New York churches were crowded on that day. The Riverside Church, St. Patrick's, the Fifth Avenue Presbyterian Church[2]—these and others reported overflow attendance at multiple services. The uniqueness of the program at Christ Church was, therefore, not in the capacity crowds nor in the Easter message, but in the fact that Ralph W. Sockman was that day preaching his fortieth Easter sermon to the congregation he had served as a min-

* Fred J. Barton (B.A. Abilene Christian College 1937, M.A. 1939, Ph.D. 1949, State University of Iowa) is dean of the Graduate School at Abilene Christian College, Abilene, Texas.

ister since 1917. He was beginning the fortieth year of what was already the longest pastorate in the annals of the Methodist Church.[3]

As early as 1924, one of Sockman's sermons had been included in Joseph Fort Newton's volume, *Best Sermons, 1924*, which introduced him as "an outstanding example of the New Preaching," and prophesied for him "a ministry . . . of wise and constructive leadership in a confused and difficult time."[4] In 1929 Sockman's Madison Avenue Church sold the home it had occupied since 1881, and purchased property one block east, at the corner of Park Avenue and Sixtieth Street.[5] In spite of the depression, the building planned for the new site was completed in 1933, the $3,000,000.00 Christ Church[6] consolidating the Madison Avenue and East Sixty-fourth Street Methodist Episcopal churches. In the first sermon preached in the new edifice, Sockman called attention to the strategic position of the church, at the geographical center of New York City and "at the gateway to America." He promised, "this is to be Christ's Church in the city of New York, limited by no local, national, nor denominational boundaries, seeking only to be a place where men may meet Christ."[7]

Newton's prophecy for Sockman has in part been fulfilled through his role in the National Radio Pulpit. In 1948 a *New York Times* reporter wrote: "If asked to guess the oldest program on the air, many listeners no doubt would think of Amos 'n Andy or the Cities' Service Hour. Actually, the honor falls to a strictly religious program—the National Radio Pulpit, which today [May 9, 1948] starts its twenty-sixth year on N.B.C." This program dates back to May 6, 1923, when S. Parkes Cadman began a series of broadcasts sponsored by the Bedford Branch of the Y.M.C.A. in Brooklyn. When the Federal Council assumed sponsorship of the program in 1928, Ralph Sockman was selected as Cadman's summer replacement in the weekly series.[8] It was but natural, therefore, that upon Cadman's death in 1936 Sockman should become the regular minister for the program.[9] The success of his efforts is evidenced by a *Time Magazine* report in 1946 which, in volume of fan mail, rated him "the No. 1 Protestant radio pastor of the U. S."[10] In 1956 the Broadcasting and Film Commission of the National Council estimated the number of listeners "conservatively at about five million."[11]

The years have further fulfilled Joseph Fort Newton's prophecy.

They have been busy, fruitful, and rewarding years. In addition to the regular weekly sermons, pastoral duties, administration of the affairs of his congregation of two thousand members, and the weekly radio sermons, he has produced fifteen books,[12] a television series of thirteen films, distributed on a sustaining basis by the National Council,[13] and a weekly syndicated column, distributed by General Features Corporation since March, 1951, and carried by a growing list of newspapers.[14] He has been associate professor of practical theology at Union Theological Seminary since July, 1950;[15] holds membership on the governing boards of seven colleges, universities, and seminaries;[16] conducts a lecture program before church, school, civic, and business groups, that in the first six months of 1956 included more than eighty speaking engagements in twenty states, the District of Columbia, and Canada;[17] plays an important role in the world-wide program of his denomination, which would more than once have made him bishop had he not declined in favor of his church and radio pulpits;[18] and participates actively in many other church and civic affairs. "Moving with relaxed urbanity through a round of activity that would faze most captains of industry,"[19] Ralph Sockman has become a twentieth century circuit rider. His circuit is the North American continent, and he makes his rounds by air.

THE MAKING OF THE PREACHER

Ralph Washington Sockman was born in Mt. Vernon, Ohio, October 1, 1889, the son of Rigdon Potter Sockman, a farmer and building contractor, and Harriet Ash Sockman. His parents as well as his grandparents, Washington and Esther Sockman, were prominent in the Methodist Church, so that strong religious influences surrounded his early life.

Sockman's speech training also began at an early age, encouraged principally by his mother. As a small boy he began giving recitations, and remembers that at least he had a loud voice![20] His first public performance apparently came at the age of six, when he recited on a children's program at church. But that performance held little foretaste of the future, as a witness reports, "he choked and stammered and almost failed!"[21] In high school, Sockman took a general liberal arts course,[22] and speech training came only in extra-cur-

ricular orations and declamations. Sockman once humorously remarked that his first audiences were his father's cows,[23] and he recalled for this writer that as he used to go back into the pasture and
drive the cows home, when nobody could hear him he would "let
off" his voice and exercise it. A friend who worked for Sockman's
father during his high school days, reports that Ralph "was a very
good student, with a wonderful memory. . . . I would often hear him
in the haymow reciting his oration, while helping with the chores."[24]
Sockman graduated from Fredericktown High School, Ohio, in
1906, probably little dreaming that in 1956 he would return to deliver the address at the fiftieth anniversary of his own commencement.

Ralph Sockman's formal speech training began at Ohio Wesleyan
University, and the years at Delaware, Ohio, were significant for his
later development as a preacher. Robert Isaac Fulton, eminent elo-
cutionist of the day, had established at Ohio Wesleyan one of the
earliest schools of elocution and oratory to receive full academic
status.[25] The college catalogue offered forty-five term hours of
credit in elocution and oratory, and Sockman accumulated thirty-
six term hours and six credits, the largest number of hours in any
one department except Greek. His formal speech courses included:
principles of elocution, argumentation and debate, rhetorical criticism, oratory, and Shakespeare; but about one-third of his credits
were earned in extra-curricular debate and other contest work.[26]
He was active in Friday evening literary societies. In his senior year
he was on the Syracuse debate team; was a member of the student
senate; and was president of the Senior Lecture Course Committee,
of the Debate and Oratory Council, of the Social Service League,
and of the Amphictyonians Literary Society.[27] These extra-class
activities, also under the direction of Professor Fulton, earned membership in Delta Sigma Rho, and are considered by Sockman to have
contributed more to his public speaking development than did the
formal courses.

The years at Ohio Wesleyan no doubt contributed significantly
to the mental powers, the physical poise, and the vocal skills which
mark the mature Sockman, but they did not make him a preacher.
Social science was his major subject interest, in which field he earned
more credits than in religion and philosophy combined.[28] Because

of his speech ability, many friends encouraged him to consider the ministry, but despite these influences, Sockman explains that while in college, "I didn't go with the group who were preparing for the ministry because I wasn't sure."

Thus it was that when Ralph Sockman came to New York in 1911, he brought with him strong religious inclinations and unusually good college training in public speaking—but no preaching experience, and he soon enrolled in Columbia University with the idea of entering the educational field. The possibility of preaching had not been entirely eliminated, however, and graduate study for the next five years was divided between Columbia University and Union Theological Seminary. This program culminated in a master's degree from Columbia, June 4, 1913, a diploma from Union, May 16, 1916, a marriage certificate with Zellah Widmer Endly, June 15, 1916, and a Ph.D. degree from Columbia, June 6, 1917.

At Columbia, Sockman's major was the history of thought and culture. He numbered among his instructors James Harvey Robinson, James T. Shotwell, and Charles A. Beard. The doctor's degree was in political science, with church history credits from Union being offered as one of the minors, and the dissertation topic being "The Revival of the Conventual Life in the Church of England in the Nineteenth Century."[29] Sockman believes that his study of history has given him a method in study. "I approach things," he said, "in a sort of historical way—get the background of it." He feels, too, that taking a doctor's degree has given him a certain amount of discipline in the preparation of both his books and sermons.

At the Seminary, Sockman's largest block of courses was in practical theology and religious education, in which he took eighteen courses for eighteen semester hours credit. The greatest concentration of credits was in church history, with twelve courses in that area, earning twenty-eight semester hours. Ten courses in the New and Old Testaments were good for twenty hours, but only two courses were taken in systematic theolgy. Sockman thus evidenced in these early years the lack of interest in theology *as such*, which has characterized his later preaching.

His principal teachers in the practical field were Harry Emerson Fosdick, Henry Sloan Coffin, G. A. Johnston Ross, and Hugh Black, to whom he feels particularly indebted for the development of his homiletic concepts and habits. With them he studied fundamentals of homiletics, sermon outlines, brief sermons, doctrinal preaching, the use of the Bible in modern preaching, public worship, and parish problems, and from them he received private criticism of his sermons.[30] Ross and Black were from Scotland, and gave him "a certain English, Scottish background." Coffin gave him "a conception of the all-round church—preacher, administrator, pastor." But, said he, "I suppose from the standpoint of just sermonizing, that Dr. Fosdick might be considered my most formative influence." The interview with Sockman was frequently punctuated with "Dr. Fosdick used to say. . . ."

Union Seminary gave Sockman an introduction to preaching, under outstanding, liberal teachers, with an emphasis upon the practical aspects of the preacher's work. In 1916 he was made assistant minister of the Madison Avenue M. E. Church,[31] but was still undecided about the future. In February, 1917, the call came to be pastor of the church, and the decision toward which his life had been inclining was ultimately made. On April 1, 1917, Ralph Sockman, now twenty-seven, preached his first sermon in his first and only pastorate.[32]

THE MAKING OF THE SERMONS

In appraising the needs of the American pulpit in 1938, Ralph Sockman used Bishop William A. Quale's definition of preaching: "Preaching is the art of making a sermon and delivering it? Why, no, that is not preaching. Preaching is the art of making a preacher and delivering that."[33] About ten years later, he wrote in a symposium on *The Ministry*: "A sermon will convey life to its hearers in proportion to the amount of life the preacher has put into it."[34]

These quotations emphasize Sockman's interest in continuing broad experience as a part of preparation for preaching. But he recognizes, too, that ample time must be allotted for the particular preparation of each sermon. He recalls an experience from his early years when he asked a famous minister how he found time, among all his other activities, to prepare his sermons. The preacher replied, "Young man, when you've preached for twenty-five years you'll get a better sermon on Sunday morning after breakfast than you do now in four days. I used to write and rewrite my sermons three or four times, . . . but now I get my text on Saturday night, mull it over in my sub-conscious mind during my sleep, go into my den or study at seven o'clock, have breakfast there, and go into the pulpit—and I preach a better sermon now than I used to in four days." Sockman related this experience to Dr. Fosdick, who replied, "I have just two things to say: first, he doesn't preach better than he did; and second, he couldn't do what he is doing now if he hadn't done that at first!"

Sockman's practice of many years standing is to devote the last three days of each week to preparation of the next Sunday morning's sermon; and he estimates that about eighteen hours of labor go into it.[35] When asked how, in his demanding schedule, he can reserve so much time for sermon preparation, Sockman remarked that every preacher must establish for himself a hierarchy of interests as a guide for his entire ministry. In this respect he has been strongly influenced by the hierarchy of loyalties outlined by Principal P. T. Forsyth of Cambridge:[36] (1) to the gospel, (2) to the local church, (3) to the church at large, and (4) to the public.[37] Such an emphasis on the gospel and the local church restrains the preacher from frittering away his time on secondary matters, and demands careful preparation of each sermon.

Sockman's preparation begins with getting subjects. He reports:

> The ideas of my sermons are sown in the summer. I have always been impressed by the statement of Dr. Harris Kirk, that a minister should let his mind lie fallow for at least one month each year. During the summer vacation I try to let my mind take in what it desires in the way of general reading. This includes biography, devotional literature, and some fiction.
>
> When I return in the fall I have perhaps seventy-five or a hundred sermon themes in my mind. Many of these may never come to fruition, but I frequently go over them to see which ones seem to be sprouting. Thus, I usually can keep my sermon subjects in my schedule about six weeks ahead.[38]

This summer harvest of ideas is supplemented throughout the year by personal and pastoral contacts, including radio audience response; by reading the Bible and such papers as the *The Christian Century* and *The Pulpit;* and by meditation. It is not his practice to carry a sermon idea note-book, except on trips to Europe and the like.

Preparation of the particular sermon begins, then, at the middle of the week, with a more or less specific subject already determined. The first part of the process closely parallels the "rough tabulation of materials and topics" recommended to college speech students by Sarett and Foster.[39] With clean sheets of paper before him Sockman begins to meditate on the subject at hand, and to make one-line notes of related ideas as they appear. The one-line-note sheets preserved with manuscripts of earlier sermons on the same or related themes, are consulted for pertinent material which may not have been used before. He explains further, that his habit "is not to read books through and catalogue their contents, but to scan over each new book and note its general subjects. Thus when I start to prepare a morning sermon, I happen to remember that various books have passages bearing on the theme. Hence I may consult a dozen different books in the course of developing each sermon. I put down one-line notations of the idea, the book, and the page."[40] The notation process continues until there are four to six pages filled with a hundred or more different ideas, related in one degree or another to the sermon theme. For example, the notes for a sermon entitled "Christian Co-existence," preached at Christ Church on July 17, 1955, consisted of six pages containing 124 separate ideas, 59 of which were brought into the sermon outline. The notes included ideas drawn from five earlier sermon folders dating from 1937 to 1954, and from three books, one of which was his own *Date with Destiny*.

As the tabulation process continues, the preacher is usually able to formulate and arrange the main heads. The next step is the selection of the notations considered pertinent to each of these headings, and their arrangement pattern. An appropriate symbol is written in the margin indicating to which point each relevant idea belongs. The process can be illustrated with a few notes from the sermon on "Christian Co-existence":

> 3—unity would be essential for the effective victory of the disciples.
> 3—could they convince the world of the oneness of the human family and yet not be one?
> —as Gandhi said, "The trouble with Xty is the Xns."
> —The Lord's own prayer.
> 2—"The closer we get to X the closer we get together."
> Int—"One Lord, one faith, one baptism."

1—Xns held the world together when the Roman empire was breaking.

When the notes have been numbered, ideas belonging to each heading are copied onto separate sheets. Each point then begins to shape up in terms of subheads and details, providing the outline from which the sermon is written. The outline is not followed slavishly, but serves merely as a suggestive guide. Ordinarily, not more than half of the outlined material finds its way into the sermon, and frequently whole points are omitted.

The outline is usually completed by Friday evening, leaving all day Saturday for writing the sermon,[41] a process which usually continues into the midnight hour. Sockman's study is in his home where he can work alone and with minimum interruptions. He writes in longhand, and remarked that he could not dictate—that the presence of another person "would just spoil it." The longhand manuscript usually runs to around twenty pages, which allows for amplification of illustrations and interpolation when the sermon is preached on Sunday morning. Apparently, Sockman writes carefully and thoughtfully, making alterations as he goes. There are few marginal or between-line changes in the manuscripts. The alterations are largely either the substitution of a more vivid word, or the rewriting of a phrase to make it more pointed or euphonious. For example, typical changes in the manuscript on "Christian Co-existence" are:

And that bond of union (holds) *undergirds* their family relationship.
. . . in joining the church we are (uniting) *linking* our lives with a living force.
. . . (the attic) childhood's attic of memories . . .
(Alliances based on fear and hatred) Fear and hatred are not adequate fusing forces.

Sockman has always written his sermons, and advises his students to do so. He believes that the practice enables him to *see* the idea and to get the precise word. Another advantage, suggested to him by Fosdick, is that the act of writing helps the flow of ideas.

The writing is usually completed around twelve or one o'clock, at which time he reads the sermon through to get it in his mind as a unit. He then retires and sleeps until seven. While resting in bed he reads and thinks the sermon through for an hour and a half before having breakfast. There is no oral rehearsal, although there was in earlier years, and no attempt is made to memorize. The post-manuscript preparation is primarily a matter of fixing ideas and their sequence in mind, and in this he prefers his longhand manuscript to a typewritten draft. At ten o'clock he listens to his transcribed radio sermon, and at ten-thirty retires to the church to make ready for the worship service, strengthened by the assurance of thorough preparation.

A unique postscript must be added to Sockman's preparation schedule. Not only is the sermon repeated at 5:00 P.M. for those who could not be accommodated at the morning hour, but from October to April or May each year the sermons preached at Christ Church are repeated on the National Radio Pulpit. One evening early in the week is usually given to revising the sermon for radio use. The Sunday morning sermons are recorded on wire, from which a secretary prepares a typewritten manuscript. Thus, Sockman reports, "I have before me both my written manuscript which I had prepared for original delivery and also the transcript of what I actually said in the pulpit. Having thus before me what I intended to say, and also, what I actually did say, I try to prepare what I should say."[42] The process is a matter of cutting a thirty-minute address to the fifteen-minute radio time limit, pointing up the transitions, and polishing the style; elements which will be noted in the next section of this study. Sockman observed that he can usually put into the radio sermon most of what he said in the pulpit, but he quotes Mrs. Sockman as saying the result is "something like the difference between a hamburger and a good steak!" Listeners to the National Radio Pulpit for the past twenty years would reply, "The hamburger has all the trimmings!"

THE SERMONS

Ralph Sockman has defined preaching as "discourse developed from divine revelation and designed to move men through and toward the divine will."[43] The preacher is conceived to be a modern prophet, whose inspiration comes through others who seek and find the revelation, through the voice of nature, through the preacher's own mystical insights, through the church, through the Bible, and through Christ as he is revealed in the Bible and experienced in daily living. It is Sockman's opinion that "mystical communion is the greatest single need of the contemporary pulpit," but he calls for a return to the Bible as "the Christian's creative and corrective source of revelation."[44] The preacher is, then, "a minister of the gospel. He is the bearer of a Book."[45] The typical Sockman sermon grows out of a biblical text. Of the thirty-five sermons preached on the National Radio Pulpit from October, 1953, through May, 1954, only two did not have a specific text. Furthermore, from one to eighteen quotations and direct references to scripture appeared in each sermon, with seven as the mean; and there were many more indirect biblical references and allusions.

It is not strange, therefore, that Sockman should call doctrine "the rugged framework of religion."[46] Doctrines are to be preached, however, "not as dry traditions but as life-giving currents of spiritual power";[47] and Sockman's sermons approach doctrine obliquely, if at all. The indirect approach to doctrine contributes a certain theological ambiguity and incompleteness to the sermons. Sockman is, nevertheless, an outspoken critic of the popularization of the pulpit in which theology is replaced by sociology and psychology,[48] and "the contents of doctrine . . . are submerged in the efforts at popular appeal." His sermons encourage men to follow the "Jesus Way of Life";[49] and those parts of the gospel are emphasized which most clearly reveal the personality of Jesus. The non-denominational character of both his church and radio pulpits has apparently led Sockman to discuss those themes which would find the widest acceptance among people of diverse faiths. Such terms as Incarnation, Resurrection, Atonement, Reconciliation, and Salvation occasionally appear, but they are not clearly defined; and "the ultimate questions, the questions concerning final life and final death, did not get much attention."[50]

Forms of support

Ralph Sockman believes with Fénelon that the preacher must prove, as well as picture and move.[51] But the rational approach to religion for which he calls[52] is largely a matter of religious experience rather than argument—a sort of "try-it-and-see" approach. In a sermon preached as early as 1925, at the time of the Scopes trial in Tennessee, Sockman expressed the philosophy which is found in all his subsequent preaching: "Christianity cannot be tried by the jury method, but by the laboratory method. . . . The Truth of the Bible is not proved by courts but by lives. . . . Man is convinced of his divine creation not by arguments . . . , but by the 'evidence of things not seen' which are within his own life when he follows in the footsteps of his Lord."[53] Sockman's frequent appeals to the Bible are more exposition than argument. He recognizes, however, that some hearers "want to know why it is in the Bible." They "want a reason for their faith."

Sockman apparently considers himself more of an *interpreter* than a *defender* of the "Jesus Way of Life"; and since "the true preacher is an artist painting pictures in the mind,"[54] the principal forms of exposition are analogy and illustration. They are frequently personal, and are drawn from all periods of his life. Some are brief; others are more detailed. The following illustrations, only two of many to be found in the same sermon, demonstrate the preacher's prolific power at this point:

> Some consciences are free as a stray dog is free. A stray dog, having no master, will likely follow any passer-by who whistles to it. Similarly many persons fall in behind any passing prejudice or whistling crowd. . . .
> Faith in God protects us with a calming sense of steadying strength. Back in 1940 I was in Mexico City on election day. From my hotel room, I could look down into Constitution Square. All day the shouting partisans surged back and forth in groups. At about four o'clock in the afternoon some bullets began to fly. But above the mob in the distance I could see the snowclad peaks of two great extinct volcanoes, Popocatepetl and Ixtacihuatl. Their majestic summits rising above the shouting turbulent crowds reminded me of the Psalmist's words: "I lift up my eyes to the hills, whence does my help come? My help comes from the Lord who made heaven and earth." The mountains stood so silent and strong in contrast to the noisy restless people and I felt like saying with Emerson, "Why so hot, little man?"[55]

This final quotation also exemplifies the effectiveness with which illustrations are interwoven with the biblical and literary quotations which form such a large part of Sockman's amplification.

The rational Sockman approach to religion leaves little room for obvious emotional appeals, and he has no place for "the superficial methods of certain flamboyant evangelists."[56] His sermons seldom call for immediate and overt response, but attempt to challenge the listener to more responsible personal and social life. This does not mean, however, that Sockman's sermons carry no emotional impact. Strong undercurrents stem from both the challenging themes discussed and the ethical qualities of the preacher himself. These are supplemented by appeals to human motivations, in which fear and hope of reward are dismissed in favor of responsibility and service. The following example provides insight into Sockman's use of motivation: The sermon answers the question, "Why is it more blessed to give than to receive?" and the first answer is that "through giving we get the satisfaction of *self-fulfillment*"; the second reason is that "*it strengthens us by standing up to life's demands*"; the third is that "we get the blessing of *extending our usefulness*"; and the fourth is that "we get the blessing of *living beyond our own years*." These challenges may be supported by strong appeals to a sense of responsibility: "Isn't there some chord in us that responds to the iron string of duty? I believe there is. I believe that strong characters want to stand up to responsibilities." Or they may be strengthened by more tender appeals to compassion: "Suppose we never had a chance to give to anyone. Suppose we could never give to our children, never see their eyes dance with joy at something we do for them. Suppose you saw a little child struck down in front of your house by a passing truck. There it lies, limp and bleeding, turning its large round eyes of pain imploringly toward you, before the tears begin to flow, and you could not give any aid whatsoever."[57] Whether or not the Sockman sermons have evangelistic appeal, the man who wants to live a fuller life will find incentive in them.

Organization

A speech teacher wrote in 1955: "Dr. Sockman . . . is a speech professor's dream in clarity of organization."[58] That statement is hardly an exaggeration. Sockman believes that "there are always enough people in your congregation who want to see the sermon structure" to justify careful attention to it.

> When I began with this church, I had the idea of a pretty precise formula. One of my laymen, a lawyer, was the son of a bishop, and after about a year of my preaching, he said,

"Sockman, I'll give you a suggestion that helped my father. My father was a professor of mathematics at Northwestern University before he became a preacher, and he wanted his sermons to be very logical. But an old man told him, 'Look here, ——, people don't remember your outline—they just remember those little emotional hot spots.' My father deliberately cultivated some emotional hot spots in his sermons, and greatly improved his preaching."

Well, Sockman reminisced, I thought, "I'll do that next Sunday." So I cultivated some hot spots, and a good old dowager here said, "Dr Sockman, we had a preacher here who told about two stories like that every Sunday. He only lasted a year!"

Sockman's sermons indicate that he reverted to his "precise formula," which is the traditional one of introduction, thesis, body, and conclusion.

The introductions vary in length, and on occasion may consist of only three or four sentences. Such brevity is not typical, however, and the introductions normally comprise from one-fifth to one-third of the entire sermon. The primary purposes of the introduction are apparently to stimulate interest and attention, to establish rapport between speaker and audience, and to announce the subject. The sermon, "Big Persons in Little Places," illustrates the pattern most frequently followed. The speaker begins by telling the story of two brothers, one of whom proved to be a "little person in a big place," and the other a "big person in a small place." This situation leads to an announcement of the general theme. God's attitude toward persons is contrasted with man's weakness in this respect, and the text, Exodus 3:4-5, is introduced by a contextual background. The relation of the text to the sermon theme is then revealed in a clear statement of the thesis: "Even little places can become holy ground on which God touches men to greatness."[59] Into this pattern are frequently inserted expressions of personal appreciation and purpose.

Almost without exception there is an explicit statement of purpose in the form of a thesis. Although the thesis may be stated more than once, its typical position makes it a transition from the introduction to the first main head of the sermon body. Sometimes it appears as an affirmative statement, as in the preceding paragraph;

sometimes it is in question form: "What are the works which Christ did and expects us to do?"[60] The thesis frequently includes words of the text or of the sermon title, and through it the sermon theme clearly emerges.

The steps by which the body of the sermon supports the theme are generally as explicit as the original purpose statement. A partitioning of the *text* sometimes provides the main heads,[61] but the topical pattern of division is typical. In the sermon "Televising the Soul," the main heads were stated in the following manner:

> First of all, we need the eyes of our hearts to be enlightened *in order to see ourselves*. . . .
> And secondly, after we have opened the eyes of our hearts to see ourselves, we are then more ready to open our eyes *to see our neighbors*. . . .
> And as the eyes of our hearts are opened to see ourselves and to see our neighbors, may they also be enlightened to see Our Heavenly Father. . . .[62]

This example also illustrates the summary and transitional elements included in the statement of the main heads, which contribute to the clarity of organization. They are normally supplemented by short summary paragraphs at the end of each division. The subheads are less obvious than the main points to which they are subordinated, but they, too, are usually not difficult to discover.

Sockman's conclusions are less well defined than the other parts of the sermon. "I never like to get through with a sermon and say, 'Now what I've been trying to say is this'—then sum it up at the end. . . . I try, when I get to the last point, to gather up what I have said, and then just hurl the last point . . . and conclude it with a fling." Of the 1953-54 sermons referred to earlier, almost half concluded with the development of the last main head. Perhaps the typical Sockman practice of transitional summaries eliminates the need for review at the end. At any rate, final summaries seldom appear except in a restatement of the text or thesis. In Sockman's opinion, such practice contributes to the movement and momentum of the sermon. The final "fling" frequently includes a quotation or an illustration. It varies in length and in method, but its purpose is invariably to stamp the central thought on the hearer's conscience. Thus, the typical Sockman sermon moves toward a climax. The theme emerges at the beginning, is pointed up in transitional elements, and builds through relevant divisions to a restatement at the end. It would be difficult for a hearer to miss the point.

Language

One critic's observation that Ralph Sockman "scintillates for the intelligentsia"[63] is perhaps more clever than just. But the description of him as a man who "looks like a successful lawyer and talks like the man next door,"[64] depends on the neighborhood. Baird has said that "his language is brisk, personal, unhackneyed, vivid, and well adapted to radio, as well as to his face-to-face cosmopolitan audiences."[65] Sockman does not refuse a word merely because it contains three or four syllables. But at the same time there is an absence of technical terms and phrases. One audience-analysis study indicates that Sockman's radio audience consists largely of people with from seven to eleven or more years of schooling, many of whom have had graduate training; as compared with Charles E. Fuller's "Old Fashioned Revival Hour," which seems to attract people with less than a high school education.[66] But sermon content and general program format are probably more responsible for this difference than the language.

Sockman's sermons abound in the use of personal pronouns. He identifies himself with his hearers and maintains intimate contact with even his radio audiences. Another frequently appearing technique is alliteration: ". . . irresponsible wildness soon wearies"; or "It [the church] offers the longest lever of helpfulness." Alliteration often makes the main heads easier to remember, as when the "three R's of Readiness for the Best" were called Responsiveness, Responsibility, and Resourcefulness. The element of style most frequently noticed by reporters is the terse, epigrammatic sentence, such as, "He was a little person in a big place"; or "A succession of 'large evenings' does not make the abundant life." But contrasting words and antithetical phrases and sentences also comprise a standing stock-in-trade: "Wishful thinking might imagine a God to die *with*, but hardly a God to die *for*"; and, "Christ fought the evil but loved the evil-doers. We fight the evil-doers and then keep the evil. We kill the warriors but preserve the war system." The speech critic knows that there is a point in speech analysis at which style and forms of support overlap or merge; and Sockman's sermons demonstrate how the happily chosen word or figure can help the speaker to prove, to picture, and to move: "Some persons are like houses with their doors and windows open in the winter time. They hold no warming convictions"; or "There must be Divine guidance in the traffic of the Milky Way."[67]

These examples of Sockman style have been taken from radio sermons, and perhaps the reader should be reminded that they were prepared for radio after having been written earlier, but preached extemporaneously at Christ Church. A comparison of these three "editions" of the same sermon reveals that the radio sermon closely follows the original manuscript, except for editing the references to local persons, times, and places, and cutting supporting details to accommodate the fifteen-minute radio time-limit. On the other hand, the extemporaneous sermon follows the longhand manuscript in only a general way. Amplification varies by expanding or reducing, or by leaving out certain details and inserting new ones. With particular reference to style, the words of the extemporaneous sermon are less specific than the others, the sentences are more loosely put together, the epigrams are less sharply drawn, and the figures less vividly portrayed. The following brief example comes from the sermon, "The Rich Full Life," preached at Christ Church, January 3, 1954, and on the National Radio Pulpit, February 7, 1954:

LONGHAND MANUSCRIPT

We cannot get the whole of ourselves into our work or our play or our human loves. The fruitless attempt results in a cramp of the soul which hardens into a permanent contracture unless we relieve it by a soul-stretch, somewhat as a tired man gives when he opens arms and legs and stretches his body.

Worship is the stretch of the soul to relieve the cramp of of our natures which have been confined to matters too small for them.

EXTEMPORANEOUS SERMON AT CHRIST CHURCH

When we try to put the whole of ourselves into any segment of our work, or of our play, or of our family loves, it cramps our nature and will contract our nature until we sometimes stretch the soul, just as a man has to stretch his arms and legs to keep from getting cramped and contracted.

Worship is the stretch of the soul toward the wholeness of life.

RADIO SERMON

We cannot put the whole of ourselves into our work, our play, or our human loves. The fruitless attempt results in a cramp of the soul which hardens into a permanent contracture, unless we relieve it by a soul-stretch, as a tired man gives when he opens arms and legs and stretches his body.

Worship is the stretch of the soul to relieve the cramp of our natures which have been confined to matters too small for them.

Delivery

Although Sockman's radio sermons are read from manuscript, he preaches extemporaneously in Christ Church. He never carries a manuscript into the pulpit with him, except for the quotations, which are deliberately read for the sake of accuracy. Sockman believes that a manuscript gets between the preacher and the people, overcoming any stylistic advantage which might be gained from sermon reading. In both in-church and radio preaching, his aim is exalted conversation. "I try to make it conversational, with just a little louder tone and more distinct utterance."

Sockman has two habits which give a certain indistinctness to his conversational speech. First, occasional phrases are thrown out at such a rapid rate that words and syllables are run together; and secondly, on long inflections the intensity level frequently drops below the threshold of intelligibility. Sockman is aware of these faults, and largely overcomes them in preaching. They appear infrequently in the extemporaneous sermons, and hardly at all in the sermons read over the radio. As a result, Sockman "is unusually effective in vocal abilities."[68] His voice uses a wide pitch and intensity range, and has many rising inflections. It is a dramatically flexible and expressive voice—a dynamic, urgent voice which says to the hearer, "This is vital. Listen!"

Ralph Sockman is a tall, well-groomed, distinguished looking man. He stands erect in the pulpit, with a quiet and contagious air of assurance. A magnetic speaker-audience contact continues throughout the sermon. A lapel microphone allows liberty of movement, but movement is not excessive. Action and gesture are not planned but are a spontaneous part of the sermon. Large, restrained and unhurried gestures are an important part of the delivery pattern. A hand may occasionally find its way into a pocket; or both hands may grasp the coat lapels. The entire experience appears effortless, and Sockman confessed to this writer that the physical act of speaking is not tiring for him—that the preparation is the wearying chore. Surely there are few, if indeed any other, American public speakers at mid-twentieth century who so completely demonstrate oral communciation at its best.

Much time must pass before Ralph Sockman's work can be fully evaluated. The estimate of his own generation is found in this citation which in 1954 accompanied an honorary degree from Columbia University, one of the fifteen such honors conferred upon him by American colleges and universities:

> *Ralph Washington Sockman*: An eloquent voice, fearless, intelligent, tolerant, and respected across the land; a scholar proudly claimed as alumnus by this university; for nearly four decades filling a distinguished pulpit in this city, applying with meaningful force to problems of the day the eternal truths of God; in the community giving generously of his talents in causes that enrich men's lives; a spiritual leader, a light that glows more brightly with the years.[69]

Footnotes

1. Ralph W. Sockman, "The Goal Beyond the Grave," Easter Sermon at Christ Church (April 1, 1956), tape transcription.
2. *New York Times*, April 2, 1956, p. 14.
3. *New York Times*, March 22, 1941, p. 18.
4. Joseph Fort Newton, ed., *Best Sermons, 1924* (New York, 1924), p. 66.
5. *New York Times*, April 29, 1929, p. 1.
6. *New York Times*, November 18, 1933, p. 16; November 27, 1933, p. 19; "Most Lavish Church is Most Democratic," *Literary Digest*, CXVII (March 17, 1934), 20.
7. *New York Times*, November 5, 1933, I, p. 5; November 20, 1933, p. 3.
8. *New York Times*, May 9, 1948, II, p. 9; September 26, 1928, p. 1; September 27, 1928, p. 31; December 6, 1928, p. 5; June 2, 1929, IX, p. 15.
9. "The Air's Oldest Pulpit," *Newsweek*, XXX (October 13, 1947), 74.
10. "Radio Religion," *Time*, XLVII (January 21, 1946), 74, 76.
11. Information in a letter to the author from Wesley B. Goodman, Associate Executive Director, Broadcasting and Film Commission, National Council of Churches of Christ, New York, April 18, 1956.
12. "Ralph W. Sockman," *Who's Who in America*, 1950-1951, XXVI (Chicago, 1950), 2850; 1956-1957, XXIX (Chicago, 1956), 2410.

13. Letter from Goodman, May 3, 1956; brochures distributed by the Broadcasting and Film Commission.
14. Information in a letter to the author from Robert L. Morgan, Assistant Editor, General Features Corporation, New York, April 27, 1956; and brochures distributed by General Features.
15. *New York Times*, January 11, 1950, p. 13.
16. *Best Sermons, 1951-52*, ed. G. Paul Butler (New York, 1952), pp. 1-2.
17. Carbon copy of official engagement itinerary.
18. *New York Times*, June 3, 1944, p. 14; June 18, 1948, p. 24; June 9, 1952, p. 25.
19. "Practical Pastor," *Time*, LV (January 23, 1950), 53.
20. Personal interview with Dr. Sockman, in New York, April 2, 1956. Subsequent details not specifically footnoted are from this interview.
21. Information in a letter to the author from Arthur O. Wyker, Mt. Vernon, Ohio, May 23, 1956.
22. Official transcript from Ohio Wesleyan University.
23. Sockman, *The Whole Armor of God* (New York, 1955), p. 56.
24. Information in a letter to the author from Mr. Tom C. Balcom, Mt. Vernon, Ohio, May 21, 1956.
25. Marie Hochmuth and Richard Murphy, "Rhetorical and Elocutionary Training in Nineteenth-Century Colleges," *A History of Speech Education in America*, ed. Karl R. Wallace *et al.* (New York, 1954), pp. 163, 171.
26. Ohio Wesleyan transcript.
27. Ohio Wesleyan annual, *Le Bijou* (1911).
28. Ohio Wesleyan transcript.
29. Official transcripts from Columbia University and Union Theological Seminary.
30. Union transcript.
31. *Current Biography, Who's Who and Why*, ed. Anna Rothe (New York, 1946), p. 561.
32. *New York Times*, February 24, 1917, p. 16; June 9, 1952, p. 25.
33. Sockman, *Recoveries in Religion* (Nashville, 1938), pp. 268-269.
34. Sockman, "The Minister's Work as Preacher," *The Ministry*, ed. J. Richard Spann (New York, 1949), p. 78. Hereafter referred to as *Spann*.
35. Sockman, "A Statement of My Method," *Here is My Method, The Art of Sermon Construction*, ed. Donald Macleod (Westwood, N. J., 1952), p. 182. Hereafter referred to as *Macleod*.
36. Spann, p. 79.
37. P. T. Forsyth, *Positive Preaching and the Modern Mind*, Yale Lectures for 1907 (New York, 1907).
38. Macleod, p. 181.
39. Lew Sarett and W. T. Foster, *Basic Principles of Speech* (New York, 1946), pp. 335-341.
40. Macleod, p. 182.
41. Charles A. McGlon, "How I Prepare My Sermons: A Symposium," *The Quarterly Journal of Speech*, XL (February, 1954), 55; Macleod, p. 182.
42. McGlon, p. 55.
43. Spann, p. 79.
44. Sockman, *The Highway of God*, Yale Lectures for 1941 (New York, 1942), pp. 77-100, 84, 89. Hereafter referred to as *Highway*.
45. Spann, pp. 73-74.

46. Interview.
47. Spann, pp. 75-76.
48. *New York Times*, February 15, 1937, p. 20.
49. *Highway*, pp. 35, 54.
50. Julian N. Hartt, "Analysis of Program Content, National Radio Pulpit; . . ." Appendix A, *The Television-Radio Audience and Religion*, Everett C. Parker *et al.* (New York, 1955), p. 421.
51. Spann, p. 73.
52. Sockman, "Higher Religion for Higher Education," *Vital Speeches*, XIV (March 1, 1948), 304-308; "Make Up Your Mind," *Vital Speeches*, XVI (October 1, 1950), 762-763.
53. *New York Times*, June 22, 1925, p. 18.
54. Spann, p. 76.
55. *National Radio Pulpit*, "The Shield of Faith," (April 4, 1954). These sermons are published in booklet form, and distributed without charge by the Broadcasting and Film Commission of the National Council of Churches, 220 Fifth Avenue, New York City.
56. Spann, p. 78.
57. *National Radio Pulpit*, "The Help That Heals" (November 15, 1953).
58. Gregg Phifer, "The Organization of Sockman's Sermons," *The Speaker*, XXXVII (March, 1955), 13-16.
59. *National Radio Pulpit*, "Big Persons in Little Places" (October 18, 1953).
60. *National Radio Pulpit*, "The Call and the Promise" (December 6, 1953).
61. *National Radio Pulpit*, "Where Faith Begins" (November 1, 1953); *National Radio Pulpit*, "To See Life Whole" (February 28, 1954).
62. *National Radio Pulpit*, "Televising the Soul" (December 27, 1953).
63. John R. Scotford, "No More Great Preachers," *The Pulpit*, XXII (March, 1951), 20.
64. "Radio Religion," 76.
65. A. Craig Baird, ed. *Representative American Speeches: 1946-1947* (New York, 1947), p. 271.
66. *The Television-Radio Audience and Religion*, pp. 220-221.
67. *National Radio Pulpit*, "The Help That Heals" (November 15, 1953); "The Sword of the Spirit" (April 25, 1954); "Ready for the Best" (January 31, 1954); "Big Persons in Little Places" (October 18, 1953); "The Whole Man in a Broken World" (November 29, 1953); "The Seeds of Hope" (November 22, 1953); "The Sandals of Peace" (March 28, 1954); "Life's Loose Ends" (October 11, 1953); "God's Guidance" (May 23, 1954).
68. Baird, p. 271.
69. *New York Times*, June 2, 1954, p. 34.

THE STATE

Albert Baird Cummins
An Analysis of a Logical Speaker

ALBERT BAIRD CUMMINS *(February 15, 1850—July 30, 1926). Born near Carmichaels, Pennsylvania; attended district schools; for three years attended Waynesburg College, Pennsylvania; financed himself by working as carpenter, farm hand, school teacher; after college continued work as carpenter, express office clerk, surveyor, and engineer; in 1873 began study of law in offices of McClellan and Hodges, Chicago; admitted to the bar in 1875; moved to Des Moines, Iowa, and in 1881 associated himself with the law firm of G. G. Wright and Sons; senior member in 1886 of same firm which eventually came to be known as Cummins, Hewitt, and Wright; chosen attorney to represent the Farmers' Protective Association in the famous barbed wire case; elected to lower house of state legislature in 1888; candidate for office of United States senator in 1894; achieved national reputation in the campaign of 1896 for his work as Republican national committeeman; candidate again in 1900 for office of United States senator; ran for office of governor; elected three times and served from 1902-1908; opposed Senator Allison in 1908 but defeated in the June primaries; upon death of Allison before general election, and after winning special primary election, appointed United States senator by the legislature and served from 1908-1926; elected president pro tempore of the United States Senate in 1919; defeated in 1926 primaries by Smith W. Brookhart, but died before his term of office expired; widely proposed in the press in 1908 as candidate for office of president of the United States; nominated in Republican national convention for this office in 1912 and again in 1916.*

Albert Baird Cummins
An Analysis of a Logical Speaker

ELBERT W. HARRINGTON*

FOR more than a quarter of a century Albert Baird Cummins battled in the political arena. At first he led the reform elements in his state; then, as governor, he not only attacked with vigor the local problems of Iowa, but he became a recognized leader on the subjects of reciprocity and the control of monopolies. Later in the United States Senate he quickly achieved a position of responsibility and prominence. Finally, he had dangled before his eyes the greatest political prize of all, the presidency of the country.

To achieve his ends he was forced at the beginning of his career to defy the leaders of his party and appeal directly to the people. At all times he relied heavily upon his ability as a speaker. He was equally at home in the hustings of the campaign, in the selected situations of occasional speaking, and in the halls of the United States Senate. Although he was not an orator of the old school, he gained both renown and respect as an effective speaker.[1]

The major reasons for his impressive record in speaking were his choice of issues which grew naturally out of his background and experiences, his thorough preparation as a speaker, and his desire to bring his audiences to a clear understanding of his themes. In these respects Cummins makes an excellent case study.

THE ISSUES HE CHOSE

Primarily Cummins was interested in domestic questions that had a governmental and economic basis; only incidentally did he

* Elbert W. Harrington (A.B. Iowa State Teachers College 1926, M.A. 1930, Ph.D. 1938, State University of Iowa) is professor of speech and dean of the College of Arts and Sciences at the University of South Dakota.

concern himself with international affairs unless, as with the tariff, he felt they affected the solution of a domestic problem.

In the field of government, he stressed the desirability and necessity of expansion. To him history presented the spectacle of socialists forging ahead; individualists holding back, with the vast mass of humanity, trusting in empiricism, advancing at one time, receding the next, but "upon the whole, enlarging the field of government, and narrowing that of the individual."[2] Yet he never became a socialist in the strict sense of the term. In 1919 he came close to adopting federal ownership as a policy for the railroads, but, to the disappointment of many of his early followers, in the final Esch-Cummins law he yielded whatever views he may have had about ownership in favor of a policy of consolidation and rate-making.

Much of this expansion of government, he felt, should occur within the national framework. Cummins was no states-righter. "The fear of centralization," said he, "is one, drawn not from a logical survey of man as he is, but from the dim traditions of a century just emerged from the long and universal reign of despotism."[3] Following this philosophy he argued to give Congress power to deal with the law of negotiable instruments, of descent of property, of marriage and divorce. He advocated national solutions to the problems of capital and labor and federal incorporation of railroads.

Regardless of the unit of government involved, Cummins insisted that it find its source in the people. Throughout his life he worked in this tradition, fighting for the Iowa primary law, finally passed in 1908, advocating the direct election of senators and nomination of the president and vice president in primaries, insisting on a strong and virile national law-making body that would not be subservient to a strong executive, supporting in a moderate way the initiative and referendum, arguing and voting for women suffrage, opposing the practice of lame duck congresses, and combating various forms of corporation control of politics and excessive expenditures for political purposes.

The proper control of corporations was one of Cummins' biggest issues. His chief concern was that business should never reach the point where it could corrupt public officials or threaten the interests of either investor or consumer. As governor he advocated that capital stock be paid for at par in money; he recommended laws prohibiting corporation campaign contributions; he inveighed against political lobbyists; he insisted that the tariff be adjusted to preserve the principle of free competition; he struck out at free passes and discrimination by the railroads among individuals, localities, and states. As senator he was one of the leaders to speak for the Federal Trade Commission and the Clayton Act. He took a principal part, following World War I, in returning the railroads to private control under a system of regulation.

Although he believed in protection, he felt that tariff duties should not be any higher than the difference between cost of production here and abroad minus the cost of transportation. Reciprocity was simply another means of regulating business. From the beginning of his senatorial career Cummins was a leader in tariff reform, and the efforts of men like him, La Follette, Beveridge, and others were notable examples of legislative debating at its best.

In international affairs he was an isolationist but not a pacifist. He entered into the war effort wholeheartedly. At the close of the war he opposed the entrance of the United States into the League of Nations. Later he supported, in a moderate way, adherence to the World Court.[4]

The above analysis outlines the ideas Cummins used for speech making. What kind of pattern do they make? How consistent are they one with another?

From a major premise that people should control the machinery of government he argued for direct primary elections, direct election of United States senators, direct nominations of the president and vice president, elimination of party caucuses, prohibition of free passes by railroads, regulation of corporate campaign contributions and lobbying, and maintenance of legislative authority against the encroaching power of the executive.

From a major premise of expanding national government he spoke for federal regulation of child labor, marriage and divorce, railroads, and capital and labor. He advocated reciprocity, tariff protection, and railroad consolidation because he believed national considerations should outweigh local ones. On the other hand, basic in his philosophy was the major premise that competition is an essential requirement of our capitalistic system. From this premise he spoke for tariff reform and the break-up of monopolies.

From a major premise that the nation should not give up any major part of its sovereignty he opposed the League of Nations, although he supported the World Court with reservations.

Aside from the criticism that he might have extended his ideas of nationalism into the area of internationalism, his ideas show a fine sense of consistency. They may be briefed in typical debate brief form, and the basic assumptions underlying the premises can stand the test of light. They form a consistent, harmonious whole. It is important that a single speech stand the test of briefing, but it is more significant that the complete philosophy of a man stand a similar test.

Preparation for Speech Making

An investigation of Cummins' background shows that he had prepared all his life to discuss these ideas.

Many factors combined to make him a democrat. Members of his ancestral stock had served in the American Revolution and had signed the Mecklenburg Declaration of Independence. His father was a farmer, carpenter, contractor, Republican, and Presbyterian.[5] Albert Baird was the oldest of eleven children. A turn at the district school and three years at Waynesburg College (Pennsylvania), during which he worked his way as carpenter, farm hand, and teacher, completed his formal education. Coming west from Pennsylvania, he worked as carpenter, express office clerk, assistant surveyor, engineer, and finally lawyer. By his own efforts he became one of the ablest attorneys of the nation.[6]

His democratic background helped him to become a reformer, but other specific circumstances also led him to assume this role. He early gained a state-wide and even national reputation for integrity, courage, and ability when he smashed the barbed wire trust as attorney for the Farmers' Protective Association. In 1888 he ran as an independent Republican for a seat in the lower house of the state legislature and won. He caught a glimpse of his life's goal as a candidate for the United States Senate in 1894. By political juggling he was set aside again as a candidate for the same office in 1900, but this time, with aroused ire, he defied the leaders of his party.

Building his own machine, he won election as governor three times before the opportunity finally came in 1908 to become United States senator. To achieve all of these ambitions he was forced to seek the support of and to unify the reform elements of his state.

Cummins' basic philosophy was thus shaped in part by forces outside of his control, but he added to these factors by acquiring a self-made general education. He never finished at Waynesburg College, and he gained his legal education in a private office; but although he was not a proverbial bookworm, he was a fairly wide general reader and in some areas a deep reader. His legal and private libraries were spoken of as the "choicest and largest in the state."[7] He turned naturally to history, politics, biography, and especially to English history. He was fond of fiction with a historical background. His speeches and his library indicate that he was not deeply acquainted with art, music, poetry, literature, or philosophy; and doubtless he could have been a better speaker had he a greater interest in these fields of learning.

His speeches invariably contained a fund of specific information. His colleague, Senator Joseph T. Robinson, spoke of Cummins' capacity for research and added, "when he arose to speak it was recognized that his address would supply valuable information."[8]

ADAPTATION TO AUDIENCES

A review of all of Cummins' speeches, both popular and in the Senate, shows that his selection of ideas for his audiences did not differ materially from the ideas he himself accepted because of natural interest and background. To his popular audiences he spoke chiefly on reciprocity, tariff reduction, regulation of business along the lines of competition, regulation of railroads, and popularization of government. To his senate colleagues he delivered major speeches on postal savings banks, the income tax, the metal schedule, the sugar schedule, the cotton schedule, the woolen schedule, the court of commerce, Canadian reciprocity, the American Tobacco Company, Panama Canal Tolls Act, the term of office of the president of the United States, the Clayton Anti-Trust Bill, railroad rates, child labor, government manufacture of munitions, armed merchant vessels, foreign policy, war with Germany, coordination of executive bureaus and agencies, federal control of railroads, the League of Nations, peace with Germany, and cooperative marketing.

These ideas grew naturally out of his background and education; yet he did not advocate these measures without some adjustment to his general audience. He stressed tariff reduction, reciprocity, regulation of business and popularization of government when these ideas were popular in his state. On the other hand, when Iowans lost interest in reciprocity, Cummins ceased to talk about the subject and even opposed President Taft on the issue. With the exception of the Transportation Act of 1920, Cummins happened to be on the popular side (with the people although not always with his party's leaders) of every major issue he discussed.[9]

In the development of his speeches the Iowa senator chose the materials and methods that revealed his message most clearly to his hearers. He used exposition to analyze a subject for his audience, to define his terms, and as argument itself; i.e., when he finished his explanation the argument was clear. In his earlier speeches, especially, he used this procedure. As he matured as a speaker, and especially in his senate speeches, he relied more on specific instances and statistics. Of all the forms of proof, these last two were most common with Cummins. To a lesser degree he used causal relations in many speeches, tracing for his hearers complex relationships. Analogy he used little, and his appeal to authority was somewhat incidental. Authorities, when he used them, were almost always living characters or those drawn from American history. The extent to which he revealed in his speeches the academic preparation for his arguments was great; his speech materials were more than merely illustrative or suggestive of this academic proof. Of a popular speech given in 1902 to the National Reciprocity Convention, *The Register and Leader* said, "It possesses more of the qualities of a legal argument than of a popular address." His colleague, Senator George Norris, was inclined to regard Cummins' attention to detail in his speeches as almost a fault.[10] He made limited use of literal analogy, and little or none of fictitious or figurative. Maxims he generally eschewed, and although he had a good sense of humor, not much of it appeared in his speeches.

Coupled with this reliance on substantial evidence was an ability to link his ideas together in a logical manner. Every speech can stand the test of rigid briefing. Senator George W. Norris said of him, "He was one of the most logical speakers I ever heard," and Senator Joseph T. Robinson spoke of his "logical mind."[11]

This kind of thinking was characteristic of his speeches taken as a whole. Each one shows a harmonious relationship to the others. He may have stressed one issue at one time of his life and another at another time, a type of inconsistency which should be commended rather than condemned, but his entire group of speeches shows that he could follow through to the full the implications of his ideas. This ability to arrive at and deal with a developed philosophy did not mean that he fully revealed to his audiences, in formal syllogistic form, all the lines of his thinking. Few speakers ever do. Only the necessary parts of his reasoning were shown.

One further characteristic should be noted. Although he had a definite philosophy that rested on general assumptions, such as faith in the dignity of man and the democratic processes, he usually dealt with minor premises and conclusions. This habit reflected the practical nature of a man who was concerned with the immediate questions of the day and their solution. Only occasionally, when the minor premise was difficult to support with specific evidence, he would retire to a more philosophical discussion of his major premise and make his point by showing the logical relationships involved.

This use of close reasoning does not mean that Cummins was unaware of the possibilities of other kinds of proof. He knew how to strengthen his arguments by a revelation of character. In earlier speeches, especially, he often merely stated the case and then gave his opinion about it. His inaugural address of 1902 is a good example. After explaining the need for various solutions, he simply gave his opinion about what should be done. Little evidence was given, and few of the recognized forms of logical proof were employed. Said Harvey Ingham, who knew Cummins well, "It was not what Senator Cummins said, but the fact that Senator Cummins said it, that was important."[12] Later on in his senatorial speeches he relied less on his reputation and literally piled up evidence to support his case.

Throughout his speeches he revealed the qualities of fairness, magnanimity, courage, utmost courtesy, and great tact and diplomacy. These traits were also shown in his correspondence; in the thousands of letters he wrote it would be difficult to find a scant half-dozen that were definitely brusque. These qualities taken together made it possible for Cummins to speak on an issue and yet usually retain the respect and friendship of men on the other side.

If need be he could lash out in stinging terms at his opposition. He was forthright in his denunciation of Joseph Cannon for what Cummins believed was an unwarranted seizure of power by the Speaker of the House. In his debate at Spirit Lake, Iowa, in 1906, with George D. Perkins, he accused this Sioux City publisher of deliberately defaming him. But such speeches were given in his earlier days. In the vast majority of his addresses, and especially those given in the United States Senate, almost the whole emphasis was on the ideas and little on the personalities of either those who espoused or opposed.

Cummins made little appeal to the feelings of his audiences. He knew he had a message. He couched it in careful terms, gave it with dignity, and expected his audience to rise to the level of his message. Senator Smith W. Brookhart said of him, "He adapted himself to his audience by bringing the audience to a clear understanding of his theme."[13]

In earlier speeches, it is true, he deliberately tried to play upon the emotions of his hearers. This trait was especially apparent in his addresses dedicating the monuments erected by the State of Iowa to Civil War veterans.[14] Here he appealed to such sentiments as love of home, family, and occasionally to religious feelings. In other speeches occur appeals to pride in the Republican party, patriotism in community, state, and nation. His later speeches lacked most of these appeals. He apparently changed deliberately, for his daughter said he often talked about his manner of speaking and inclined more and more to a simple, direct style.[15]

Had he deliberately sought to cultivate these types of appeal, he certainly missed many opportunities. He made slight use of poetry.[16] The Bible and other religious materials were neglected. Relatively little appeal was made directly to the motives of self-preservation or property. Seldom did he attempt to arouse his audience to anger or indignation.

Summary and Conclusions

Cummins' approach to the subject matter of his speeches can now be summarized. He was well stocked in resources from which to draw his arguments, resources which rested on background, general education, and the ability to gather data. His keen analytical mind made it possible for him to progress from point to point in a logical manner, both in the formulation of a general philosophy and in the preparation of each individual speech. He was careful to show the relationships of ideas in a particular speech, but he tended to emphasize minor premises, or immediate issues, without revealing directly the more general assumptions upon which they rested.

Primarily the logical speaker, he was aware, in a measure, of the value of other kinds of proof. In his earlier speeches he tended to rely on his reputation as a form of support. The character traits that he exhibited were those that were natural to the man, and he emphasized ideas rather than personalities. He never made much attempt to stir the feelings of his audience. The appeals he made were invariably on a high plane, and the motives he appealed to generally grew naturally out of the logical nature of the argument.

Cummins was a successful speaker and leader, and although he did not entirely neglect the non-logical supports, he gained his success primarily by appealing to the reason of his audiences.

Footnotes

1. In 1906 Cummins wrote, "I have been speaking on an average of twice a day, probably, for two months, and about the only weapon I have to fight with is my voice." Letter to T. F. Gunn, May 31, 1906, *Personal Letters*, XVI, 114. These letters are with the Cummins' papers in the Department of History and Archives, Des Moines.
2. Address to graduating class, Highland Park College of Law, Des Moines, May 3, 1899, *Progress*, I; copy in *Newspaper Clippings*, I. Ten volumes of *Newspaper Clippings* were compiled by Miss Anna Cummins, sister of Senator Cummins, who also acted as his secretary. Some volumes have no page numbers.
3. Address delivered before the law class at the State University of Iowa, June 22, 1886. See pamphlet among Cummins' papers in the State Department of History and Archives, Des Moines.
4. For a more detailed account of Cummins' ideas, see the author's "A Survey of the Political Ideas of Albert Baird Cummins," *The Iowa Journal of History and Politics*, XXXIX (1941), 339-386.
5. John W. Jordan and James Hadden, *Genealogical and Personal History of Fayette and Greene Counties, Pennsylvania* (New York, 1912), III, 872-875.
6. For greater detail of his early life and legal and political experiences see "A Survey of the Political Ideas of Albert Baird Cummins," 339-357. Comments on his ability as a lawyer may be found in letters to the author from Senator George W. Norris, Gardner Cowles, Harvey Ingham, and others. These letters are now with Cummins' papers, State Department of History and Archives, Des Moines.

7. Benjamin F. Shambaugh, *Biographies and Portraits of the Progressive Men of Iowa* (Des Moines, 1899), II, 91. The author spent several days examining the private library and discussing with Miss Anna Cummins, a sister, and Mrs. Kate Rawson, the daughter, the reading habits of the senator.

8. Letter to the writer, dated April 22, 1937, now with Cummins' papers, State Department of History and Archives, Des Moines.

9. For a more detailed account see the author's "Albert Baird Cummins as a Public Speaker," *The Iowa Journal of History and Politics*, XLIII (1945), 212, 213, 228-230.

10. *The Register and Leader* (Des Moines), December 11, 1902. Letter to the writer from Senator George W. Norris, dated May 14, 1937.

11. Letters to the writer from George W. Norris, dated May 14, 1937 and from Joseph T. Robinson, dated April 22, 1937.

12. Address to the Twenty-ninth General Assembly, in *Iowa Documents,* 1902, I, No. 2, 1-3. Letter to the writer from Harvey Ingham dated March 23, 1937.

13. Letter to the writer dated March 26, 1937.

14. See *Dedication of Monuments Erected by the State of Iowa to Iowa Soldiers* (Des Moines, 1906).

15. Interview by the writer with Mrs. Kate Rawson, Des Moines, June 12, 1937.

16. Cyrenus Cole felt that Cummins' taste for poetry was on a rather low level. See his *I Remember I Remember* (Iowa City, 1936), p. 206.

*The Political Speaking of
Robert M. La Follette*

ROBERT M. LA FOLLETTE *(June 14, 1855—June 18, 1925). Born in Dane County, Wisconsin; attended local schools; Wisconsin Academy, 1873-1875; University of Wisconsin, 1875-1879; studied the typical classical curriculum; member of the Athenian debating society; acted in off-campus theatrical productions; edited a student newspaper; won the Inter-State Oratorical Contest, 1879; admitted to the bar, 1880; district attorney, Dane County, 1881-1884; United States House of Representatives, 1885-1891; campaigned against the regular Republican organization in Wisconsin and made unsuccessful bids for gubernatorial nomination in 1896 and 1898; as governor, 1901-1905, launched the progressive movement in Wisconsin, establishing the direct primary, equal taxation of public utilities, a merit system for state employees, and state regulation of railroad rates; served in the United States Senate, 1905-1925; was a leader of the insurgent, progressive forces in the Republican party, favoring regulation of railroads, stricter anti-trust laws, lower tariff rates, civil liberties, and measures designed to aid agriculture and labor; actively sought the presidential nomination in 1912, but was unsuccessful when Theodore Roosevelt took over the insurgent movement and launched the Progressive party; opposed American participation in the war, 1917, and voted against the Treaty of Versailles and the League of Nations, 1919; successfully opposed actions to unseat him, resulting from his opposition to the war, 1917-1919; resumed leadership of Republican progressives, 1920-1925; instituted Teapot Dome investigation, 1922; was Independent Progressive candidate for president, 1924, gaining nearly five million popular and thirteen electoral votes; honored by the United States Senate, 1959, as one of the five outstanding senators in American history.*

The Political Speaking of Robert M. La Follette

GORDON F. HOSTETTLER*

THE end of the nineteenth century and the first decades of the twentieth witnessed a rising discontent in the United States. Men were coming to realize, more and more, that their political and economic systems fell somewhat short of the assumed perfection. It was becoming increasingly apparent that government, local and national, was dominated by machine rule; that these machines acted to serve the special interests of "Big Business"; and that the common man, farmer and worker, was largely disregarded in the framing and administration of laws.

In the decades following the Civil War the Republican party, symbol of freedom and national feeling, gained almost complete ascendancy in politics. Simultaneously the nation entered into a period of unparalleled economic expansion. Railroads spread rapidly over the continent, and industrial corporations of unprecedented size and power put in their appearance. The dominant Republican party espoused the cause of this rising industrialism, and the results were not always in the public interest. "Land grants, franchise steals, favorable court decisions, supple politicians, appeared in bewildering array. Long before the country realized it, the government was being used, not in the interests of the many, but in the interests of the few."[1]

Inevitably, reform movements arose to express popular protest—first, in third parties; then, personified by Bryan, among the Democrats; finally, in the Republican party itself. Dolliver and Cummins

* Gordon F. Hostettler (A.B., B.S. Kent State University 1940, M.A. 1942, Ph.D. 1947, State University of Iowa) is professor of speech and chairman of the Department of Speech and Dramatic Arts at Temple University.

of Iowa, Norris of Nebraska, Clapp and Nelson of Minnesota, Beveridge of Indiana, Johnson of California, Bristow of Kansas, Borah of Idaho, La Follette of Wisconsin—these were men who sought to reform the Republican party, to make it progressive, to establish it as an agent through which more representative government and more effective regulation of corporations could be attained. The first of these men to embrace progressivism, perhaps the most intelligent, certainly the most indefatigable and uncompromising was Robert M. La Follette.

Senator Borah posed well the problem for the rhetorical critic when he said: "It's hard to say the right thing about Bob La Follette. You know, he lived one hundred fifty years."[2] He referred, of course, to the fact that the irrepressible Wisconsin leader was in the forefront of almost every political struggle from 1900 to 1925. Direct primaries, railroad regulation, taxation, finance, tariffs, social and labor legislation, foreign policy—all were pertinent to his purposes and all felt the impact of "Battling Bob." Perhaps no political figure of our century lost so many battles and won so many wars. Every presidential year, for example, the La Follette-controlled Wisconsin delegation would present a platform to the Republican national convention; and regularly, dominated by conservatives, the convention would defeat the proposals by overwhelming votes. Yet, in 1920, when still another La Follette document was rejected, the Wisconsin spokesman could note that eleven of the thirteen 1908 planks and fourteen of the eighteen 1912 proposals had been enacted into law.[3]

La Follette is an eminently qualified personality for consideration in a volume devoted to public address. More than for most leaders, his speaking and his political career were inseparable. His abilities on the platform made possible his career; and his career was largely determined by the results of his speeches. It is not too much to say that without his platform ability La Follette never could have achieved his political successes. He found the press, for the most part, loyal to business interests and regular Republicanism and, therefore, hostile to him. He was forced, as a result, to resort to direct oral communication to put his ideas before the public, and his successes depended almost wholly upon his ability to convince voters in face-to-face situations.

Early Influences and Speaking Experiences

The necessity of having to rely upon speech certainly was not distasteful to La Follette. From early boyhood he displayed a growing interest in and ability for the public platform. With speech-making central to politics, entertainment, and personal recognition in nineteenth century mid-America, his desire to excel as a speaker was something of a natural phenomenon, akin to ambitions which motivated Beveridge, Dolliver, Borah, Bryan and others of that generation. Particular circumstances of boyhood, however, may have played a special role in La Follette's case. With his father dead and his mother remarried, there is ample evidence that his boyhood was lonely. Thus, the praise and recognition which he gained from childish endeavors in recitations may have been given special emphasis in his mind. Mrs. La Follette must have gained impressions of her husband's childhood directly from him, and one is struck by the emphasis which she places upon his early speaking experiences and the satisfaction he derived from them. She writes, for example, that although he did not excel at traditional spelling bees, "he always had a 'star' part on these occasions, for he was in great demand as a speaker and actor."[4] La Follette's recollections of speakers heard in his youth indicate his interest in their speech techniques and his belief that speaking was essential for personal recognition.[5] His sister recalled that in 1878, after hearing an eloquent Memorial Day speaker, he clutched her by the arm and earnestly declared, "Jo, I can do that—some day they will be coming out to hear me speak."[6]

During his senior year in college, 1879, he received dramatic confirmation that he had unusual ability in speech and that it could win flattering attention for him. With a penetrating analysis of Iago, he entered into oratorical competition and won successively the contest at the University of Wisconsin, the state championship, and the Inter-State Contest in which winners from six states met in Iowa City. When the triumphant orator returned to Madison, he was greeted by the student body headed by a brass band, conducted in a victory parade to the campus, and presented with gifts at an impromptu rally. In the evening he was regaled by an extraordinary gathering in the assembly chamber of the state capitol, where he was congratulated formally by the university regents and leading citizens of Madison. Such attention, now reserved for athletes on the American campus, would tend to convince almost any young man that speaking ability was a prime key to success.[7]

Entering law practice after college, La Follette continued to enhance his reputation through speech by frequently addressing audiences at county fairs, holiday gatherings, and political rallies. In 1880 he was elected district attorney of Dane County, and in 1884 he won the first of three terms in Congress. Little in the record of these years indicates that he would become a militant leader of progressivism. He appears, rather, as a young man, ardent in support of regular Republican doctrine, who was determined to gain personal acclaim by virtue of his growing ability in public speaking. Looking back upon his years in the House, La Follette himself wrote: "The alignment of forces was not so clear to me then as it is now, but I knew well enough where the leaders stood."[8]

His early campaigns in Wisconsin, however, forced him to adopt a basic technique of political action which became highly important in later life. When he first ran for public office and, again, when he declared for Congress, he was opposed by the forces of Colonel E. W. Keyes, Madison postmaster and Republican state leader. In later years, La Follette pictured this opposition as his first encounter with the boss system and his reaction as his first "insurgency."[9] His account seems exaggerated. Certainly no fundamental issue divided him from Keyes as was the case in his progressive years. Opposition to him came, most likely, as a result of natural antagonisms which arise among loyal party workers when a newcomer desires office without first serving in the ranks. None the less, lacking support by the local organization, he was forced to carry his campaigns directly to the people. He tirelessly canvassed the district, talking to farmers in the fields and addressing audiences, large and small, wherever he could find them. He learned he could win by convincing voters through direct, oral communication. He developed a conviction which stayed with him all his life. Going to the people was a chief La Follette characteristic. In his own words: "I had gone behind all this organization and reached the voters themselves. Whatever success I have attained since then has been attained by these simple and direct means."[10]

A dramatic encounter in 1891 foreshadowed La Follette's revolt to progressivism. Summoned to a private meeting with Senator Philetus Sawyer, undisputed leader of Wisconsin Republicans, La Follette claimed he was offered a bribe to influence decisions of his brother-in-law, Robert Siebecker, the presiding judge, for a series of cases in which Sawyer stood liable for considerable sums. La Follette recoiled in hurt amazement and anger. When Siebecker, giving no reason, withdrew from the cases, Sawyer published a denial that he had attempted to influence the judge through La Follette. The latter immediately issued a statement revealing his version of the meeting—and the state was rocked by the controversy that ensued.[11] The press came to the support of the powerful Sawyer. La Follette found himself the object of social and political ostracism. Whatever hopes he had for public life seemed gone beyond recall. The winter of 1891-92 found his spirits at lowest ebb. Many long nights were spent in his study as he considered his situation and reviewed the political scene. For the first time he began to see clearly the implications of the alliance between corporate interests and politics. He decided to fight. As he put it: "So out of this awful ordeal came understanding; and out of understanding came resolution. I determined that the power of this corrupt influence . . . should be broken."[12]

The Sawyer incident, of course, can not be viewed as the only causative agent which led La Follette to progressivism. It acted rather as a catalyst, bringing to focus facets of his personality and factors inherent in his background.[13] Of the influences which played upon him, brief mention can be made of the high ethical standards taught by his mother; the rural environment of his youth when the Granger Movement was stirring; and the education he received at the University of Wisconsin. "It has always seemed to me," wrote Mrs. La Follette, "that the experience of the Granger Movement . . . did more than even Bob himself realized to shape his political career."[14] Of the University, La Follette said: "I owe what I am and what I have done largely to the inspiration I received while there. It was not so much the actual courses of study . . . it was rather the spirit of the institution."[15] This spirit, from all accounts, was embodied in President John Bascom who stressed high ethical standards for personal conduct, democratic ideals for government, and the duty of citizens for responsible participation in political affairs.[16]

These were themes which La Follette drove home in almost every speech.

LA FOLLETTE'S PROGRAM

After his year of decision, of course, La Follette's ideology and program were extended and refined; but thereafter he had a basic point of view with which to measure new issues and proposals. Succinctly stated, his aim was to divorce special interests, especially those of business, from control of government and to restore government to the control of the whole people. As he phrased it: "The essence of the Progressive movement, as I see it, lies in its purpose to uphold the fundamental principles of representative government."[17] Since most leaders of his party were frankly allied with the rising corporations, he could look forward only to long and continued struggle; and conflict after conflict was exactly what he encountered to his death. Espousing the direct primary to replace the cumbersome and corrupt caucus system, he engaged in three bitter battles to gain the governorship before he was successful in 1900. By the time of his election, he was demanding equal taxation of corporations, and soon he was seeking regulation of railroad rates by the state. Re-elected twice, his terms as governor were fraught with hectic intra-party conflict, including an outright bolt of the stalwarts in 1904, before he saw his total program enacted into law. From 1906 until 1925, the object of ostracism and contempt, he carried on his relentless crusade in the Senate. He came to be known, significantly, as "Battling Bob."

Throughout his life he was regarded by many as a dangerous radical, a member of the lunatic fringe. This reputation was inevitable since he stood in opposition to almost all that characterized political life in his day. Yet there is more than a little irony in his being so classified. For La Follette and the other progressives were not innovators. They proposed no radical change in American society. In fact, they were true conservatives in the sense that they invoked the basic ideas of the founding fathers and called for America to return to the old ways when, at least in theory, each man stood on his own feet, neither seeking nor securing special privilege from government. As Chief Justice Warren expressed it: "La Follette believed implicitly in . . . the system of free enterprise, but he believed it belonged to the people . . . and that every hindrance should be removed from it . . . so that it might produce a better life for every man."[18] From this viewpoint La Follette was a defender of capitalism against itself. He advocated more democracy for capitalism, not a new society. He visited Russia in 1923, but was disappointed in what he saw. Lincoln Steffens, a traveling companion, quoted him as saying, "Marx is not the way to do it."[19] "If I were a citizen of Russia," La Follette wrote, "I should resist the communistic dictatorship as vigorously as I have endeavored to resist the encroachment upon our democratic institutions in America. I hold that government by one class . . . is tyranny."[20] His attitude was underlined in 1924 when he repudiated a communist dominated convention, desiring to use his name, by bluntly stating: "Communists [are] the mortal enemies of the progressive movement and democratic ideals."[21]

As a product of and spokesman for the West, La Follette could have held no other views. Frontier tradition, still active, gave paramount importance to the ideals of democracy, but frontier economic conditions had been superceded by a new agriculture. The farmer of La Follette's day, as now, was no longer a self-sufficient producer. He was a businessman growing a money crop so that he could purchase equipment and supplies for his farm and family. He was committed to basic capitalistic tenets. His complaints arose because credit, necessary for any businessman, was difficult to secure; because interest rates were high; because corporations, particularly railroads, occupied favored positions in the market place; and because his product was subject to hazards of weather and blight. His demand was for equal opportunity in the market and equal treatment by government.[22]

La Follette reflected, spoke for, and led the farmer-businessman of the Midwest. He was at once a Jeffersonian and Hamiltonian—Jeffersonian in his idealism and concepts of democracy; Hamiltonian in his practical and specific approach to political and economic problems. Did the caucus system defeat the will of the majority? Then establish direct primaries and give each voter equal voice in selecting candidates. Were railroads taking advantage of their natural monopoly, charging excessive rates and securing favorable tax structures? Then enforce tax laws without favor and establish scientific regulation by government, insuring thereby reasonable rates to shippers and fair profits for the roads. Were corporations merging and combining to become so large as to threaten free competition in the markets? Then enforce the Sherman Anti-Trust Act, amending it where needed, to prevent monopoly, force competition, and secure a fair price for all. Were tariff rates so high that favored producers, especially trusts, could secure excessive profits by the elimination of foreign competition? Then provide a tariff commission which would determine exactly the difference in production costs here and abroad and permit no more than that difference in a tariff schedule. These were the practical solutions which La Follette sought. In each instance the problem posed was one of deep concern to the farmer-businessman, and the specific solutions appealed to his practical mind. As Nye puts it, "La Follette was closer to the people and closer to the Midwest than any politician after Bryan."[23] For him audience adaptation was a minor rhetorical problem, for he thought and reacted as did his auditors.

No issue of his day better displays his reflection of the farmer as businessman than does the tariff. He frankly accepted the basic concept of protection. He believed that high labor costs in the United States made it necessary to safeguard our standard of living. Significantly, he wanted the same protection for farmers as for manufacturers. As a member of Congress, he proposed an increase in tobacco duties, a position undoubtedly related to the fact that his constituents then grew over one-half of Wisconsin's annual crop. The McKinley Tariff of 1890, which La Follette helped write, was the first to attempt comprehensive protection for agricultural products, and it was this feature of the bill which he stressed when he addressed the House.[24] When progressive Republicans openly broke with Taft over the Payne-Aldrich Act of 1909, La Follette led the revolt in the Senate; but his aim was only to prevent increases and to reduce others to equal differentials in production costs.[25] In 1911, he was bitterly opposed to reciprocal trade treaties with Canada, proposed by Taft, on grounds that duties on farm products would be reduced.[26] He voted for the Democratic Underwood Act in 1913, despite misgivings in regard to agricultural reductions, and he automatically opposed the Fordney-McCumber Act of 1921 when high rates were re-established.[27] In his speeches and votes he accurately echoed midwestern sentiment.

His closeness to the people of his region, however, was at once a major source of his platform effectiveness and a severe limitation upon his leadership at the national level. Nye phrases it well: "His inability to adjust to changing political and human situations narrowed his appeal. His thinking was midwestern—typically so . . . He lacked what historians call the 'world view'. . . ."[28] Probably the best illustration of this basic weakness is to be found in his views of foreign policy. He was one of the "little group of willful men," so designated by Wilson, who by filibuster in 1916 prevented passage of the Armed Ship Bill. He voted against war with Germany, against conscription, and against American participation in the League of Nations. He did not seem to understand that the world of 1919 was vastly different from the world which, throughout most of his life, had permitted American isolation. He failed to appreciate, in its broadest scope, the responsibility inevitably devolving upon the United States for the preservation of western civilization. He was suspicious of any American involvement which might divert attention from domestic reform. In fairness, it must be added that once war was declared La Follette voted for all measures necessary for its successful prosecution, dissenting only to specific provisions and offering amendments when he felt vested interests were securing unwarranted concessions. It is also true that some of his suspicions regarding the war aims of the allies were confirmed in later years. None the less, his position was essentially misguided; but, again, it approximated that of his constituents. Isolationism then, as now, largely centered in the Midwest.

La Follette's unremitting courage, determination, and self-confidence, all deep aspects of his personality, were revealed at their best during the war years. War hysteria swept the nation and it focused with full force upon him for his votes against the Armed Ship Bill and the Declaration, his criticism of certain provisions of war measures, and, most important, a misquotation of a speech he delivered in St. Paul. He was quoted by the Associated Press as having said, "We had *no* grievances against Germany," when in fact he had not used the word "no."[29] Vicious cartoons, editorials, public meetings heaped vituperation upon him. "Chief apostle" of the "white rabbits

of pacifism" and "one of a little band of perverts" were typical
appellations hurled at him.[30] Theodore Roosevelt called him "the
Grand American neocopperhead" and one of the "Huns within our
gates."[31] As he left the Senate, after voting against the declaration of
war, a stranger stepped up and handed him a rope.[32] More serious,
as a result of the St. Paul speech, action was brought in the Senate to
unseat him, a move which was enthusiastically endorsed by groups
throughout the nation. Against this attack and avalanche of vilifica-
tion, La Follette stood fast, certain that in time he would be vindicated. "I can't quit," he wrote his former law partner, "when there
is more to fight for and more to fight against than ever before."[33]
And fight he did, in the Senate and its committees, criticizing war
measures and defending his, and others', right and duty to dissent.[34]

The reaction was typical for Battling Bob. Satisfied to live with
his own conscience, he fought tenaciously for truth as he saw it.
"Once convinced of the necessity of a reform," wrote his wife, "he
could not be driven from his course."[35] Personal gain, the majority
view, blandishments of friendship—none could sway him. Compromise was rarely acceptable. In his own words: "In legislation *no
bread* is often better than *half a loaf*. I believe it is usually better to
be beaten and come right back at the next session and make a fight
for a thoroughgoing law than to have written on the books a weak
and indefinite statute."[36] Time after time, in his Wisconsin fight, he
could have settled for compromise measures, but he drove on until
his reforms were adopted totally. Without this unflinching approach
he could not have succeeded so well.[37]

Arranged against him, throughout his life, were the entrenched
interests of party and business. His opponents commanded powerful
weapons—money, the press, social prestige—and all were deployed
against him. La Follette had to be tough, within and without, to
carry his reforms to fulfillment. But perhaps he made too much
virtue of virtue. Professor Hofstadter criticizes the progressives in
that "they set impossible standards, that they were victimized . . .
by a form of moral absolutism" which led to "ruthlessness in political life."[38] In some respects, La Follette was a case in point. "A
friend who declines to follow his leadership," noted one critic, "can
no longer be recognized by him as a friend."[39] More than a few men,
Irvine Lenroot being most notable, who fought side by side with

La Follette in early battles, found themselves alienated from him in later years because they could not accept his views on other issues. His uncompromising attitude, therefore, was a source of both strength and weakness. It brought him loyal, even dogged, support from many, but he was "too inflexible, too rigid, too much the lone wolf to become the prairie Jackson that the midwest progressive tradition demanded."[40]

SPEECH METHODS

Despite such limitation, La Follette was a consummate politician. He understood that direct contact with people was the only realistic basis for political success. He flooded the voters with copies of his speeches, special reports, government bulletins, and letters. He helped found three newspapers, and in 1909 became the publisher of *La Follette's Magazine*. Nor did he ignore the efficacy of sound organization. He built up a tight-knit, loyal body of followers, and maintained close touch with them, in every part of the state. So efficient was his organization that it rivaled and resembled in some ways the stalwart machine which he broke.[41]

But it was primarily public speaking which brought success to La Follette. For sheer effort, some of his campaigns have rarely been equalled in our history. Defeated for the gubernatorial nomination in 1896, he set out the next year on an off-year campaign, delivering long speeches, day after day, at county fairs for the most part, to educate the farmers in regard to machine politics and, the remedy, the direct primary. In time his views were accepted, and "Bob always felt," his wife recalled, "that he never made any speeches that produced better results."[42] In 1904, after four years of deadlock with a conservative legislature, La Follette, now governor, stumped the state for forty-eight days, averaging more than eight hours a day on the platform, to win the progressive legislature he needed to have his program finally adopted. Again, in 1914-15, after the stalwarts had recaptured the governorship, he returned to the state throughout the winter to re-establish the people's faith in progressivism. And again, in 1922, with his senatorial seat at stake and his war record under scathing assault, Old Bob returned to the hustings, speaking three and four times daily for six weeks, to win the largest majority in the history of his state.

On the national level, too, La Follette relied primarily upon speech to convey his ideas to the people. The Senate itself was a sounding board, but adjournments found him constantly upon the chautauqua circuits. His topic was "Representative Government," a lecture which dealt with "the struggle between democracy and privilege," and which was revised each year in light of political developments. Year in and year out, his audiences were large and enthusiastic, and in his opinion his chautauqua addresses "were the most practically effective work I have done, in a national way, for the Progressive movement, though it cannot well be separated from my work as a public official."[43]

What, then, was the nature of La Follette's speeches? What specific techniques did he employ to win political success? A comprehensive evaluation need not be attempted here. Space contravenes and, more important, Carroll P. Lahman has already published a detailed and excellent criticism of the Senator's rhetorical methods.[44] This account, therefore, can be completed by a general description and evaluation.

A significant feature of La Follette's speaking was his careful and meticulous preparation. He wrote: "I have no sympathy with, nor confidence in, the fellow who pretends that he gets the best results on the inspiration of the moment. He may have a flash of mental ecstasy while under the intellectual stress of speaking, but he is more likely to have a brain fluke—with a mediocre result."[45] His methods coincided with his theory. He "always dreaded making a speech," his daughter reported, "which he had not had time to prepare carefully."[46] And preparation was to him, primarily, a search for facts and understanding. Testimony on the point is legion. "No public man of his day," said Mark Sullivan, "equalled him in the energy with which he dug into economic data."[47] Woodrow Wilson declared: "He is strong because he studies every angle of every question. When he gets up to speak he knows what he is talking about."[48] It was, for example, Old Bob's grubbing for facts—and a speech he made in the Senate—that brought about the investigation and disclosures in the famous Teapot Dome scandal.[49] Secretaries, research clerks, friends, members of his family—all served to gather materials for him, "but he never took his speeches . . . 'ready made' from another hand."[50] The work and speech was his own; and long hours were spent, night after night, when he faced an important address, legislative debate, or campaign. Indeed, his wife felt that "at times . . . he was overzealous, too cautious, in making his preparation. His standard was perfection; he wanted to be sure his proof was invulnerable."[51] The perfectionist attitude was admitted. "I always hate a speech after I make it," he wrote, "and don't see how I or anybody could ever have thought it was even tolerable."[52]

By any measure, the outstanding characteristic of La Follette's speeches was his use of factual material. His mastery of subject matter was not for himself alone. His facts went into his speeches for the benefit of his auditors. His arguments were close-knit and detailed. His appeal to voters was pre-eminently rational, not emotional as was Bryan's; and his essential method was inductive. If classical rhetoric stresses the canon of invention, La Follette was a classicist *par excellence.* He flooded audiences, two and three hours at a time, with statistics and examples. Voting records, tax rates, tariff duties, railroad rates, interest tables, wage rates—these were the materials from which he built to his generalizations and conclusions. In 1903, for example, he sent the legislature a table for 151 Wisconsin towns showing that railroad freight rates were higher for them than for comparable towns in Iowa and Illinois. When he was accused of having selected a biased sample, he sent in a 181 page table, listing *every* Wisconsin village and showing higher rates.[53] The table became an important part of his basic campaign manuscript in 1904 when he went to the people for a third term as governor and for a legislature to support him. Rate after rate was read to his audiences to gain approval of his plan for regulation. "It was said after his campaign," the *New York Times* reported, "the people of Wisconsin knew more about railroad rates than the rest of the people of America combined."[54] In 1909, when Senator Aldrich claimed the cotton schedule of his tariff bill did not increase duties, La Follette took the Senate floor for a speech lasting the better part of three days. He had had hundreds of small samples of cotton cloth put through customs, each being marked according to existing rates and then according to those in the proposed bill. He stood at his desk, exhibiting sample after sample, and completely demolished the Aldrich position.[55] Of this speech, Beveridge wrote: "It was murder and sudden death today. La Follette tore the cotton schedule to

pieces. I told [Senator] Dillingham that even if La Follette were
the devil himself, his statements were unanswerable. Aldrich has
utterly lost his composure."[56] And so it was with almost all of La
Follette's speeches. He exhibited what Justice Warren calls "an old
fashioned faith in the sovereign power of reason in human affairs."[57]

La Follette's heavy reliance upon fact and tight argument was a
corollary of his abiding faith in the sound judgment of the people.
In his wife's words: "Bob was always conscious of the native power
of the plain people to grasp thought. It never occurred to him to
speak 'down' to his audiences or to consider any theme beyond their
reach."[58] In public speech and private letter, La Follette reiterated
his faith that, given the facts, the people would choose the truth.
"He trusted the people," said Lincoln Steffens, "as no other leader
has trusted them."[59] A critic has suggested that the progressives' confidence in the people was misplaced.[60] La Follette's faith may have
reflected more of sentiment than reality; but from his experience the
belief could be justified. After all, rank and file voters *did* respond to
his methods. He won Wisconsin and held loyal support, the war ex-
cepted, until his death.

It would be a major misconception, however, to envision La
Follette as presenting dry fact and statistic alone. He did not fit the
stereotype of the college professor. The secret of his ability to maintain rapt attention for long hours lay in his highly effective techniques of audience adaptation. His arguments and facts were related
directly and specifically to ideals and motives of his auditors. It was
more than the helpful fact that he reflected and articulated the basic
views of the Wisconsin farmer-businessman. It was that he deliberately interpreted his arguments for his hearers in terms of their
interests and desires. The value of farm land in relation to taxes, the
price of wheat in relation to railroad rates, the cost of food and
supplies in relation to tariff duties, the importance of true represen-
tation in government to the voter—these were the aspects of his
argument that were stressed. "He always thought of economic problems in their concrete relation to human experience," his wife wrote,
"and his imagination invested abstract figures with power to stir an
audience."[61] Appeals were centered upon immediate auditors. When
the primary was the issue, his election statistics included those of
the town in which he spoke; when it was railroad regulation, actual

rates paid by local farmers and shippers were cited. On the chautauqua circuit in 1907, he hit upon the idea of sending his secretary
about the towns to gather information on local economic conditions
for incorporation into his addresses.[62] He invited audience participation. He asked questions which could be, and were, answered in
unison. He would pretend he had no time to develop some point
and then would respond to the cries of "Go on, Bob!" In 1897,
during his off-year campaign of education on the primary, he drove
home his thesis with such skill, using the same words, that often audiences would chorus with him.[63]

His manner was simple, direct, intense, earnest. Audiences caught
the spirit of his grim determination and his boundless confidence.
He was at his best when speaking extempore. He usually began a
campaign with a manuscript, and at early meetings, without actually
reading, would follow his text closely. "Very soon, however, he
would get into a heart-to-heart way of talking to his audience. Then
he would be moved by much the same spirit as when in the company
of family and friends."[64] It was then that his arguments were best
enlivened with anecdote and wit[65] and that his motive appeals,
altruistic and selfish, were most effective. Then his very real identification with his hearers brought the interreaction of speaker and
audience to its height. "When he saw earnest faces looking puzzled,"
his wife recalled, "he would repeat his arguments in different form
and use further illustrations until he saw they understood and were
convinced."[66] This was audience adaptation at its best.

Special attention should be given to a unique political and rhetorical device which originated with La Follette. Reference is to his
use of what he termed "the roll call." He first employed it in 1904 to
help convince Wisconsin voters that progressives should be sent to
the legislature to enact his program. He would explain in detail the
significance of votes recorded in previous legislative sessions and
then, imitating the monotonous voice of a reading clerk, would call
the roll and answer for each legislator. Then would come the questions: "Did your representative vote in your interests or for the
railroads? Did he favor you or special interests?" The technique
effectively dramatized the issues. Often stalwarts who had opposed
the Governor would be on the platform, and some of them would
quietly slip out of the hall as their records were exposed. Calling the

roll became a standard part of La Follette's chautauqua addresses. He sought every opportunity to put the Senate on record so that he could report the votes of his colleagues across the country. Fellow senators reacted bitterly to his exposure of their votes. Sometimes, as a personal favor, he was asked to omit it in certain cities or states. He always refused. His use of the roll call has been credited with helping to retire more than a few of his conservative opponents. "I have always believed," said Mrs. La Follette, "the institution of the roll call . . . was one of the greatest services Bob has rendered."[67]

Another important element of La Follette's speaking, one which helped make his mass of fact and argument palatable, was his delivery. A vibrant, flexible voice and strenuous, continuous, meaningful bodily action were his basic assets. Both, no doubt, were derived in part from his youthful activity in the theater. His powers of pantomime and mimicry were used to excellent effect. He could be the very personification of the crafty machine politician as he argued for the primary. His mobile features portrayed every shade of emotion; he knew the value of the pause. He dramatized his message. He was always moving—all over the platform—and his hands were never still. After his introduction, his coat came off as he went to work. When he quit several hours later he was usually wringing wet. Continual action became so much a part of his method that in 1924, when a broadcast tied him to a microphone, he told his audience: "I have been advised . . . that if I bellow too loudly, the radio doesn't get it . . . I have got to shoot right at this thing. What I like when I am speaking to an audience is freedom; I like the freedom of the stage; I like the freedom that comes from not being tied down to a miserable manuscript."[68]

A speaker's use of language is often an important clue to his success or failure. It may be significant, therefore, that style is rarely mentioned by those who have commented on La Follette's speaking. If the function of language is to communicate, this omission may be a tribute to his oral style. For his words and sentences fitted the seriousness of his message and his intent. As a young man he strove for effect through words. His success with Iago stemmed largely from his ability in this respect,[69] and there are traces of his concern for phrases and figures in his House speeches and even in his "Menace of the Machine," the speech which marked the beginning of his fight for Wisconsin. When the issue was drawn, however, La Follette became more concerned with arguments and voters than with words. Language in his speeches was simple and direct. He spoke in the vernacular of the people of the Midwest.

What, finally, shall we say about Robert La Follette? His speeches were as long as colonial sermons; but his audiences demanded more. Extraordinary audience adaptation, direct style, and vigorous delivery drove home the facts, statistics, examples, and arguments which he heaped upon his auditors. He was honest, sincere, and fair. He was of and spoke for the plain people of the West; and he fought all his life, with courage and confidence, for the democracy in which he believed. Public speaking was his chief weapon, and from many points of view, he was classical rhetoric in action.

He accomplished much. The loyalty of Wisconsin and the votes of almost five million Americans which he received in 1924 are a tribute to his life work and his hold on the common people. "The real leader of progressivism, and its greatest, was Robert Marion La Follette. . . . He had what the others lacked, expressed the tradition best, gave it its wisest and clearest direction, and when he died, it died with him."[70] In Old Bob's desk, after his death, a small piece of paper was found on which he had written: "I would be remembered as one who in the world's darkest hour kept a clean conscience and stood to the end for the ideals of American democracy."[71] We may also with profit remember him as a man who demonstrated that public speaking, as he used it, can be a real force in American life.

Footnotes

1. Benjamin De Witte, *The Progressive Movement* (New York, 1915), p. 14.
2. *New York Times*, June 19, 1925.
3. Belle C. and Fola La Follette, *Robert M. La Follette* (New York, 1953), II, 997.
4. *Ibid.*, I, 19.
5. Robert M. La Follette, *La Follette's Autobiography, A Personal Narrative of Political Experiences* (Madison, 1913), pp. 15-17, 22-24, 33-36. Permission to cite passages from this volume has been graciously given by Miss Fola La Follette, the Senator's daughter.
6. B. and F. La Follette, I, 28.
7. For a comprehensive account of La Follette's college career, his speech training, and the Inter-State Contest, see: Carroll P. Lahman, "Robert M. La Follette as

Public Speaker and Political Leader, 1855-1905" (doctoral dissertation, University of Wisconsin, 1940).

8. *Autobiography*, p. 126.

9. *Ibid.*, pp. 8-14, 45-47, 63-65.

10. *Ibid.*, p. 13.

11. For La Follette's account of the meeting, see: *Ibid.*, pp. 138-59. See also B. and F. La Follette, I, 95-98.

12. *Autobiography*, p. 164.

13. In this regard, La Follette himself wrote: "Sooner or later I probably would have done what I did in Wisconsin. But it would have been later. It would have been a matter of much slower evolution." *Ibid.*, p. 146.

14. B. and F. La Follette, I, 24.

15. *Autobiography*, p. 26.

16. For a discussion of Bascom's influence, see: Charles McCarthy, *The Wisconsin Idea* (New York, 1912), pp. 21-24.

17. *Autobiography*, p. x.

18. Earl Warren, "Freedom Itself Is Radical—An Appreciation of Robert M. La Follette, Sr.," *The Progressive*, XIX (August, 1955), 15.

19. *The Letters of Lincoln Steffens* (New York, 1938), II, 631.

20. *Washington Herald*, December 16, 1923, as cited by B. and F. La Follette, II, p. 1082.

21. *Ibid.*, II, p. 1102.

22. Russel B. Nye, *Midwestern Progressive Politics* (East Lansing, 1951), pp. 1-27.

23. *Ibid.*, p. 223.

24. *Congressional Record*, XXI, pt. 4, pp. 4474-4475.

25. He told the Senate: "I want to give every industry in this country that protection which is necessary to measure the difference in the cost of production between this and the competing foreign country." *Ibid.*, XLIV, pt. 2, p. 2037.

26. *Ibid.*, XLVII, pt. 3, pp. 2396-2398.

27. For a summary of his tariff views, see *Autobiography*, pp. 98-114.

28. *Ibid.*, p. 223.

29. The speech was delivered September 20, 1917, but it was not until May 23, 1918, that the Associated Press admitted its error and apologized. Nye (p. 316) calls the incident "one of the most blatant offenses against the truth in the history of American journalism."

30. B. and F. La Follette, I, 629, 645.

31. *Ibid.*, II, 771-72.

32. *Ibid.*, I, 666.

33. Letter to Gilbert Roe, June 16, 1917, as cited in *ibid.*, II, 738.

34. For a typical La Follette response, see his speech, "Free Speech in Wartime," in *American Public Addresses, 1740-1952*, A. Craig Baird, ed., (New York, 1956), pp. 244-48.

35. B. and F. La Follette, I, 75.

36. *Autobiography*, p. 268.

37. For detailed accounts of the Wisconsin fight, see Allen F. Lovejoy, *La Follette and the Establishment of the Direct Primary in Wisconsin, 1890-1904* (New Haven, 1945); Albert O. Barton, *La Follette's Winning of Wisconsin* (Des Moines, 1924); B. and F. La Follette, pp. 116-187.

38. Richard Hofstadter, *The Age of Reform* (New York, 1955), pp. 15-16.

39. Fred E. Haynes, "La Follette and La Follettism," *Atlantic Monthly*, CXXXIV (October, 1924), 538.
40. Nye, p. 198. See also Kenneth W. Hechler, *Insurgency* (New York, 1940), p. 84.
41. See Robert E. Maxwell, "La Follette and the Progressive Machine in Wisconsin," *Indiana Magazine of History*, XLVIII (March, 1952), 55-70; Nye, p. 222; Hofstadter, p. 267; Lovejoy, p. 69.
42. B. and F. La Follette, I, p. 123.
43. *Autobiography*, p. 305.
44. "Robert M. La Follette," in *A History and Criticism of American Public Address*, ed. W. N. Brigance (New York, 1943), II, 942-967.
45. Letter to Isabel Bacon La Follette, April 30, 1925, as cited by B. and F. La Follette, I, 51.
46. *Ibid.*, II, 762.
47. *Our Times* (New York, 1926), II, 215-16.
48. *Milwaukee Journal*, January 13, 1913, as cited by B. and F. La Follette, I, 460.
49. See *ibid.*, II, 1044-54.
50. *Ibid.*, I, 348.
51. *Ibid.*, I, 51.
52. Letter to his family, March 14, 1919, as cited in *ibid.*, II, 949.
53. *Ibid.*, I, 157-58.
54. June 19, 1925.
55. *Congressional Record*, XLIV, pt. 3, pp. 2731-2752.
56. Letter to Mrs. Beveridge, June 4, 1909, as cited by Claude G. Bowers, *Beveridge and the Progressive Era* (New York, 1932), p. 345.
57. P. 16.
58. B. and F. La Follette, I, 44.
59. Letter to Mrs. La Follette, June 20, 1925, cited in *ibid.*, I, 652.
60. Hofstadter, pp. 18-21.
61. B. and F. La Follette, I, 70.
62. La Follette to Mrs. La Follette, April 9, 1907, cited in *ibid.*, I, 231.
63. Lovejoy, p. 39.
64. B. and F. La Follette, I, p. 71.
65. Spontaneous humor often crept into his speeches, but the seriousness of his approach minimized humorous appeals. His formal addresses were devoid of stories and flings. He thought it was dangerous for a public figure to gain the reputation of being a wit. *Ibid.*, I, 71.
66. *Ibid.*, I, 193.
67. *Ibid.*, I, 173.
68. Speech at Kansas City, October 13, 1924, as cited in *ibid.*, II, 1136.
69. Years later, C. W. Thompson, in the *New York Times*, quoted a long passage in which Iago is compared to Richard III, and then commented: "This may not be great literature. It is, however, a remarkable example of the sustained carrying on of what the old rhetorics used to call the figure of antithesis. . . . The words are Anglo-Saxon and strike with the force of a broad-axe." September 7, 1924, Sec. IV, p. 6.
70. Nye, pp. 206-07.
71. B. and F. La Follette, II, 1174.

Theodore Roosevelt
The Preacher Militant

THEODORE ROOSEVELT (*October 27, 1858—January 6, 1919*). *Born, New York City; son of Theodore Roosevelt, wealthy merchant of Dutch extraction, and Martha Bullock Roosevelt; privately tutored for most of his early education; traveled in Europe 1868-1869, in Europe, Egypt, and the Holy Land, 1872-1873; at fifteen began serious study under Arthur Cutler for entrance into Harvard; at Harvard, 1876-1880; elected to Phi Beta Kappa; expressed indebtedness to A. S. Hill, professor of English, but regretted his lack of interest in forensics and writing themes; at Columbia Law School, 1880; representative to New York State Assembly, 1882-1884; delegate to Republican national convention, 1884; defeated as candidate for mayor of New York City, 1886; United States Civil Service Commissioner, 1889-1895; president of Police Commission, New York City, 1895-1897; assistant secretary of the Navy, 1897-1898; Lieutenant-Colonel of the First United States Volunteer Cavalry (Rough Riders) in Spanish-American War, 1898; Governor of New York, 1899-1900; Vice-President, March 4-September 14, 1901; succeeded to the presidency of the United States upon the assassination of President McKinley, September 14, 1901; elected President, 1904; awarded Nobel Peace Prize, 1906; retired from presidency, March 4, 1909; hunted in Central Africa, 1909-1910; traveled in Europe, lectured at Oxford University, Sorbonne, Berlin, and Christiania, Norway, March to June, 1910; candidate for Republican nomination for president, 1912; bolted the Republican party and became unsuccessful Progressive party candidate for president, 1912; explored the Brazilian jungle, 1913-1914; was refused permission to raise and equip a division of volunteers for service in France in World War I, 1917; spoke in behalf of vigorous war effort by United States, 1917-1918; died at Oyster Bay, New York, January 6, 1919. Contributed numerous articles to magazines; editorial writer for* OUTLOOK, *1909-1914;* METROPOLITAN, *1917;* KANSAS CITY STAR, *1917; author of numerous books.*

Theodore Roosevelt
The Preacher Militant

CARL A. DALLINGER*

W HEN the measure of a man's influence has been taken and the
dominant theme of his message has been found, it is likely we will
discover a prevailing perspective in his analysis of the issues he
confronted, a basic approach in his encounter with men and ideas.
Considered from this point of view, Owen Wister's comment brings
into focus what was probably Theodore Roosevelt's most prominent characteristic as a speaker. "If they treated Theodore as they
deal with certain composite substances in chemistry, . . . and melted
him down and down until nothing remained at the bottom of the
crucible but his ultimate, central, indestructible stuff, it's not a
statesman they'd find, or a hunter, or a historian, or a naturalist—
they'd find a preacher militant."[1] Roosevelt himself attested:

> My duty was to stand with everyone while he was right, and
> to stand against him when he went wrong. . . . When a busi-
> ness man or labor leader, politician or reformer, is right, I sup-
> port him; when he goes wrong, I leave him. . . . So long as
> they work for evil, smite them with the sword of the Lord and
> of Gideon! When they change and show their faith by their
> works, remember the words of Ezekiel: "If the wicked will
> turn from all the sins he has committed, and keep all my
> statutes, and do that which is lawful and right, he shall
> surely live. . . ."[2]

Appeals to high motives are familiar techniques used by advocates
to support their contentions, but Roosevelt made morality the central issue. No matter what problem was under discussion, ultimately

* Carl A. Dallinger (A.B. Park College, 1934, M.A. 1938, Ph.D. 1952, State University of Iowa) is associate professor of speech and communication skills, and coordi-
nator of the Communication Skills Program at the State University of Iowa.

135

he reduced the alternatives to a dichotomy between good and evil, and challenged his audience to stand for some idealistic principle.

What, then, were the precepts with which Roosevelt admonished his listeners? From whence did these doctrines arise? How did he apply them to the practical problems he faced? What was the response of his hearers? The answers to these questions will be the center of interest in this brief study of Roosevelt.

ROOSEVELT'S DOCTRINES

Although he was much concerned with reform in his career, it was not out of any one consuming mission to which he devoted his whole life that Roosevelt's doctrines arose. Nor was he a visionary who spoke in a speculative mood. Rather it was with what he called "realizable ideals" that Roosevelt challenged his countrymen. "I have always had a horror of words that are not translated into deeds, of speech that does not result in action—in other words, I believe . . . in preaching what can be practiced and then in practicing it."[3] He condemned those who advocated ideals "which the preacher and the hearer know cannot be followed, which they know it is not intended to have followed."[4] His was a philosophy capable of adjusting to the give and take of practical politics, but it was not biased against any particular group or class. It was a creed by which all controversies could be judged.

Representative of Roosevelt's tendency to focus on moral issues was his approach to the 1896 political campaign. Speaking on October 15 before the American Republican College League in Chicago, he challenged the college man to spend "every faculty and power he possesses . . . in behalf of the cause of righteousness."[5] He contended: "Our foes are waging a campaign which is at bottom waged primarily against morality and ability. . . . They use free silver as a cry because they hope therewith for the moment to mislead some honest men. . . . At bottom what they most desire is to strike down the men who by virtue of leadership in any walk of life . . . tend by their efforts to raise the whole community upward. . . ."[6] And near the conclusion of his speech: "We believe that the campaign should be waged on the moral, even more than the material issue."[7] In his letter of acceptance of the vice-presidential nomination, Roosevelt defined similarly the fundamental issue of the campaign of

1900.[8] Not that the practical arguments were ignored, for they were not. For example, in Detroit, September 7, 1900, Roosevelt refuted one by one Bryan's pronouncements on free silver, economic conditions in the country, and the danger of militarism, imperialism, and expansionism.[9] But Roosevelt's penchant to argue from moral grounds was consistent.

Righteousness, right, morality were, to Roosevelt, self-defined terms, cast largely in the pattern of traditional American protestantism. More particularly, he was inclined to identify "right" with *his* stand on a question, as was demonstrated in the questioning of Roosevelt during the trial of Barnes vs. Roosevelt:

> Q. How did you know that substantial justice was done?
> Mr. Roosevelt. Because I did it, because . . . I was doing my best.
> Q. You mean to say that when you do a thing thereby substantial justice is done?
> Mr. Roosevelt. I do. When I do a thing I do it so as to do substantial justice. I mean just that.

Pringle, his biographer, comments: "This was the essence of Theodore Roosevelt's philosophy, the conviction of righteousness that strengthened him in his moments of inner doubt. Justice was an essential part of righteousness."[10]

The meaning of these basic tenets was not derived out of any complex weighing of varying degrees of morality. Common understanding was assumed through reference to traditional Christian concepts. Said Roosevelt: "The doctrine that I preach . . . is a doctrine that was old when the children of Israel came out of Egypt; a doctrine as old as our civilization; . . . the doctrine that teaches us that men shall prosper as long as they do their duty to themselves and their neighbors alike; the doctrine that we shall believe as long as we believe in those archaic rules of conduct which were set down in the Sermon on the Mount."[11]

But we must not overlook the practical side of Roosevelt's idealism. His entrance into politics provides early testimony to this tempering quality in his outlook. Here was a well-born young man, financially independent, whose rearing and environment set him apart from the ward heeler, the political boss who met with his henchmen over a saloon. But if this were the way to become a mem-

ber of the governing class, Roosevelt would take it.[12] In a time
when bossism was the order of the day in politics, he had no other
choice if he wanted to make a career of public life. So his years as
an office holder present an interesting study of a man who balanced
his ideals against the practical problem of getting a job done, working as far as his conscience would let him with men who did not
share his outlook, but who often controlled the means by which a
task could be accomplished.

Out of this experience Roosevelt evolved his two gospels, the
"gospel of morality" and the "gospel of efficiency." In public life,
he held:

> A man must not only be disinterested, he must be efficient. If
> he goes into politics he must go into practical politics, in order
> to make his influence felt. . . . He must not lose his own high
> ideal, and yet he must face the fact that the majority of the
> men with whom he must work have lower ideals. . . . He
> must realize that political action, to be effective, must be the
> joint action of many men, and that he must sacrifice somewhat
> of his own opinions to those of his associates if he ever hopes
> to see his desires take practical shape.[13]

These precepts Roosevelt not only practiced but preached. He
inveighed against critics who do not translate their words into action. One of the most complete developments of this theme was his
William Belden Noble lecture on "Applied Ethics" delivered at
Harvard University, December 14, 1910. In it he said:

> The only value in a speech comes from there being the effort
> made with measurable success to translate the words into deeds.
> Of course, the man who preaches decency and straight dealing
> occupies a peculiarly contemptible position if he does not try
> himself to practice what he preaches; and, on the other hand,
> the men who listen to him—you here—should realize that if
> they treat listening to a lecture about their duties as a substitute
> for performing their duties they would better have stayed at
> home.[14]

Urging men to get into the hurly-burly of political life and practical affairs, he gave his highest praise to those "men who have
spoken to us through deeds and not words, or whose words have
gathered their especial charm and significance because they came
from men who did speak in deeds."[15]

To morality and efficiency Roosevelt added the virtue of manliness. His pursuit of this ideal in his own life, his policies, and his exhortations of the American public extended to the point that some of Roosevelt's critics charged him with pugnaciousness, even jingoism. Individually and as a nation he admonished us to be strong. "No people has ever yet done great and lasting work if its physical type was infirm and weak. Goodness and strength must go hand in hand if the Republic is to be preserved. The good man who is ready and able to strike a blow for the right, and to put down evil with the strong arm, is the citizen who deserves our most hearty respect."[16] His efforts on behalf of preparedness while he was Under-Secretary of the Navy prior to the Spanish American War, his participation in that war, the display of strength in sending our battle fleet on a mission around the world while he was President, and his bitter criticism of Woodrow Wilson in failing to push military preparation prior to World War I were all expressions of Roosevelt's belief in the virtue of strength on a national scale. To him, strength and courage, individual and collective, were fundamental American ideals.

Roosevelt also staunchly upheld the virtues of family life, particularly the responsibility of rearing children. Failure in these duties was fraught with danger to the commonwealth. Decrying the fact that the birth-rate had fallen below the death-rate in certain areas and among certain classes of the population, in his sixth annual message he admonished: "Surely it should need no demonstration to show that wilful sterility is . . . the one sin for which penalty is national death, race death; a sin for which there is no atonement; a sin which is the more dreadful exactly in proportion as the men and women guilty thereof are . . . those whom for the sake of the State it would be well to see the fathers and mothers of many healthy children."[17] In this message, as in some of its predecessors, "marked by interminable observations on the moralities,"[18] Roosevelt spelled out what he considered to be an essential virtue of American life. His position was conservative, not subject to much argument.[19] Nor did Roosevelt discuss this subject as often as some others. Rather, the importance of the family in American life was assumed.

That a moralistic orientation was dominant in Roosevelt's thinking is commonly agreed among those who have studied his life and works. As Gifford Pinchot put it: "The final test with Roosevelt was always—Is it right? And when he had concluded what was right in any given set of circumstances his action followed simply and certainly. . . . This view of himself as the servant of righteousness was thoroughly characteristic of Roosevelt."[20]

SOURCES OF ROOSEVELT'S MORAL PRECEPTS

Why a man holds the ideas he does can be only partially explained. The uniqueness of the man himself best accounts for some of his attitudes and ideas. It could have been partially a matter of metabolism that gave Roosevelt the boundless energy he seemed to possess. Achievement is likely to result from the conspiring of will power and drive with natural endowments, factors which we cannot fully assess. But we can also discern some external influences which seemed to help shape the fabric of Roosevelt's thinking and develop his moral sensitivity.

Parental influence apparently was strong. Some striking parallels exist between Roosevelt and his father. That Theodore had a deep affection and admiration for his father is evident from his description of him as "the best man I ever knew. He combined strength and courage with gentleness, tenderness and great unselfishness. He would not tolerate in us children selfishness or cruelty, idleness, cowardice, or untruthfulness. . . . With great love and patience, and the most understanding sympathy and consideration, he combined insistence on discipline. . . . [But] he was the only man of whom I was really afraid. I do not mean it was a wrong fear, for he was entirely just, and we children adored him."[21] Sufficiently successful in business to give his family the comforts of gracious living in the city, summers in the country, extended travel abroad, and still leave his children independent in means, the elder Roosevelt also took an active interest in reform movements. He taught a mission class regularly on Sundays, a practice continued by the younger Roosevelt for three years prior to going to college and during his four years at Harvard. Reforms and charities concerned with the welfare of children were of particular interest to Roosevelt's father.[22] Religious habits, marked by morning and evening prayers and regular attendance at Sunday services, were observed in the Roosevelt household.[23]

Undoubtedly many of Roosevelt's contemporaries were reared in similar family patterns without acquiring the characteristics which marked Roosevelt so distinctly. It is not surprising, however, to find in the mature Roosevelt a disposition to set questions in a moralistic framework and a proclivity for reforms. These seeds were planted and nurtured in his boyhood; they seemed to flower in his public life.

Although the reading a man has done may have a strong influence in shaping his outlook, Pringle, Roosevelt's biographer, comments: "It is not too safe to attribute the characteristics of adult years to the books and magazines of childhood. Nearly every boy and girl of the Victorian era read the same moral rubbish. Some of them grew up to be statesmen. . . . Others became editors of the *Police Gazette*, and worried, when the twitch of conscience came, over their own depravity."[24] Despite the skepticism of Pringle, it is clear that some of Roosevelt's reading stimulated his moralistic interests. He singles out for special comment, *Our Young Folks*, a magazine which he read as a boy, preserved in bound volumes, and reread as an adult. He found the stories in the magazine interesting and designed to teach "manliness, decency, and good conduct."[25] Whether *Our Young Folks* significantly modified Roosevelt's ideas and attitudes or whether he read this magazine because he found it congenial to the interests he had already acquired is a moot question. Nevertheless, in Roosevelt's mind its influence was important.

Apparently the personality and writings of Jacob Riis also had considerable impact upon Roosevelt. During his first years in politics Roosevelt tells us that he was not "alive to social and industrial needs."[26] But by the time he became Police Commissioner of New York City, *How the Other Half Lives* by Jacob Riis had impressed him with the squalor in the tenements to the point that he turned to Riis for guidance in attacking the conditions in those areas of the city.[27] Through his writings and personal influence Riis succeeded in sensitizing Roosevelt to social conditions.

One other writer mentioned specifically as contributing significantly to Roosevelt's ideas on the business and economic life of the nation was Herbert Croly. In *The Promise of American Life*, Croly attempted to analyze the position of the man of wealth and the corporation in American social, political, and economic life in the light of our democratic ideals. The following excerpt strikes the keynote of the book: "The Promise of American Life is to be fulfilled—not merely by a maximum amount of economic freedom, but by a certain measure of discipline; not merely by the abundant satisfaction of individual desires, but by a large measure of individual subordination and self-denial. . . . The automatic fulfillment of the American national Promise is to be abandoned, if at all, precisely because the traditional American confidence in individual freedom has resulted in a morally and socially undesirable distribution of wealth."[28] This appraisal of our economy according to moral and social principles found a sympathetic response in Roosevelt and was reflected in the economic reforms he espoused.[29]

Manliness, another virtue stressed by Roosevelt, probably was an outgrowth of his struggle for health. Embarrassed by his puniness and inability to hold his own physically with boys of his age, at fourteen Roosevelt began to take boxing lessons to overcome his physical weakness, an interest which was sustained even into his years as President. His physical activity extended to hiking, tennis, horseback riding, ranching, hunting, exploring, and from it all evolved his gospel of "The Strenuous Life," or as Roosevelt preferred it, "The Vigor of Life."[30] But he was concerned not only with physical health and vigor. Spiritual implications were involved. Having reviewed his exploits, Roosevelt commented: "I have mentioned all these experiences . . . because out of them grew my philosophy—perhaps in part caused by my philosophy—of bodily vigor as a method of getting that vigor of soul without which vigor of the body counts for nothing."[31]

Any attempt to explain this man and his ideas is destined to be incomplete. Roosevelt crossed the American scene at the point when the stimulus to industrialization and the building of railroads was far enough removed from the Civil War so that they were no longer endowed with immunity because they were important to the war effort. The nation could turn its attention to the corruption, exploitation, abuses that had grown up with rapid industrial expansion. The time was ripe for social, political, economic reform.[32] Freed from the compromises sometimes necessitated by the burden of earning a living, yet not so truly wealthy that he was fully a part of the monied aristocracy, Roosevelt was in a position to look analytically and critically at American life, point out the deficiencies he saw, and challenge his listeners to apply moral principles to all phases of their individual and corporate lives. In a sense Roosevelt had the degree of independence, the range of experience, the touch of flamboyance, and the idealism which marked him as the "typical American," and gained for him acceptance from a large segment of the public. The stage was set for someone to attack the social and political ills resulting from the exploitation and abuse of power by those in control of the wealth and industry of the country. In a sense, then, Roosevelt spoke what his audience was ready to hear. He became one of the dominant voices in American politics during the first decade of this century because of a unique blending of his insights and abilities with the particular circumstances and tone of the times.

Virtues Applied to Issues

The sermonic tone that dominated Roosevelt's speaking can be illustrated from his pronouncements on some of the principal issues he faced. A continuing controversy through most of Roosevelt's public life was the proper role of government in business, finance, and industry. The power of organized wealth in government had become so great that, in the opinion of some observers, this country was never closer to social revolution than during the presidency of Roosevelt. He is credited with contributing substantially to the prevention of that disaster.[33]

Unlike some of his contemporaries, Roosevelt did not condemn wealth as such; rather he focused upon the abuse of the power and prestige wealth brings. In his speech, "The Man with the Muck-Rake," frequently selected as most representative of Roosevelt,[34] he condemned those who were indiscriminate in their attacks upon men of wealth.

> We can no more and no less afford to condone evil in the man of capital than evil in the man of no capital. The wealthy man who exults because there is a failure of justice in the effort to bring some trust magnate to an account for his misdeed is as bad as, and no worse than, the so-called labor leader who clamorously strives to excite a foul class feeling on behalf of

some other labor leader who is implicated in murder. One attitude is as bad as the other, and no worse; in each case the accused is entitled to exact justice. . . .[35]

Calling upon his audience "to discriminate in the sharpest way between fortunes well won and fortunes ill won," he exhorted them
to "strive to bring about clean living and right thinking."[36]

This is a recurrent theme in Roosevelt's speeches. The issues were
drawn in terms of evil, justice, honesty. We do not get a careful
analysis of the distribution of wealth, a citing of facts and figures
concerning corporations and their activities. Rather there is a piling
up of admonitions against the irresponsible stirring up of discontent,
accompanied by appeals for justice, honesty, and righteous living.
The central issue in Roosevelt's mind was not economic or legal,
but moral.

Reform in government, the extension of the civil service system,
and the correlate denunciation of the spoils system also occupied a
considerable portion of Roosevelt's attention. In an address on
"Americanism in Municipal Politics," while he was chairman of the
New York City police board, he demonstrated his inclination to
make the fundamental consideration a moral issue when he said,
"to sum up then, let me speak once more of the need of a radical, a
thoroughgoing Americanism and the need of the common virtues
for the solution of our municipal problems."[37] To those who expected him to pattern the New York City police force after those
of Berlin, London, or Dublin, he responded, "I was going to model
it largely upon certain of the elementary virtues advocated in the
Old and New Testament."[38] To this same group he said, "There
are certain audiences before which I feel that it is especially incum-
bent upon me always to lay especial stress upon the fact that they
must be decent and straight. There are other audiences, like this,
where I know that it is entirely needless to make an appeal for
decency and righteousness and where I make my appeal purely that
you shall be effective, that you shall be efficient."[39] In this dichoto-
mous approach to audiences he not only presented his analysis of
the issues involved in reform, but also his general tendency to view
questions from a moral perspective.

How heavily Roosevelt sometimes loaded his speeches with appeals to virtue is found in his review of the accomplishments of the

Fifty-first Congress, particularly its passage of a copyright law. "It was a measure of justice and right; a measure demanded by honor and honesty; one of those measures which distinctly raise the national tone; which give us cause to feel a just pride in the manliness and high-mindedness of the American people."[40] In one sentence he has packed practically all of the gospel he preached again and again, which he related to almost every specific question he discussed.

The process by which he converted military preparedness and war into virtues is one of the more interesting facets of Roosevelt's mind. Pacifism might seem more congenial to one so moralistically inclined. Quite the opposite was the case. Few men in our history have pressed more ardently for making our nation militarily strong or have romanticized war as much as this leader of the Rough Riders. Of all the bromides associated with Roosevelt, "Speak softly, but carry a big stick" is probably most frequently remembered by Americans. When asked what title or honor he would prefer above all others, he replied, "Major-General in United States Army in active service."[41] To Roosevelt, leading the charge up San Juan Hill in the Spanish-American War was one of the most glorious moments of his life.[42]

The "peace of righteousness" became the keynote of Roosevelt's message concerning war, peace, and the principle upon which this nation should conduct its international affairs. On his scale of values, he held: "No triumph of peace is quite so great as the supreme triumphs of war. . . . It is true that no nation can be really great unless it is great in peace; in industry, integrity, honesty. . . . But it is also necessary that the nation should have physical no less than moral courage; the capacity to do and dare and die at need, and that grim and steadfast resolution which alone will carry a great people through a great peril."[43] To Roosevelt, the Revolutionary War, the War of 1812, the Civil War, the Spanish-American War, all were righteous wars against oppression and injustice. The men he eulogized—Washington, Lincoln, Grant, Dewey—were measured ultimately by their soldierly virtues or their leadership in a military struggle for righteousness.[44] This principle led him to advocate preparedness ardently, to denounce President Wilson bitterly for his policies prior to and during World War I.

Here was the application of the virtue of manliness to national and international affairs. Policies and actions, no matter how righteous, just, or well intentioned, availed little if they could not be sustained by physical strength. To brag and posture without the ability to back up words with force, individually and as a nation, or to be abject and weak in the face of injustice was contemptible to Roosevelt. In the summary of his writings on "America and the World War" he revealed the extent of his scorn for the pacifists: " 'Blessed are the peacemakers,' not merely the peace-lovers; for action is what makes thought operative and valuable. Above all, the peace-prattlers are in no way blessed. On the contrary, only mischief has sprung from the activities of the professional peace-prattlers, the ultrapacifists, who, with the shrill clamor of eunuchs, preach the gospel of the milk and water of virtue. . . ."[45]

War was the way to peace, in the mind of Roosevelt, if war was necessary to establish justice and righteousness. So he exhorted individuals to manliness, the nation to preparedness, and in our foreign policy to make only those commitments and pronouncements we are prepared to sustain with military power.

Nor did he believe that the United States would develop a warlike spirit or engage in unjust war.[46] Almost by definition its cause would be righteous. The issue to be decided was simply, "Is our stand just, is it right?" With an affirmative answer, essentially on our terms, then war became an expression of our national greatness and an opportunity for individual heroism of the highest order.

Roosevelt applied his ethical precepts to the use of speech itself. Recognizing oratory as one of the foremost gifts admired in a democracy, and the desirability of a "leader of opinion" being able "to state his views clearly and convincingly," he set these limitations on this gift:

> But all that the oratory can do of value to the community is to enable the man thus to explain himself; if it enables the orator to persuade his hearers to put false values on things, it merely makes him a power for mischief. . . . The phrasemaker, . . . however great his power, whose speech does not make for courage, sobriety, and right understanding, is simply a noxious element in the body politic, and it speaks ill for the public if he has influence over them. To admire the gift of

oratory without regard to the moral quality behind the gift is to do wrong to the republic.[47]

His comments about journalists were even more decisive. Thus, the means of discussing issues were measured by ethical standards. In this, as in other questions, the problem was reduced to a moral concern.

Roosevelt did not specifically relate the virtue of family life to the economic and political issues he discussed, nor would it have been essentially logical for him to do so. Such a virtue is more a general concern of our society. Not that families and family life have no economic and political consequences; witness the contemporary concern about the rapid rise in the birth rate and the impending crisis of overpopulation in such nations as China, India, Russia, possibly in the United States itself. But Roosevelt's was a different day, and the rearing of large, healthy families was, in his thinking, fundamental to our society. In "The Strenuous Life," which stands alongside the "Muck-Rake" speech as one of his more significant utterances, Roosevelt pulled together the virtues that constituted his creed of Americanism.

> In the last analysis a healthy state can exist only when the men and women who make it up lead clean, vigorous, healthy lives; when the children are so trained that they shall endeavor, not to shirk difficulties, but to overcome them. . . . The man must be glad to do a man's work. . . . The woman must be the housewife, the helpmeet of the homemaker, the wise and fearless mother of many healthy children. . . . When men fear work or fear righteous war, when women fear motherhood, they tremble on the brink of doom. . . .[48]

Fifty years later the problem might have appeared different to Roosevelt, at least as far as the birth rate is concerned, but he was speaking in the context of frontiers still to be won, of congestion in cities that posed grave social problems but not imminent overpopulation. In this admonition he was simply reiterating a commonly accepted tenet in the American Credo.

SUMMARY

In this brief study of Roosevelt, no attempt has been made to analyze in detail the logic, the forms of support, the rebuttal of opponents he presented in hundreds of speeches. Nor has any effort been made to duplicate the able analyses of his career as a speaker by William A. Behl and Richard Murphy.[49] Rather, an attempt has been made to focus on the dominant tone of Roosevelt's message to the American people.

We have seen Roosevelt as a militant preacher, exhorting his fellow countrymen to follow the elementary virtues of justice, righteousness, manliness, and decent, courageous, healthy family life. These were not simply the emotional appeals used by Roosevelt to provide motivation for the logic he employed, the action he desired. These were the yardsticks in his thinking by which specific questions were measured. Ultimately he reduced the argument to a moral issue and on these grounds took his stand and challenged his listeners.

In the preface of one of the volumes of Roosevelt's *Works*, William Allen White characterizes effectively the impact of this man as a speaker on his contemporaries:

> This is a book of sermons. . . . There is a husky Old Testament flavor about these homilies. . . . Their exegesis is forthright: Be good and you will be useful and so should be happy. . . . Like Isaiah . . . they are addressed to men in the mass, to a nation; to a civilization; to an age—these sermons of the Preacher. Their form is not rhetorically interesting, nor is the language of the dissertations beautiful or eloquent. . . . Conviction comes largely by two devices: vigorous declaration and diverting repetition. Over and over the theme is hammered into the mind and heart of the multitude: Be good, be good, be good; live for righteousness, fight for righteousness, and if need be die for it. Nothing else matters but to be militantly decent.[50]

Footnotes

1. Owen Wister, *Roosevelt: The Story of a Friendship* (New York, 1930), p. 232.
2. Theodore Roosevelt, *Autobiography* (New York, 1914), pp. 155-156.
3. *Ibid.*, p. 174.
4. Theodore Roosevelt, *Realizable Ideals* (San Francisco, 1912), p. 5.
5. Theodore Roosevelt, "The Menace of the Demagogue," speech before the American Republican College League, Chicago, Illinois, October 15, 1896, *Works of Theodore Roosevelt* (National Edition; New York, 1926), XIV, 260. Hereafter all references to the *Works of Theodore Roosevelt* will be identified as *Works*, with the particular volume indicated. The National Edition of Roosevelt's *Works* printed in 1926 is identical in content with the Memorial

Edition published 1923-1925. Notes in both editions indicate that the texts of speeches and articles were taken from primary sources and appear to be consistent with these primary sources.

6. *Ibid.*, pp. 260-261.

7. *Ibid.*, p. 273.

8. Theodore Roosevelt, revised draft of a letter "To Hon. Edward O. Wolcott, chairman, committee on notification of vice president, Oyster Bay, N. Y., September 15, 1900," Manuscript Division, Library of Congress, Washington, D. C., p. 3. See also Roosevelt, "The Issues of 1900," *Works*, XIV, 361.

9. Theodore Roosevelt, manuscripts of "Detroit Speech, Sept. 6, 1900," Manuscript Division, Library of Congress, Washington, D. C. See also Roosevelt, "The Prophecies of Mr. Bryan," *Works*, XIV, 373-385. The manuscripts of this speech indicate that it was to be delivered September 6, 1900; the text in the *Works* states the speech was delivered in Detroit, September 7, 1900.

10. Henry F. Pringle, *Theodore Roosevelt* (New York, 1931), p. 446.

11. Roosevelt, "Property and the State," speech at the Independent Club, Buffalo, New York, May 15, 1899, *Works*, XIV, 328.

12. Roosevelt, *Autobiography*, pp. 56-59.

13. Theodore Roosevelt, "The Manly Virtues and Practical Politics," *Forum*, XVII (July, 1894), 551-552.

14. Roosevelt, "Applied Ethics," lecture at Harvard University, December 14, 1910. *Works*, XIII, 597.

15. Theodore Roosevelt, "True American Ideals," *Forum*, XVIII (February, 1895), 750.

16. Theodore Roosevelt, "Professionalism in Sports," *North American Review*, CLI (August, 1890), 187.

17. Roosevelt, "Sixth Annual Message," December 3, 1906, *Works*, XV, 377-378. Also, *Congressional Record*, Fifty-Ninth Congress, Second Session, XLI, Pt. 1, 29.

18. Pringle, *Theodore Roosevelt*, p. 359.

19. Wister, *Roosevelt: The Story of a Friendship*, pp. 233-235.

20. Gifford Pinchot, "Roosevelt as President," *Works*, XV, xxxiv.

21. Roosevelt, *Autobiography*, pp. 7-8.

22. *Ibid.*, pp. 9-11.

23. *Ibid.*, pp. 10-12.

24. Pringle, *Theodore Roosevelt*, p. 24.

25. Roosevelt, *Autobiography*, p. 17. See also p. 27.

26. *Ibid.*, p. 63.

27. *Ibid.*, pp. 173-174. Also Roosevelt, "Americanism in Municipal Politics," speech before the Liberal Club, Buffalo, New York, September 10, 1895. *Works*, XIV, 203-204.

28. Herbert Croly, *The Promise of American Life* (New York, 1909), p. 22.

29. Roosevelt, *Autobiography*, p. 79.

30. *Ibid.*, p. 52.

31. *Ibid.*, p. 51.

32. Vernon Louis Parrington, "The Beginnings of Critical Realism," *Main Currents in American Thought*, III, 1860-1920 (New York, 1930), *passim*.

33. *Encyclopedia Britannica*, XIX (1956), 538.

34. For example, the speech appears both in A. Craig Baird, *American Public Addresses* (New York, 1956), pp. 211-219, and Wayland Maxfield Parrish and Marie Hochmuth, *American Speeches* (New York, 1954), pp. 482-491.

35. Theodore Roosevelt, "Original draft of President's address at the laying of the cornerstone of the House of Representatives Office Building, April 14, 1906," Manuscript Division, Library of Congress, Washington, D. C., p. 14. See also Roosevelt, "The Man with the Muck-Rake," *Works*, XVI, 420.

36. Theodore Roosevelt, "Address of President Roosevelt at the laying of the corner stone of the Office Building of the House of Representatives, Saturday, April 14, 1906," Manuscript Division, Library of Congress, Washington, D. C., 9 DR and 12 DR of the revised galley proof. See also the original draft of this speech (fn. 35), p. 21, and *Works*, XVI, 421, 423-424.

37. Roosevelt, "Americanism in Municipal Politics," speech before the Liberal Club, Buffalo, New York, September 10, 1895, *Works*, XIV, 201.

38. *Ibid.*

39. *Ibid.*, p. 200.

40. Roosevelt, "The Fifty-First Congress," speech before the Federal Club, New York City, March 6, 1891, *Works*, XIV, 131.

41. Pringle, *Theodore Roosevelt*, p. 589.

42. *Ibid.*, pp. 193-196.

43. Roosevelt, "Washington's Forgotten Maxim," speech before the Naval War College, June, 1897, *Works*, XIII, 185-186.

44. Roosevelt, *Works*, XIII, 420-429, 430-441, 500-505.

45. Roosevelt, "Summing Up," *Works*, XVIII, 164.

46. Roosevelt, "Washington's Forgotten Maxim," speech before the Naval War College, June, 1897, *Works*, XIII, 182.

47. Roosevelt, "Citizenship in a Republic," address delivered at the Sorbonne, Paris, April 23, 1910, *Works*, XIII, 516-517.

48. Roosevelt, "The Strenuous Life," speech before the Hamilton Club, Chicago, April 10, 1899, *Works*, XIII, 320-321.

49. William Behl, "The Speaking and Speeches of Theodore Roosevelt," (doctoral dissertation, Northwestern University, 1942); "Theodore Roosevelt's Principles of Speech Preparation and Delivery," *Speech Monographs*, XII (1945), 112-122; "Theodore Roosevelt's Principles of Invention," *Speech Monographs*, XIV (1947), 93-110. Richard Murphy, "Theodore Roosevelt," in *History and Criticism of American Public Address*, III, ed. Marie Kathryn Hochmuth (New York, 1955), 313-364.

50. William Allen White, "Saith the Preacher," *Works*, XIII, xi.

William Jennings Bryan
Crusader for the Common Man

WILLIAM JENNINGS BRYAN *(March 19, 1860–July 26, 1925)*. *Born at Salem, Illinois; participated in declamation, oratory, and debate at Salem High School, at Whipple Academy, 1876-1877, and at Illinois College at Jacksonville, 1877-1881; active in literary and debating society at college and winner of second place in Illinois intercollegiate oratorical contest in junior year; A.B. (highest honors and valedictorian) Illinois college and winner of second place in Illinois intercollegiate oratorical law at Jacksonville, 1883-1887; then at Lincoln, Nebraska; elected to Congress by Democrats of Nebraska in 1890, 1892; defeated for United States senator, 1894; editor* OMAHA WORLD HERALD, *1894-1896; nominated by Democrats for presidency in 1896 at convention where he represented Nebraska's silver delegation; traveled extensively to deliver unparalleled number of campaign speeches; defeated by McKinley; lectured on bimetallism, 1897-1898; Democratic candidate, 1900, defeated by McKinley-Roosevelt ticket; established the* COMMONER *at Lincoln in 1901; nominated a third time by Democrats, 1908; defeated by Taft; tour of world, 1905-1906; instrumental in securing nomination of Woodrow Wilson in Democratic convention of 1912; Secretary of State, 1913-1915; resigned because of lack of sympathy with Wilson's policy after sinking of "Lusitania"; supported Wilson's nomination in Democratic convention of 1916; prosecutor for state in Scopes trial in Dayton, Tennessee; lecturer on Chautauqua circuit and at religious assemblies. Author of* THE FIRST BATTLE, *1896;* SECOND BATTLE, *1900;* SPEECHES OF WILLIAM JENNINGS BRYAN, *2 vols., 1913;* MEMOIRS OF WILLIAM JENNINGS BRYAN, *1925; many articles and editorials. Significant speeches include "The Tariff," Mar. 16, 1893; "Bimetallism," Aug. 16, 1893; "On Income Tax," Jan. 30, 1894; "Cross of Gold," July 8, 1896; "Imperialism," Aug. 8, 1900; "The Value of an Ideal," 1901; "The Prince of Peace," 1904; "Shall the People Rule?" Aug. 12, 1908; "Lincoln as an Orator," Feb. 12, 1909.*

William Jennings Bryan
Crusader for the Common Man

MARGARET WOOD*

WILLIAM JENNINGS BRYAN said that no one could question the truth of Daniel Webster's statement that eloquence consisted in the man, in the subject, and in the occasion.[1] Was Bryan, three times an unsuccessful candidate for president, an eloquent speaker by some or any of the tests of effective speaking? Have his ideas, which some say form the bridge between Andrew Jackson and Franklin Delano Roosevelt, stood the test of time? For more than thirty-seven years Bryan spoke for his party, voicing his belief in the inherent dignity of the common man. Without wealth, except his own earnings, without holding political office, except for four years in Congress and two years as Secretary of State, and without professional success as a lawyer, he had a powerful influence upon the Democratic party and upon subsequent legislation.

Contemporaries referred to Bryan as the silver tongued orator, the boy orator of the Platte, or the Gladstone of America, and contradictorily as anarchist, imposter, and demagogue. The *New York Times* considered Bryan's maiden effort in Congress the best tariff speech in ten years.[2] The *New York Tribune* regarded Bryan as one of the few good elocutionists in the House but his address on bimetallism "more sentimental than argumentative, more forcible than convincing, and more rhetorical than logical. . . ."[3]

Charles E. Merriam of the University of Chicago, who said Bryan's gift of oratory was beyond question the most notable factor in his political leadership,[4] defended him as effectively as H. L. Mencken condemned him. Henry Steele Commager called Bryan

* Margaret Wood (B.A. Grinnell College, M.A. 1938, Ph.D. 1950, State University of Iowa) is professor of speech at Northern Illinois University.

the last great spokesman of the America of the nineteenth century who "was always in command of his subject as well as of his audience. . . ."[5] Richard Hofstadter wrote that Bryan lacked steadfast and self-confident intelligence.[6]

TRAINING FOR PUBLIC ADDRESS

As a young boy, Bryan's interest in public speaking was encouraged both by his father and his mother. From his father, a lawyer and a judge, Bryan developed a respect for good speaking and a familiarity with the Bible which he nourished throughout his life and which he revealed in his speeches. He said that his first audience was his mother, to whom he declaimed his lessons as he stood on a walnut table about two feet square.

Bryan received a classical education typical of the early training in liberal arts colleges in Illinois. While still at Whipple Academy, he was elected to Sigma Pi literary society where he gained valuable experience in recitations, declamations, orations, and debates. He continued this type of competitive participation in college. In his junior year he represented Illinois College in the intercollegiate oratorical contest at Galesburg, winning second place with his oration, "Justice." He placed great value upon declamations, essays, and orations but considered debating superior training for public speaking because of its requirements of preparation and its opportunities for renown.[7] As editor of *The World's Famous Orations*, Bryan showed in his introductory remarks that he was familiar with addresses of antiquity and that "Nowhere is so much information crowded into the same number of words as in a memorable speech." Bryan, who admired Bancroft's address of 1835 on "The People in Art, Government and Religion," was probably influenced by the historian's belief in the union of moral force and popular government.[8]

At the age of sixteen when he attended his first national convention, Bryan became a student of the effective speaking of others. He also tested his ideas and improved his style by writing. In addition to his conventional training in speaking throughout high school and college, Bryan gained further experience as a lawyer, a politician, and a platform lecturer.

BASIC IDEAS

Bryan experienced the impact of the Industrial Revolution, the depressions of 1873 and 1893, the rise of the Populist movement, the trend toward imperialism influenced by the war with Spain, the catastrophe of World War I followed by decisions concerning peace, and the growing conflict between science and religion. What were Bryan's basic assumptions on the issues which he propounded consistently?

Democracy against plutocracy

Steeped in Jacksonian and Jeffersonian philosophy, he was primarily the defender of the masses. The organized source of Bryan's concept of the common man was the Populist and Progressive movements, motivated by the Grangers, the Greenbackers, and the Farmers' Alliance, which originated to meet the decline of rural America. Bryan stated that "if you legislate to make the masses prosperous, their prosperity will find its way up through every class which rests upon them."[9] Debate upon this controversial point was renewed in the 1930's.

Bryan was also the interpreter of the Yankee-Protestant political tradition which felt that government should guard the moral character of individuals.[10] Successful industries, large corporations, and political bosses that could not be explained by personal character mystified both the Populists and Bryan. From 1898-1914 major consolidations took place in steel, oil, tobacco, and utilities. When the cost of living soared, the public placed the blame upon trusts. Concern for the farmer and the working class shifted to concern for the taxpayer and the middle class. Bryan believed that competition should be restored and regulated. Variations of his motto that "a private monopoly is indefensible and intolerable"[11] appeared in the Democratic platforms of 1900, 1904, and word for word in the platform of 1908. At the Conference of Natural Resources at the White House in 1908 he uttered his historic phrase, "There is no twilight zone between the nation and states. . . ."[12] While the country has favored democracy over plutocracy, it has not been a partisan question but a national policy.

Tariff for revenue only

Although Bryan opposed tariff for protection, he favored it for revenue.[13] His thinking, like that of his father, was based on the Jacksonian philosophy of distributing the cost of government as widely as possible. Bryan proposed lowering tariff on raw materials and necessary items but keeping it higher on luxury items in order to take revenue from those able to pay and to stimulate competition and production of cheaper consumer goods. His argument was sound when judged by modern economic theory such as is embodied in the Reciprocal Trade Agreements Act of 1934. Because he failed to take into account the borrowing and expansion policy of the farmers, crop failures caused by drought, increased railroad rates, and the fact that the price of farm products was also determined by the world market, he oversimplified the cause of depression. But his underlying principle that the burdens of taxation should be equalized was vindicated.

Free coinage of silver

Because unjust deflation of prices favored the creditor class, Bryan wanted to cheapen the value of money by issuing silver. The money lenders interpreted this demand as division of property. Although Bryan correctly recounted symptoms of discontent, he oversimplified by laying the inequalities at the feet of the supporters of the gold standard. The real cause was not gold but the fact that currency could have no elasticity as long as it was bound to any standard which was scarce. But he was not wrong in his concept that a dollar approaches "honesty" as its purchasing power approaches stability.[14] Essentially the conflict concerning the "honest" dollar remains unresolved, although most of the demands of the Populists and the Democrats whom Bryan led have been incorporated into later laws and policies.

In later years Bryan said that free coinage of silver was not an end in itself but a means to an end—the relief of poverty by placing more money in circulation.[15] The end was partially accomplished by the unexpected increase in the production of gold. In addition, the great increase in the population of cities provided a market for agricultural products. Twenty years later, flexibility was achieved by the Federal Reserve note, based, not on gold, but on the supply of economic goods. Thus the currency could expand and contract as the volume of business rose and fell.

Income tax

Another outgrowth of Populist proposals, the income tax, Bryan presented solely as an issue between the rich and poor. Proponents felt that a greater measure of opportunity might be restored to the individual through the revival of the Civil War income tax on wealth. The well-to-do called it "rank class legislation" and called Bryan and his followers socialists and communists. Although Bryan preferred a graduated tax, he accepted the Wilson Tariff Act with its income tax rider "as offering a more equitable plan for making up the deficit in our revenues than any other which has been proposed."[16] Bryan's three platforms contained an income tax plan. His basic ideas have become an accepted type of taxation.

Anti-imperialism and peace

As an outgrowth of isolationism and ruralism, the Populists were more nationally minded than non-militaristic. Like the Populists, Bryan thought imperialism, tainted by association with England, the natural enemy of the free silverites, and linked with a protest against British colonial policies in South Africa, benefited Wall Street only. Bryan's "Naboth's Vineyard" speech crystallized his belief that self-determination was the right of all people: "Our national idea is self-government . . . we cannot ignore it in dealing with Filipinos."[17] Paradoxically, he favored the treaty to cede the Philippines to the United States because he thought it safer "to trust the American people to give independence to the Filipinos than to trust the accomplishment of that purpose to diplomacy with an unfriendly nation."[18] The moral earnestness of his thinking, growing out of religious conviction, strengthened his attack on imperialism. But Republican prosperity lost the anti-imperialism issue for Bryan. His ideas finally won acceptance because, by an Act of Congress and Proclamation of Franklin Delano Roosevelt, the Philippines became a free and independent nation.

Combined with Bryan's isolationism and nationalism were an earnest desire for peace and an abhorrence of dictation over others. What may have begun as opposition to vested interests was nourished by Christian pacifism. He considered militarism "nothing less than a challenge to the Christian civilization of the world."[19] It was to this belief of his fellow men that Bryan often appealed as did Woodrow Wilson.

Inspired by commissions of inquiry in disputes between capital and labor, Bryan drafted a plan for a similar court of arbitration for international disputes.[20] He negotiated thirty peace treaties and twenty ratifications with foreign powers, but the fact that he sent a warship to Haiti to protect economic interests deepened Latin American hostility to the United States. Although not a consistent pacifist when national honor was in question, Bryan was the first man in public office to attempt to put the ideas of peace advocates into political action.

Bryan, like Abraham Lincoln rather than Edmund Burke, stated that a candidate should follow the dictates of his party and its voters rather than urge personal views that had not been submitted to constituents. "I believe in the right of the people to instruct their delegates, and when a delegate is instructed, the instruction is binding upon him."[21] This is still a moot question among statesmen.

In his last years Bryan became more evangelist and less politician as he attempted to meet the threat of scientific realism. Somehow he did not succeed in relating his religious fundamentalism to the problems and attitudes of the twentieth century.

DEVELOPMENT OF HIS IDEAS

Factual and logical elements

Although Bryan was censured for lack of evidence and faulty reasoning, his congressional debates contradicted the charge. These speeches were primarily logical developments substantially supported by evidence. In the Democratic convention and political campaigns in Nebraska, he had formulated and tested his theories of free trade and protection. In his maiden speech on the tariff, most of his reasoning was cause and effect; that is, the alleged effect of the protective tariff and the actual effects on the manufacturer, consumer, and laborer. He supported his contentions with authorities acceptable to both political parties.[22] In support of the income tax, he showed that the principle of maximum exemption and minimum rate of taxation was not new but accepted universally: he cited its use in this country for ten years as well as its use in six other countries where the tax was higher than the proposed 2 per cent.[23]

In contrast to Bryan's congressional debates, his tariff address in 1908 contained less factual evidence because it was a campaign speech delivered to a mixed audience quite unused to contemplating the technical aspects of tariff. Although his attack on imperialism in 1900 was a passionate appeal rather than a logical argument, he used definition to show that imperialism was forcible annexation or monarchy as contrasted with expansion, which was mere acquisition of territory or democracy. As examples of the latter he named the Louisiana territory, Florida, and Texas.[24] With the exception of his justification of the Mexican annexation, his use of history was commendable.

The argument of his Cross of Gold speech consisted of contradictions, definitions, and dichotomies, the latter often specious because of improper division. His belief that legislation to make the masses prosperous would eventually improve all classes resting upon them[25] was debatable, but Bryan failed to establish its causal relationship with the currency question.

Both in his congressional debates and in his campaign speeches, Bryan used numerous examples for clarification. He used analogy for the same purpose. He compared the consumer with the fulcrum which was crushed by the tariff lever used to raise prices.[26] One of his famous analogies illustrated the advantages of bimetallism by comparing it with a river. Just as the river fed from two sources instead of one was less likely to fluctuate in volume, so the dollar resting upon two metals was less variable in purchasing power than the dollar which depended upon one metal.[27] This was a combination of authority and analogy because it was a theoretical advantage stated by a European writer on political economy.

Bryan demonstrated that he could argue effectively in the House or when he presented close reasoning to hostile audiences. His congressional addresses also displayed his skill in rebuttal. Although he cited instances and clarified argument by analogy, he also relied heavily upon historical precedent. Sometimes he neglected to point out causal relationships, and analogies were more figurative than literal.

Emotional and personal elements

Perhaps because Bryan was generally regarded as an honest man of good will, he used a minimum of personal justification in his speeches. "I would be presumptuous, indeed, to present myself against the distinguished gentlemen to whom you have listened if this were a mere measuring of abilities; but this is not a contest between persons,"[28] he said, as he tried to arouse the dissatisfied silverites without offending the gold supporters. By asserting that the question was not a matter of persons but of principles, he transcended personalities to discuss philosophy.

His congressional speeches did not lack humor. His satire on Raines as the "last rose of summer,"[29] or the fact that Bryan was delighted to hear about protective tariff from its highest source in Maine and Massachusetts because it became diluted and often polluted when traveling to Nebraska lightened a rather factual speech.[30] When Cockran suggested that taxation was a badge of freedom, Bryan countered "let me assure my friend that the poor people of this country are covered all over with the insignia of freemen."[31]

Although Bryan's congressional addresses appealed to patriotism and justice, his non-legislative speeches abounded with examples of exaggerated emotional entreaty. At the Chicago convention, for instance, Bryan associated the belief that the government had the right to coin and issue money, with Thomas Benton, who had compared Andrew Jackson's stand on that issue with Cicero's destroying the conspiracy of Catiline and saving Rome.[32] Thus he gracefully identified his opponents with conspiracy and allied his belief to that of a man admired by the Democrats. His conclusion was an appeal to patriotism in the face of the traditional enemy, England. He played upon nationalism to wipe out sectional feelings. He succeeded in making the campaign a crusade as he changed a great economic and political question to a moral one. But he successfully blended conservatism in spirit with radicalism in conviction and purpose. His ideas of surrendering the right of self-government by placing legislative control in the hands of foreign powers was semantically unsound since he exaggerated the issue as black or white.

In his speech in Madison Square Garden, Bryan immediately dispelled any idea of a crusade by admitting that he could not make magnanimous guarantees such as transferring the reward of industry to the lap of indolence.[33] In his conclusion he tried to unite sectional interests, for he brought greetings to the East from the West and the South together with an invitation "to accept the principles of a living faith rather than listen to those who preach the gospel of despair. . . ."[34]

His speech on imperialism justified his agreeing to the ratification of the treaty with Spain. This justification was needed, for accusations concerning his attitude had been made. He called upon nationalism when he argued that "for more than a century this nation has been a world power."[35] When he contrasted democracy of his party on the one hand and plutocracy of the Republicans on the other, he was making a partisan appeal directed to the common man, but it was an unsupported and invalid appeal.

Although Bryan could and did blend logical and emotional elements for persuasive purposes, he played upon the popular attitudes of his constituents concerning security, sectionalism, and nationalism. He could well have omitted some exaggerated dichotomies and impassioned appeals. Bryan directed affirmative attention to himself only when he needed to mitigate animosity. Both in congressional addresses and in campaign speeches he associated himself with acceptable causes and directed his appeals for justice and patriotism to the common man. He was inventive enough to combine fact and reasoning with emotional entreaty for a persuasive effect upon audiences inside and outside Congress.

STRUCTURE OF SPEECHES

Although Bryan's speeches did not always conform to traditional principles of organization, they were usually well-adapted to the specific audience. His congressional addresses were often refutatory in arrangement, with his ideas organized topically as he interwove refutation with his main contentions. Some non-legislative speeches were also rebuttals; others developed in problem-solution fashion. His Chicago speech of 1896 was not a model of organization. It was often difficult to tell whether he was attacking the Republicans or the gold Democrats or both. Although he was the fifth speaker in the debate on the currency question, there was some evidence that he welcomed this opportunity to exhibit party leadership and to be considered a candidate for the presidency. In the light of his purpose, then, he wanted to introduce the principal planks of his party within his time limit. Thus he had difficulty organizing his speech to meet several objectives.

Bryan's introductions varied in length and type, depending upon his analysis of the audience. In his congressional speech on bimetallism, for instance, the introduction had to be long, as Bryan attempted to placate the Cleveland Democrats and at the same time remind the representatives of their responsibility to their constituents. His conclusion was a lengthy emotional challenge, for this was his first stand against the Cleveland Democrats, and he had to make his feeling strong. In his acceptance speech of 1896, his introductory remarks denied that he was attacking the rights of private property. Bryan affirmed "that property rights, as well as the right of persons, are safe in the hands of the common people."[36] Thus he recognized objections raised by critics at Madison Square Garden.

Bryan's method of unfolding material and his treatment of relevancy were heavily governed by his sensitivity to the temper and interests of his audience. The type and length of his introductions depended upon whether he spoke in the House, where the question was already in debate, or whether he felt it necessary to conciliate his audience. His speaking usually reached a climax so that he concluded, not with a summary, but with a well-calculated emotional exhortation. Bryan was more concerned with unity of mood than with conventional arrangement of material.

LANGUAGE

Bryan exhibited the typical flights of imagery, connotative language, and heightened emotional style to which listeners of the latter part of the nineteenth century were accustomed. Like the earlier speeches of his contemporary political opponent, Albert J. Beveridge, Bryan's first speeches were elaborate in style compared with his subsequent ones. With the criticism of the press and the rise of realism and intellectualism, he may have sensed the trend toward more simplified oral expression.

Concreteness and figurativeness

Because of his concrete and homely expressions, Bryan succeeded in making complex subjects interesting and understandable to his constituents. He referred to the protective tariff as the type which "can get the most feathers off the goose with the least squawking." He declared that "the laborer has been used as a catspaw to draw chestnuts out of the fire for the manufacturer."[37] He warned metaphorically that "if there is poison in the blood of the hand it will ultimately reach the heart," and he vowed that scripture had "no Gatling gun attachment."[38]

Simile and analogy were effectively used. He created his famous definition of a business man by consecutive similes.[39] His analogy to blood poisoning was well-handled: ". . . remedies increase in severity as their application is postponed. Blood poisoning may be stopt by the loss of a finger today; it may cost an arm tomorrow or a life the next day. So poison in the body politic cannot be removed too soon. . . ."[40]

Biblical allusions

Bryan declared that the best quotations were from Holy Writ because people were more familiar with the Bible than with any other single book.[41] Many of his references were biblical: "You shall not press down upon the brow of labor this crown of thorns, you shall not crucify mankind upon a cross of gold."[42] He concluded his acceptance speech of 1908: ". . . by assuring to each the enjoyment of his just share of the proceeds of his toil, no matter in what part of the vineyard he labors, or to what occupation, profession or calling he devotes himself."[43]

Exaggeration

Bryan was justly criticized for purple passages. He spoke of the producer of wealth who "goes forth into a night illuminated by no star; he embarks upon a sea whose farther shore no mariner may find; he travels in a desert where the ever-lasting mirage makes his disappointment a thousandfold more keen."[44] Some of his sentences were so embroidered that they detracted from his central idea. Invoking the memory of the leadership of Jefferson and Jackson, Bryan questioned the Democratic party: "Standing upon this victory-crowned summit, will it turn its face to the rising or the setting sun?"[45] Numerous cliches and excesses individually regrettable in his Cross of Gold speech were minimized by the total emotional intensity and apparent sincerity of the speaker.

Connotation

Bryan's choice of connotative words helped him reach the populace. He was unwilling to "make merchandise of human blood," and he argued that "it is not necessary to own people in order to trade with them." He referred to the "gunpowder gospel" and was disinclined to "civilize with dynamite and proselyte with the sword."[46]

Bryan recognized the danger of slanted phrases used by others. "The poor man is called a socialist if he believes that the wealth of the rich should be divided among the poor, but the rich man is called a financier if he devises a plan by which the pittance of the poor can be converted to his use." Or he observed that "the man who wants the people to destroy the Government is an anarchist, but the man who wants the Government to destroy the people is called a patriot."[47]

Parallelism

When Bryan wanted to defy forcefully, he sometimes coupled short sentences with parallel structure. "We have petitioned, and our petitions have been scorned; we have entreated, and our entreaties have been disregarded; we have begged, and they have mocked when our calamity came. We beg no longer; we entreat no more; we petition no more. We defy them."[48] A combination of antithesis and parallelism was rhythmically excellent: "They call that man a statesman whose ear is tuned to catch the slightest pulsation of a pocketbook, and denounce as a demagogue anyone who dares to listen to the heart-beat of humanity,"[49] or "In a monarchy the king gives to the people what he believes to be a good government, in a republic the people secure for themselves what they believe to be a good government." Some of his parallelisms were quotable. Notable were: "Force can defend a right, but force has never yet created a right,"[50] or "People do not eat in proportion to their income; they do not wear clothing in proportion to their income; they do not use taxed goods in proportion to their income."[51]

Although Abraham Lincoln never spoke over the heads of his audience, he was not commonplace. Sometimes in trying to reach the masses, Bryan stooped to the vernacular. But he did know the importance of specific expressions and connotative words. Because of his use of antithesis and parallel structure, he was epigrammatic. For an espoused lover of peace, Bryan relied on a number of military metaphors and allusions. His equable nature, however, discouraged undue invective or irony. As Bryan said of Lincoln, "he gave felicitous expression to the thoughts of his followers."[52]

EFFECTIVENESS

Bryan, a national figure at thirty-six, was never out of the limelight until his death twenty-nine years later. The recorded praise of friends and enemies testified to his impact as a speaker. Possibly his speech at the convention in Chicago was not responsible for Bryan's nomination for the presidency in 1896, but it was the highlight of the convention.

In spite of an unfriendly press, Bryan's oratory helped him reach the people. "As each important speech is virtually a product of the entire life of the speaker . . . ,"[53] Bryan's effectiveness was a result of encouragement of his family, early training in college and extracurricular speaking, a splendid memory, and considerable writing both for the newspaper which he edited and for the *Commoner*. In addition, attending his first national political convention when he was sixteen, experimenting with ideas on the hustings and lecture platform, Bryan prepared for important speaking events. He admitted using the closing sentence of his Chicago address, "You shall not press down upon the brow of labor this crown of thorns, you shall not crucify mankind upon a cross of gold," at Crete, Nebraska. He tested this metaphor at that time in a debate with John Irish, a noted gold orator.[54] He said that he answered extemporaneously at the convention insofar as arrangement was concerned. From writing and committing speeches to memory, Bryan progressed to speaking from notes, unless the speech was of official importance.[55]

When Bryan did not read his addresses, critics praised his delivery. His most severe critics usually agreed that nature had given him a magnificent voice, which he used without effort in auditoriums many times the size of the House or without the aid of any mechanical device to reach 30,000 people in the open air.[56] In spite of his vocal intensity, Bryan achieved conversational effectiveness. Although it was agreed that his diction was easily understood, the *New York Times* commented that he said 18 *and* 69 instead of *1869* and that he elided some syllables such as *vir-chally* and *inter-nashnal*.[57] Bryan's platform appearance[58] and endurance and his quiet but forceful gestures enhanced his speaking. He had excellent bodily restraint and his gestures were well-coordinated with his thinking.

Did Bryan lose the presidential office but save the issues? The income tax law which he helped to write in 1894 was adopted as an amendment in 1913. He proposed the election of senators by direct vote as early as 1890. As Secretary of State in 1913 he signed the proclamation that made his proposal a part of the Constitution. He also helped to create the cabinet post of Secretary of Labor, to abolish government by injunction, to prohibit child labor, and to secure an eight-hour day. He first declared against monopolies in 1899 and wrote an anti-trust law into four Democratic platforms. By 1914 Woodrow Wilson incorporated Bryan's remedy for trusts into a Message to Congress. In 1898 Bryan urged the nation to declare its purpose to give independence to the Philippines. By 1916 he saw his ideal written into the Jones Bill, passed by both Houses and signed by President Wilson. His peace pacts originated from the idea of solving labor disputes through arbitration. As Secretary of State, he signed the first peace treaty in 1913. The principles which Bryan advocated were sustained by the passage of the Neutrality Bill by Congress in 1936. Most of the issues which Bryan supported were vindicated by time or continue to be fundamentals of social and economic democracy debatable today. Bryan's concept of individual freedom refused to accept either socialism or plutocracy.

Although Bryan clung obstinately to the issue of free silver, he failed to show how it could alleviate the problems of the nation. The currency question may have been partially solved by the discovery of gold which brought inflation, the eventual goal of the free silverites.

Recognized generally as a good and earnest man, Bryan had deficiencies that prevented him from attaining first rank as a speaker.

In his solicitude for the Cubans and the Filipinos, he ignored some of the problems of the Southern states. He was not concerned with the fact that state constitutions violated the federal Constitution which said that the Negro's franchise was not to be abridged. Bryan was consistent in most of his beliefs, although in the final analysis when he had to choose between nationalism and peace, he moved toward nationalism.

"A molder of thought is not necessarily an originator of the thought molded,"[59] said Bryan. While he did not have an inventive mind, he courageously championed ideas which he felt were paramount issues because they expressed the feeling of the masses. Probably his most original and successful contribution was the adoption of the arbitration treaties. He was more of an evangelist than a political scientist, more interested in faith than in fact. He could usually detect and analyze symptoms of problems and sometimes create devices to cure them. He could not develop acceptable ways of carrying out the reform. Although he captured the thinking of the agrarian West and South and usually translated the thinking of the common man into platform issues, he did not appeal to those who looked for speculative curiosity and deep thought.

Bryan, the man, was generally identified with social progress, world peace, and human brotherhood. Although he had courageous defensive instincts, good refutatory techniques, and moral earnestness, he lacked ability to analyze deeply enough to originate ideas. Failing to question his own aphorisms, he tended to support the obvious. He appealed to the common man and to specific groups but not to the intellectuals and to divergent groups. His propositions and his language indicated a partisan and sectional point of view, and his organization of speech materials was not always effective. Bryan could fight for a just eradication of an evil, but he could not campaign with sustained philosophic eloquence. His strength as an orator lay primarily in his sincerity of motives, his superb delivery, and his ability to clarify and simplify an issue.

Footnotes

1. *The World's Famous Orations*, ed. William Jennings Bryan (New York, 1906), I, x (Introduction).
2. *New York Times*, March 17, 1892, p. 3.

3. *New York Daily Tribune*, August 17, 1893, p. 1.

4. Charles Edward Merriam, *Four American Party Leaders* (New York, 1926), p. 76.

5. Henry Steele Commager, "William Jennings Bryan," *There Were Giants in the Land* (New York, 1942), p. 99.

6. Richard Hofstadter, *The American Political Tradition* (New York, 1948), p. 199.

7. William Jennings Bryan and Mary Baird Bryan, *The Memoirs of William Jennings Bryan* (Great Britain, 1925), pp. 40-60.

8. *The World's Famous Orations*, pp. xvi-xvii. "If it be true that the gifts of the mind and heart are universally diffused, if the sentiment of truth, justice, love, and beauty exists in everyone, then it follows as a necessary consequence that the commonest judgment in taste, politics, and religion is the highest authority on earth and the nearest possible approach to an infallible decision." George Bancroft, "The People in Art, Government, and Religion," *Modern Eloquence*, ed. Thomas B. Reed (Philadelphia, 1900), VII, 73.

9. William Jennings Bryan, "In the Chicago Convention" (July 8, 1896), *Speeches of William Jennings Bryan*, (New York, 1911), I, 248. Hereafter cited as *Speeches*.

10. "The success of our government depends upon the independence and the moral courage of its citizens." "I Have Kept the Faith" (1904), *Speeches*, II, 53.

11. "At the New York Reception" (August 30, 1906), *Speeches*, II, 78.

12. "The Conservation of National Resources" (May 15, 1908), *Speeches*, II, 399.

13. "The Tariff" (March 16, 1892), *Congressional Record*, XXIII, pt. 3, 2129.

14. "Bimetallism" (August 16, 1893), *Congressional Record*, XXV, pt. 1, 401.

15. "At the New York Reception" (August 30, 1906), *Speeches*, II, 75.

16. "An Income Tax" (January 30, 1894), *Congressional Record*, XXVI, pt. 2, 1656.

17. "Naboth's Vineyard" (1898), *Speeches*, II, 8.

18. "Imperialism" (August 8, 1900), *Speeches*, II, 21.

19. "I Have Kept the Faith" (1904), *Speeches*, II, 52.

20. ". . . I am here because I want this Interparliamentary Union to take just as long a step as possible in the direction of universal peace." "At the Peace Congress" (July 26, 1906), *Speeches*, II, 229.

21. "I Have Kept the Faith" (1904), *Speeches*, II, 55, and "The voters are the sovereigns; the officials are the servants, employed for a fixt time and at a stated salary to do what the sovereigns want done, and to do it in the way the sovereigns want it done." "Shall the People Rule?" (August 12, 1908), *Speeches*, II, 100-101.

22. "The Tariff" (March 16, 1892), *Congressional Record*, XXIII, pt. 3, 2128-2132.

23. "An Income Tax" (January 30, 1894), *Congressional Record*, XXVI, pt. 2, 1655.

24. "Imperialism" (August 8, 1900), *Speeches*, II, 26.

25. "Cross of Gold" (July 8, 1896), *Speeches*, I, 248.

26. "The Tariff" (March 16, 1892), *Congressional Record*, XXIII, pt. 3, 2130.

27. "The Silver Question" (August 10, 1896), *Speeches*, I, 269-270.

28. "Cross of Gold" (July 8, 1896), *Speeches*, I, 238.

29. "The Tariff" (March 16, 1892), *Congressional Record*, XXIII, pt. 3, 2133.

30. *Ibid.*, 2124.

31. "An Income Tax" (January 30, 1894), *Congressional Record*, XXVI, pt. 2, 1656.

32. "Cross of Gold" (July 8, 1896), *Speeches*, I, 243.

33. "The Silver Question" (August 10, 1896), *Speeches*, I, 250-252.
34. *Ibid.*, 289.
35. "Imperialism" (August 8, 1900), *Speeches*, II, 39.
36. "The Silver Question" (August 10, 1896), *Speeches*, I, 252.
37. "The Tariff" (March 16, 1892), *Congressional Record*, XXIII, pt. 3, 2129-2133.
38. "Imperialism" (August 8, 1900), *Speeches*, II, 43-44.
39. "The Cross of Gold" (July 8, 1896), *Speeches*, I, 240.
40. "Shall the People Rule?" (August 12, 1908), *Speeches*, II, 117.
41. *The World's Famous Orations*, p. xv.
42. "The Cross of Gold" (July 8, 1896), *Speeches*, I, 249.
43. "Shall the People Rule?" (August 12, 1908), *Speeches*, II, 119.
44. "Bimetallism" (August 16, 1893), *Congressional Record*, XXV, pt. 1, 402.
45. *Ibid.*, 411.
46. "Imperialism" (August 8, 1900), *Speeches*, II, 41-44.
47. "Bimetallism" (August 16, 1893), *Congressional Record*, XXV, pt. 1, 401.
48. "The Cross of Gold" (July 8, 1896), *Speeches*, I, 241.
49. "An Income Tax" (January 30, 1894), *Congressional Record*, XXVI, pt. 2, 1658.
50. "Imperialism" (August 8, 1900), *Speeches*, II, 30-34.
51. "The Tariff" (August 21, 1908), *Speeches*, I, 311.
52. "Lincoln as an Orator" (February 12, 1909), *Speeches*, II, 423.
53. *The World's Famous Orations*, p. xvii.
54. Bryan, *The Memoirs*, p. 103.
55. *Ibid.*, 114-152.
56. Gerald W. Johnson, *The Incredible Tale* (New York, 1950), pp. 8-9; *New York Times*, March 17, 1892, p. 3; *New York Daily Tribune*, August 17, 1893, p. 1.
57. *New York Times*, August 13, 1896, p. 1.
58. *New York Times*, July 11, 1896, p. 1 and August 13, 1896, p. 1.
59. "Lincoln as an Orator" (February 12, 1909), *Speeches*, II, 423.

The Speaking of Albert J. Beveridge

ALBERT JEREMIAH BEVERIDGE *(October 6, 1862—April 27, 1927). Born on a farm in Highland County, Ohio; moved with family because of economic reverses to farm near Sullivan, Ill.; entered Asbury College (now DePauw University), Greencastle, Ind., 1881, on a $50 loan; supported himself in part by winning oratorical and literary prizes; graduated 1885; practiced law in Indianapolis, 1886-1899; elected United States senator from Indiana, 1899 and 1905; showed passion for first-hand information by traveling to Philippines before taking Senate seat, to Siberia during Russo-Japanese conflict; joined Theodore Roosevelt in bolting Republican party for Progressivism, 1912; made temporary chairman and keynote speaker for Progressive national convention, 1912; defeated as Progressive candidate for governor of Indiana, 1912, and United States senator, 1914; returned to Republican party, 1916; defeated for United States senator, 1922; active speaker in almost every political campaign from 1884 to 1924; in demand throughout his adult life as occasional speaker. Author of several books, including* THE RUSSIAN ADVANCE *(1903),* THE YOUNG MAN AND THE WORLD *(1905),* THE BIBLE AS GOOD READING *(1906),* AMERICANS OF TODAY AND TOMORROW *(1908),* WHAT IS BACK OF THE WAR *(1915), and* ART OF PUBLIC SPEAKING *(1924); most ambitious and successful work was* LIFE OF JOHN MARSHALL *in four volumes (1916-1919); at time of his death had almost completed two volumes of projected four-volume work on Lincoln.*

The Speaking of Albert J. Beveridge

Halbert E. Gulley*

ALBERT J. BEVERIDGE became a national political figure at the turn of the twentieth century. In 1896, the Republicans wanted former President Benjamin Harrison of Indianapolis to close the party's campaign in Chicago Auditorium. He declined, recommending Beveridge, whose speech received wide notice and at least Republican acclaim. In 1898, before Boston's Middlesex Club and in his "March of the Flag" speech opening the Indiana Republican campaign, Beveridge boldly advocated a new policy of American imperialism. In 1899, at 36, he was elected to the United States Senate. His vault to prominence was due in large part if not primarily to "rare ability as a public speaker."[1]

For the first twelve years of the new century, the political newcomer spoke frequently and effectively in the Senate, where he was one of the foremost spokesmen for the insurgency which culminated in the Progressive party. After 1912, in spite of the failure of Progressivism and his continuing defeat at the polls, he retained his national reputation as an orator. He never completely regained the confidence of some Republican leaders, however, and his earlier brilliance was less lustrous as the voters repeatedly denied him office and as he turned his talents to writing historical biography.

While his influence was greatest as a senator, Beveridge was a leading political speaker for more than a quarter of a century. As a college student he stumped Indiana for Blaine in 1884, and thereafter participated energetically in almost every political campaign until his death. He was always a sought-after speaker in state and national contests. In the campaign of 1908, for example, he was one of the Republican stump speakers most in demand, alongside Presi-

* Halbert E. Gulley (B.Ed. Southern Illinois University, 1940, M.A. 1941, Ph.D. 1948, State University of Iowa) is professor of speech at the University of Illinois.

dent Roosevelt, Taft, Hughes, and Lodge.[2] He delivered the key-note address for the Progressive party convention of 1912, and when an assassin wounded Roosevelt, Beveridge filled the candidate's next speaking engagement.

Although his courtroom speaking was limited to the ten years before he entered the Senate and his legislative speaking to his two terms in Washington, Beveridge gave occasional speeches throughout his life. In later years, he spoke on "The Bible as Good Reading" and "The Art of Public Speaking." His last important address was given in Philadelphia in 1926, on the occasion of the sesquicentennial of independence.

From childhood Beveridge aspired to become a speaker, since "oratory was the road to distinction."[3] In his youth, he frequently participated in speaking programs, debates, and plays,[4] and undoubtedly studied the advice and speech models in *McGuffey's Readers*.[5] Leaving his home in east central Illinois to enter DePauw University,[6] he determined to improve his speaking. Often he rose at four in the morning, went into the woods or along the railroad tracks at the edge of town to practice his speeches or exercise his voice, and returned to his rooming house in time to read Shakespeare or perhaps orations or essays for an hour before breakfast.[7] Because his family could not give him financial support, to earn money he entered oratorical contests offering cash prizes.[8] He won almost all the prizes during his DePauw days, climaxing his victories by placing first in the Interstate Oratorical Contest in 1885. In these exercises he learned respect for diligent practice and endless work as prerequisites of success.

LINES OF THOUGHT

Maturing in the period of the clash with Spain, Beveridge in his speeches gave expression to the popular defense of developing national power and championed the extension of the nation's influence beyond its borders. He believed justifiable any policy glorifying his country.

His was an intense nationalism; he felt that the strength and the increasing fortunes of the Republic depended upon continuous commercial development. If colonization, or even conquest, of the islands of the sea were necessary to provide the markets and resources for American prosperity and supremacy, then he was for that, too. "The commercial extension of the Republic," he wrote his friend, George Perkins, "has been my dream since boyhood."[9]

In a speech eulogizing Grant, Beveridge in 1898 sounded a clear call for imperialism modeled after that of Britain. Grant, he asserted, "never forgot that we are a conquering race and that we must obey our blood and occupy new markets, and, if necessary, new lands."[10] His reasons for wanting Americans, as the "chosen people of God," to offer what he called a nobler civilization to the "debased and decaying races" were practical if not original: to gain consumers for American overproduction and to win raw materials for American exploitation. These aims he stated frankly. Nor did Beveridge ever doubt the basic wisdom of such a foreign policy. He favored acquisition of the Philippines, rejoiced in our possession of Hawaii and Puerto Rico, and openly hoped that some day Cuba would want an even closer relationship to the United States. After the first world war, Beveridge bitterly opposed entering the League of Nations, calling internationalism inimical to national safety. His objection was not to extension of responsibility, however, but to surrender of sovereignty.

A necessary corollary of the commercial imperialism Beveridge advocated was efficient business organizations. He believed in big business. He defended trusts as combinations delivering more and better goods at lower prices; destruction of trusts would condemn "good" as well as "bad" organizations. The elimination of "bad" trusts, he argued, should be accomplished through governmental regulation. This latter view seemed extremely progressive to the commercial interests supporting him, and Beveridge drifted further and further from grace. With straightforward, almost naive honesty, he decided that the abuses of big business could be corrected and that the parasites of greed, dishonesty, and deception could be removed without destroying business itself. His attacks in the Senate on unsanitary meat, on the exorbitant profits of the tobacco trust, and on immoral child labor profiteering were merciless and eloquent. Yet he retained his faith in business, even after his excursion into Progressivism.

Another of his fundamental beliefs was that the question of states' rights had been forever determined by the Civil War. He favored centralized power.

SUPPORT

In substantiating these lines of thought, Beveridge recognized that the aim of speaking is to produce an effect consistent with the speaker's purpose. Hence he appreciated the need for audience analysis. In exhorting the lawyer to study the jury, he wrote: "When the time comes for you to address that jury you must thoroughly understand each man. This not that you may influence him, or 'play upon' him, or resort to any of the devices of the baser sort. It is that you may know how best to get the truth of your case to him."[11] An audience, he felt, "is a composite person; therefore what will please, persuade, or convince an individual will do the same with a collection of individuals."[12]

Beveridge tried hard to be the kind of speaker who would be trusted by his audiences. He made a trip to the Philippines before taking his Senate seat, and hence his maiden speech carried more than ordinary weight; he stressed that he had seen these conditions with his own eyes. Audiences learned that Beveridge could be depended upon for a skillful speech built on hard work.

Moreover, his dedication and sincerity were unchallenged. He consistently refused political contributions for his personal use. When he returned $10,000 that George Perkins had sent him, Perkins recalled no other instance of a political candidate turning down a contribution "after he had his hands on it."[13] Beveridge's defense of imperialism and big business seemed to reflect honest conviction, just as did his attacks on such abuses as unjustified profit and child labor. In 1912, he was willing to support the insurgent Progressive party only if its creators intended to make it a permanent force for liberalism and not a temporary political expedient. Also, he frequently argued in ways detrimental to his political fortunes. In opposing premature statehood for Arizona and New Mexico, for example, he ignored strong Republican forces, and his courageous speeches against the meat and tobacco interests incurred the wrath of powerful party supporters. Thus, Beveridge confirmed in practice his own advice to the speaker; speak only when conviction impels. "This means, of course, utter sincerity. Never under any circumstances or for any reward tell an audience what you, yourself, do not believe or are even indifferent about. To do so is immoral and worse—it is to be a public liar."[14]

On the other hand, certain factors lessened his trustworthiness. Many Senators resented his rashness in speaking a few days after taking his seat, when custom required an initial period of respectful silence. Moreover, he was not always content to follow the grooves of party regularity and Senate procedure. Some of his colleagues considered him egotistical, and even his speaking skill alienated some of his less fluent peers. Many considered him "the boy orator" until he was middle-aged, perhaps because his arguments seemed less important to him than his balanced, rhythmical phrasing. Apparently he gave the impression that he was straining to impress with elegant language. Certainly he took extreme positions; his positively-worded declarations were often immediately delightful to the cheering galleries but may not always have survived the sober reflections of his colleagues. In his first Senate speech, for example, he called the Pacific "our ocean" and said the "mission of our race" in Asia was to be "trustee, under God, of the civilization of the world." The challenge, he proclaimed, "is racial. God has not been preparing the English-speaking and Teutonic peoples for a thousand years for nothing but vain and idle self-contemplation and self-admiration. No! He has made us the master organizers of the world to establish system where chaos reigns. . . . And of all our race He has marked the American people as His chosen nation to finally lead in the regeneration of the world. This is the divine mission of America. . . ." Without America, he asserted, "the world would relapse into barbarism and night." By what method was the world to be restructured in the American image? "Pray God the time may never come when Mammon and the love of ease shall so debase our blood that we will fear to shed it for the flag and its imperial destiny."[15] These were strong words.

A reporter's appraisal suggests that poor judgment and exaggerated language reduced Beveridge's credibility:[16]

> The duty of dispensing flowers of rhetoric [in the Fifty-ninth Congress] will be discharged on the Democratic side by Senator Rayner and on the Republican side by Senator Beveridge. . . .

There is this difference between Rayner and Beveridge, that Rayner's part will not be confined to the dispensing of rhetoric. Rayner has a habit of emotional eloquence which is as thoroughly confirmed in him as is the same habit in Beveridge. But, in addition to that, he is a man whose judgment is respected and whose utterances, despite the fervid form in which they are sometimes couched, command attention and are thoughtfully digested. This is not always the case with Beveridge. . . .

Beveridge came to the Senate heralded by a great reputation as a "boy orator." Some men live down that reputation; Bryan did, for instance. Beveridge has never lived it down. He is a great weaver of words, and Mr. Dooley appreciatively and admiringly remarked of his first speech in the Senate, " 'Twas a speech ye cud waltz to." And yet his word symphonies do not profoundly move men. . . .

If there were both positive and negative facets of his personal trustworthiness, the impact of his rational proof was less ambivalent. For logical support, Beveridge was able to array impressive fact, instances, and testimony. In his "March of the Flag" speech, he swiftly developed instances of our territorial expansion beyond the thirteen states in the Northwest, Louisiana, Florida, Texas, the Southwest and California. The Senate speech on the Philippines presented a series of quotations from persons Beveridge had interviewed in the Far East, merchants, educators, planters, a railroader, a physician, and others. During a lengthy Senate speech on child labor, he combined facts on the number of employed children with a series of affidavits sworn to by eyewitnesses of undesirable working conditions. Cumulatively, these instances supported his condemnation of "child *slavery* in the mines, factories, and the sweat shops of the nation." He cited sworn statements of despicable practices, interspersing his own comments: ". . . the pouring of cold water on little children to keep them awake after they had worked *standing on their feet ten hours. . . .* A girl not nine years old, who for *three cents an hour* begins work at half past six at night and works until half past six in the morning. . . ."[17] There were many other cases, and the detailed descriptions were not without emotional impact.

Beveridge often used specific instances to establish a generalization. This form blended with his use of parallel constructions and repetition of key words, as illustrated in his tribute to Frances E.

Willard: "In her life's work we see restored to earth that faith which, whenever man has let it work its miracle, has wrought victory here and immortality hereafter. Such was the faith of Joan, the inspired maid of France; such was that of Columbus, sailing westward through the dark; such was the exalted belief of those good missionaries who first invaded our American wilderness to light with their own lives on civilization's altar the sacred fire that never dies."[18] Analogy he used less often.

In refuting opponents, Beveridge believed courtesy more effective than recrimination. Denounce the opposition, he said, "only when there is real and blazing cause for such scourging, which seldom is the case."[19] A campaign speech of 1916 illustrates his practice. The speech was almost wholly an answer to Democratic claims and an attack upon the Wilson administration, but he was careful not to assail President Wilson personally.[20]

Beveridge employed extensive refutation in his "March of the Flag" speech. To the charge that we should not govern the Philippines without their consent he responded weakly: "We govern the Indians without their consent, we govern our territories without their consent, we govern our children without their consent." More telling were the rhetorical questions that followed: "Would not the people of the Philippines prefer the just, humane, civilizing government of this Republic to the savage, bloody rule of pillage and extortion from which we have rescued them? . . . Shall we turn these peoples back to the reeking hands from which we have taken them? Shall we abandon them, with Germany, England, Japan, hungering for them? Shall we save them from those nations to give them a self-rule of tragedy?" Then he attempted to heighten the effect by appealing to pride in national glory: "Will you say by your vote that American ability to govern has decayed . . . that you are an infidel to American power and practical sense? . . . Will you remember that we do but what our fathers did—we but pitch the tents of liberty farther westward, farther southward—we only continue the march of the flag?"[21]

Such emotional exhortation occurs throughout Beveridge's speeches in the Senate, on the stump, and on special occasions. Impressed with America's heritage, greatness, and destiny, he expressed his intense feeling in appeals to pride in past glories and to responsibility for the nation's preservation and future dominance. A Chicago political speech of 1900 forecast America as benevolent emperor of the world:

> Men—patriotic, brave, and wise—have sought to stay that tremendous purpose of destiny, but their opposition was as the finger of a babe. . . . For God's hand was in it all. His plans were working out their glorious results. And just as futile is resistance to the continuance today of the eternal movement of the American people toward the mastery of the world. This is a destiny neither vague nor undesirable. It is definite, splendid, and holy. When nations shall war no more without the consent of the American republic; what American heart thrills not with pride at that prospect? . . . When governments stay the slaughter of human beings, because the American republic demands it; what American heart thrills not with pride at that prospect? . . . When any changing of the map of earth requires a conference of the powers, and when, at any Congress of the nations, the American republic will preside as the most powerful of powers and most righteous of judges; what American heart thrills not at that prospect? And yet, that prospect is at hand, even as I speak. It is the high and holy destiny of the American people, and from that destiny the American bugles will never sound retreat. "Westward the star of empire takes its way."[22]

He employed appeals to sympathy, as in his pleading to end child labor, and throughout his career, of course, he pointed to the motive of personal gain through commercial expansion. In his perorations, Beveridge often stressed pride in country, frequently referring also to the Bible or the blessings of Deity. Perhaps his most dramatic use of such a conclusion occurred in his keynote speech for the Progressive party convention. "Never doubt," he said, "that in the end, the hand from above that leads us upward will prevail over the hand from below that drags us downward. Never doubt that we are indeed a nation whose God is the Lord." He closed the speech with the third verse of the "Battle Hymn of the Republic," changing the pronoun "my" to "our": "For the call that comes to us is the call that came to our fathers. As they responded so shall we. 'He hath sounded forth a trumpet that shall never call retreat, He is sifting out the hearts of men before His judgment seat. O, be swift our souls to answer Him, be jubilant our feet, Our God is marching on.' " After the wild cheering had died away, delegates in the front of the hall began to sing the "Battle Hymn" and the band joined in.[23]

Beveridge's high seriousness in these matters is indicated by the almost total absence of humor in his speeches. He insisted that the great speeches of all time were serious, not frivolous.[24]

LANGUAGE

The language of the first political speeches heard by young Albert Beveridge reflected the post-Civil War superpatriotism and emotionalism of Illinois and the north. Speakers indulged in exaggerated, over-colorful language, judged by the standards of a later day. Beveridge could hardly have escaped this influence. His early speeches strained for elegance. Purple passages cost him the usual price of accurate expression and clear meaning. Some of his sentences, frequently described as over-rhetorical, achieved rhythm, parallelism, and emphatic repetition at the expense of meaning. In his "Answer to Altgeld," for example, he declared: "A Republican is the optimist of freedom. A Republican has faith in the future. A Republican has the imagination of logic, the hope that creates, the belief that builds. Democracy is a perpetual groan of calamity; Republicanism an eternal smile of joy." He ended with an even more strained bid for immediate effect and apparent disregard for semantics: "Across the distant years ring happy bells of joy, welcome echoes of the reaper's song, gleaning the future's golden fields. Hail, mutual confidence returned! The Nation omnipotent and immortal! Hail, republic of the future, with the flag of liberty floating o'er it. 'Hail Columbia! Happy land!' Hail, the glad dawn whose early twilight Washington saw, a thousand years."[25]

Fortunately, Beveridge early recognized the artificiality of such language. Even in college he had wondered why the speaker should not speak as if addressing a large, collective individual.[26] In March, 1900, after he had spoken in the Senate on Puerto Rico, Senator Pettus ridiculed him by saying the assembly had had a "wonderul declamation" from "our great or-a-tor." Each sentence of Pettus was followed by shouts of laughter as experienced Senators enjoyed the characterization.[27] The rebuke must have impressed Beveridge with the intended lesson, for in the fall of that year his article on public speaking in a popular magazine stressed the importance of simple, straightforward expression. "The mature mind cannot endure Ingersoll's rhetoric," he wrote, "pleasing as was its music." Furthermore, he advised the speaker: "Seek only to be clear. Nothing else is important." Sentences should be short, words in the main Anglo-Saxon. In this connection he showed his sensitivity to audience analysis; native words should be employed because "these are the words of the people you address" and will be "most influential with them."[28]

Beveridge tried to apply this philosophy in his speeches. He wrote his friend Rothschild that the days of the spell-binding, "touch to tears" speech were over and that his tendency was "toward simplicity of style and the elimination of mere phrase."[29] The shift was not easy, nor did he ever completely change. The fondness for parallelism and repetition remained, although his utterances gained in simplicity and directness.

Late in life, Beveridge remained convinced that every sentence should be so clear "that the dullest or most uninformed person in the audience cannot fail to understand the meaning of what is said." Uncommon or ornate words should be shunned, since "if you are not understood or are misunderstood, the purpose of the speech has failed." At the same time, he thought he could justify a certain loftiness of expression. The speech should be pitched on the highest plane. "The heart and mind of the humblest man yearns for better and nobler things," he insisted, "and the mass instinct and intellect tend upward."[30]

This compromise between direct, clear simplicity and some degree of nobility describes rather adequately Beveridge's mature style, although he seems never to have eschewed completely his earlier ornateness. Characterized by short, emphatic sentences, repetition of key words, rhythm, balance, and antithesis, the opening of his Progressive keynote speech typifies his use of language at its best: "We stand for a nobler America. We stand for an undivided nation. We stand for a broader liberty, a fuller justice. We stand for social brotherhood as against savage individualism. We stand for an intelligent cooperation instead of a reckless competition. We stand for mutual helpfulness instead of a mutual hatred. . . . We battle for the actual rights of man."[31]

ARRANGEMENT

Beveridge often began his speeches without any attempt to orient the audience or to establish a receptive attitude. He had a penchant for terse openings, perhaps because he interpreted the times and the American audience as demanding, as he said, that the speaker get to the point due to the rapidity of life.[32] This interpretation, however, hardly seems to justify his failure, in many instances, to adapt to the particular speech situation. His stump speeches and occasional addresses frequently opened with several sentences characterizing the subject matter of the speech. The tribute to Frances E. Willard began: "Mr. President, from the beginning woman has personified the world's ideals. When history began its record it found her already the chosen bride of Art. . . ."[33] The opening sentences in a campaign speech of 1902 were: "The day of passion in politics is past. The day when prejudice controls elections is gone."[34] These introductions might have been delivered before any audience in the United States. His failure to modify them for specific listeners may be explained partially by his fastidious preparation and perhaps by verbatim memorization. Furthermore, he seems to have felt on important occasions that he was addressing a whole nation, that his arguments would be considered by people not immediately present.

Exceptions to this method occurred when Beveridge debated in the Senate. In his maiden speech he explained that he had been asked to report his observations in the Philippines and that he rose because of the "hurtful resolutions" that had been introduced.[35] When he spoke on child labor in 1907, he began with the satirical comment that the Senate, which had just voted itself salary increases, might now pass to other matters "of almost as much importance to the nation." He added: "It is to call attention of this body and of the country to what I deem, and think that I shall be able to show, is one of the gravest conditions which confronts this Republic that I have risen this afternoon to speak."[36] But even in debate his introductions did not always acknowledge the immediate audience. He began a speech on Puerto Rico in 1900 without any attempt at adaptation.[37] Undoubtedly his speeches would have gained in effectiveness, and might not have been criticized as "orations," had he made a greater effort to reach his hearers by referring directly to them at the moment of beginning.

The disposition of materials within Beveridge's speeches varied, naturally, with the purpose of the address and type of support. His political speeches were often developed topically so that he could comment on the principal issues of the campaign. Although he had no set division of the speech reserved for refutation, occasionally the topics were cast as refutations of opposition arguments. One possible shortcoming in organization was his frequent failure to use clear transitions.

DELIVERY

Beveridge considered delivery "barely second in importance" to the subject matter of a speech, "since it must be spoken well and agreeably in order to reach and impress the hearers, or even to be understood by them."[38] He advocated direct, conversational delivery. His counsel in 1900 sounds much like the advice being given young speakers today: "Whenever a speaker fails to make his audience forget voice, gesture and even the speaker himself, whenever he fails to make the listeners conscious only of the living truth he utters, he has failed in his speech itself, which, then, has no other reason for having been delivered than a play or any other form of entertainment."[39] He added that the best speakers have ordinary voices and speak conversationally, in a business-like fashion. Almost in the same breath, he suggested that a high-minded seriousness of purpose carries with it "an impressiveness in bearing and delivery." This statement may explain the characteristic sobriety bordering on pomposity of his Senate speeches.

His concept of conversational delivery grew out of his analysis of the audience. The audience, he reasoned, is only a larger "collective individuality." What would please one person, therefore, should have the same effect upon a group. "Hence, one readily deduces that a simple, quiet and direct address, a straightforward, unartificial, honest manner, without tricks of oratory, is the most effective method of lodging truth in the minds of one's hearers."[40]

Beveridge frowned upon excessive physical action during delivery of an address. "The speech," he thought, "is supposed to be an intellectual performance, not a physical feat. You are a teacher, not an acrobat."[41] That he did not always follow his own counsel is suggested by one report of his actions in the Senate: "He wags his head, shakes his fist, slaps his hand, bangs his desk and tests the capacity of his vocal organs in a way utterly to exhaust his listeners, if not himself."[42]

In appearance, Beveridge was of medium height, rather thin, but of muscular build and straight carriage. His eyes and face were expressive. He was active physically, seeming always to be in a hurry. "He is forever gliding restlessly about the Senate corridors, half the time at a hitching skip that is little short of a run. Then he pulls himself together, pulls down his cuffs and flies to the opposite extreme."[43]

When he rose to speak in the Senate, Beveridge was determined to look the part of a senator. His appearance was conspicuous and caused comment. He was called the fashion plate of the Senate of his day[44] and its "criterion in the art of tailoring."[45] Beveridge said to Robert M. La Follette, when the Wisconsin Progressive first took his seat, "Robert, you are now a Senator of the United States; dress the part."[46]

Beveridge's voice was described by a classmate as "curiously clear and penetrating . . . a voice of command . . . like a trumpet."[47] A reporter during his Senate days thought it was "rather metallic and not very flexible."[48]

Perhaps Beveridge did not fully attain the conversational directness or the quiet manner he recommended. His insistence on proper dress made him conspicuous and caused some unfavorable reaction. When he spoke, however, he drew full Senate galleries and large political audiences.

Speech Preparation

Few speakers have prepared their speeches with the meticulous care that Beveridge lavished on his. He advised the speaker to "master his subject. That means that all facts must be collected, arranged, studied, digested. . . . Take nothing for granted . . . check up and reverify every item. This means painstaking research, to be sure, but what of it?"[49]

Beveridge had remarkable energy and his speeches reflected careful research methods.[50] Of his speech on child labor, Swift wrote: "By a mountain of labor he gathered the facts and delivered a speech . . . exhaustive of the question."[51] Typical was his preparation for a Senate speech on the Lorimer case; he collected every precedent "that could be found on this subject in all countries, ancient and modern."[52]

After an intensive search for materials, Beveridge composed, revised, and rewrote the speech until it pleased him. He thought a speech should be rewritten many times, "the oftener the better."[53] He customarily showed the completed manuscript to trusted friends for criticism, and recommended this procedure to others.[54] Apparently he carried this practice to wearisome extremes for Roosevelt expressed a reaction when he sent one of his own speeches to Henry Cabot Lodge with the comment: "It is too much to expect you to keep in mind the different speeches that I make;—thy servant is not a Beveridge and does not expect such things."[55]

Beveridge often memorized his final version, since he felt that important occasions demanded a finished oration and only accurate reproduction could do justice to an immense preparation. He realized, however, that memorization tended to make delivery "rigid, whereas it ought to be flexible"; hence he advised that this method be restricted to worthy occasions.[56] Nor was he obliged to memorize in order to make a creditable speech; he was widely noted as a Senate debater and a ready respondent of hecklers at political meetings.

Concerning spellbinders Ernest Fremont Tittle observed, "if they go up like a rocket, they come down like a stick, leaving no permanent light in the sky." Whether this figure fits Beveridge is open to dispute. As he played an important part in the political and legislative battles of his day, perhaps his light is not wholly extinguished. He had convictions; he had the courage to express them; he fought boldly and energetically for reforms he believed to be in the public interest. His most trusted weapon was the spoken word. Born without influence or money, but endowed with ability and courage, he labored long at his speeches and delivered a product which received the enthusiastic acclaim of his audiences, whether or not they were converted. He wanted above all to be a speaker. In that, he succeeded.

Footnotes

1. Albert Shaw, *Review of Reviews*, LXXV (June, 1927), 609-11.
2. Letter from Theodore Roosevelt to Henry Cabot Lodge, October 21, 1908, in *Selections from the Correspondence of Theodore Roosevelt and Henry Cabot Lodge* (New York, 1925), II, 323.
3. Unpublished Beveridge autobiography MS; cited by Claude G. Bowers, *Beveridge and the Progressive Era* (Cambridge, 1932), p. 10.
4. The most thorough study of his speech training has been made by Herold T. Ross, "The Oratorical Career of Albert Jeremiah Beveridge" (unpublished doctoral dissertation, State University of Iowa, 1932). See also Ross, "Education of an Orator," *Quarterly Journal of Speech*, XVIII (February, 1932), 70-82.
5. Late in life, Beveridge wrote that he recalled the *Readers*. Mark Sullivan, *Our Times* (New York, 1927), II, 14 fn.
6. Indiana Asbury College until 1884.
7. Recollections of a college classmate, David Graham Phillips; cited in "Beveridge the Unsquelchable," *Current Literature*, XLI (November, 1906), 510.
8. Albert J. Beveridge, *The Art of Public Speaking* (Boston, 1924), p. 10.
9. May 3, 1898; quoted by Bowers, p. 70.
10. Albert J. Beveridge, *The Meaning of the Times* (Indianapolis, 1908), p. 42.
11. Albert J. Beveridge, "The Young Lawyer and His Beginnings," *Saturday Evening Post*, CLXXIII (October 27, 1900), 3.
12. *The Art of Public Speaking*, p. 11.
13. Josephus Daniels, *The Wilson Era: Years of Peace* (Chapel Hill, 1944), p. 82.
14. *The Art of Public Speaking*, p. 20. Beveridge goes on to take a stand on a controversy still current: "The practice in high schools and colleges of appointing debating teams to support or oppose propositions, regardless of what the debaters believe, is questionable—indeed, bad, I think. It merely teaches intellectual dexterity while inducing moral indifference. Might it not be better to let students study the subject and select the side they believe to be right and sound? Is it not risky to ignore the ethical?"
15. *Congressional Record*, XXXIII, pt. 1 (January 9, 1900), 704 ff.
16. Charles W. Thompson, *Party Leaders of the Time* (New York, 1906), pp. 137-138.
17. *Congressional Record*, XLI, pt. 2 (January 23, 1907), 1552 ff.
18. *Ibid.*, XXXIX, pt. 3 (February 17, 1905), 2782.
19. *The Art of Public Speaking*, p. 45.
20. *Chicago Daily Tribune*, October 6, 1916, p. 17.
21. *The Meaning of the Times*, pp. 49-50.
22. *Chicago Tribune*, September 26, 1900, p. 2.
23. *Chicago Daily Tribune*, August 6, 1912, p. 2.
24. Albert J. Beveridge, "Public Speaking," *Saturday Evening Post*, CLXXIII (October 6, 1900), 2.
25. *Chicago Tribune*, October 30, 1896, p. 2.
26. "Public Speaking," *Saturday Evening Post*, p. 3.
27. *New York Daily Tribune*, March 31, 1900, p. 3.
28. "Public Speaking," *Saturday Evening Post*, p. 2.
29. March 26, 1902; quoted by Bowers, pp. 177-178.

30. *The Art of Public Speaking,* pp. 34-37.
31. Albert J. Beveridge, *Pass Prosperity Around* (New York, 1912), p. 2.
32. "Public Speaking," *Saturday Evening Post,* p. 2.
33. *Congressional Record,* XXXIX, pt. 3 (February 17, 1905), p. 2781. In contrast, each of the other three speakers who paid tribute to her in the Senate that day, Senators Cullom, Hopkins, and Dolliver, started out by referring to the occasion and the immediate situation.
34. *The Meaning of the Times,* p. 200.
35. *Congressional Record,* XXXIII, pt. 1 (January 9, 1900), p. 704.
36. *Ibid.,* XLI, pt. 2 (January 23, 1907), 1552.
37. *Ibid.,* XXXIII, pt. 8 (March 29, 1900), A279.
38. *The Art of Public Speaking,* p. 50.
39. "Public Speaking," *Saturday Evening Post,* p. 2.
40. *Ibid.,* p. 3.
41. *The Art of Public Speaking,* p. 52.
42. "The Senate's Child Laborer," *The Independent,* LXII (February 14, 1907), 380-381.
43. *Ibid.*
44. "The Breaking and Mending of Beveridge," *The Independent,* CXVIII (May 14, 1927), 503.
45. "The Senate's Child Laborer," *The Independent,* LXII (February 14, 1907), 380-381.
46. Sullivan, III, 215 fn.
47. "Beveridge the Unsquelchable," *Current Literature,* XLI (November, 1906), 512.
48. Thompson, p. 139.
49. *The Art of Public Speaking,* p. 26.
50. Frank A. Munsey, "A Brilliant Type of the Young Man in Politics," *Munsey's Magazine,* XXIV (December, 1900), 461.
51. Lucius B. Swift, "Senator Beveridge of Indiana," *Review of Reviews,* XLII (October, 1910), 431.
52. Letter, Beveridge to Roosevelt, March 3, 1911. Roosevelt Papers, Library of Congress.
53. *The Art of Public Speaking,* p. 28.
54. *Ibid.*
55. Letter, Roosevelt to Lodge, October 16, 1906. In *Selections from the Correspondence,* II, 247.
56. *The Art of Public Speaking,* pp. 31-32.

The Political Speaking of
William E. Borah

WILLIAM E. BORAH (*June 29, 1865—January 11, 1940*). *Born in Jasper Township, Fairfield, Illinois; attended country school; the Enfield (Illinois) Academy (a Cumberland Presbyterian institution), and the University of Kansas for parts of two years; largely self-educated; active in numerous debating societies; admitted to bar and practiced at Lyons, Kansas for two years; relocated in Boise, Idaho in 1890; practiced law there until 1907; gained recognition for participation in three sensational murder trials; sought after as a speaker, debater, and campaigner; represented Idaho in Senate from 1907 until his death; remembered as an isolationist and an independent; opposed participation of United States in League of Nations and World Court; spoke against the New Deal and involvement in war in Europe; reported to be one of the most eloquent speakers in the Senate during his period.*

The Political Speaking of William E. Borah

WALDO W. BRADEN*

THE SPEAKER IN A DEMOCRATIC SOCIETY

WILLIAM E. BORAH held in reverence the Constitution, especially the First Amendment which he regarded "as more sacred" than any other provision. He believed that around the great principles of free speech, free press, and the right of peaceable assembly "the whole cause of free government has been successfully organized and fought."[1] Out of his respect for representative government and for the rule of the people he built a philosophy of public address as well as a political creed.

Borah argued that democratic society places upon the political speaker the paramount responsibilities of guarding the liberties of the people, of warning them when freedoms are challenged, and of organizing resistance at moments of crisis. He eloquently expressed his philosophy as follows:

> So long as all sovereignty rests with the people, so long as the enactment of good laws and the enforcement of all law depend so largely upon the intelligence and conscience of the citizen, we cannot dispense with those who speak with wisdom and power to the multitude. . . . They are the tribunes of the people. . . . There can be no graver responsibility than that of directing the people in the use of the instrumentalities of government.[2]

He reasoned that "the tribune of the people," to be worthy of trust, was compelled to speak out—even when he was a minority of

* Waldo W. Braden (B.A. Penn College 1932, M.A. 1938, Ph.D. 1942, State University of Iowa) is professor of speech and chairman of the Department of Speech at Louisiana State University.

one; as a result he often directed his addresses in the Senate to much larger audiences than those who crowded into the chamber. When an issue stirred public interest he supported his senatorial utterances with speeches to rallies, to dinners, to distinguished societies, and in fact, to any organization that promised an attentive audience. He never permitted a lecture bureau to sell his services. Always the lone wolf, he insisted on doing his own booking and on making his own arrangements.

To Borah, the orator-statesman was more than a mouthpiece of the people, a slave to their wishes. He is quoted as saying: "I hold with Burke that I owe my constituents my time and energy, but that I owe my judgment only to myself. My constituents elect me to exercise my own best judgment."[3] This philosophy obligated him to strive for artistic excellence in order to insure a fair hearing for his cause.

The senatorial speaking of Borah inspired such superlative evaluations as "the best orator in the Senate,"[4] "the most successful debater,"[5] and "one of the few . . . who measures up to pre-Civil War giants."[6] But from the Idaho senator's point of view he most nearly achieved his own ideal before popular audiences.[7] Hence the present article is devoted to a consideration of his speaking outside the Senate.

TRAINING

William E. Borah did not have the advantage of an extensive formal education. He spent his first seventeen years on a typical southern Illinois farm near Fairfield in Wayne County. In his home he encountered few books and magazines and only an occasional newspaper. But he learned early to read the Bible, which had a foremost place in the family. His father, a devout elder of the neighborhood Cumberland Presbyterian Church, worked hard to provide food, clothing, and moral instruction for the ten children. In later years the Senator often recalled how the elder Borah argued that "the mistakes of the great men of the Civil War came from their blind partisanship."[8] From his father, Borah learned his first lessons in Republican politics.

Borah acquired his elementary education at the little one room Tom's Prairie country school, taught by teachers who were poorly trained, underpaid, and overworked. The school term lasted no more than six months. The future senator and his twenty-five or thirty school mates were forced to rely on their own initiative when they wanted more than the rudiments of the three R's. With considerably more difficulty Borah pieced together a secondary education, consisting of a year at Southern Illinois Academy at Enfield, a term in the Lyons, Kansas, Public School, and part of a year as a subfreshman at the University of Kansas. During these years, he studied arithmetic, history, Latin, English grammar, and government.[9]

Following his subfreshman year, Borah returned to the University of Kansas for part of a year of college. In spite of his selection of the Latin-Scientific course, he chose not to follow the prescribed subjects, but to enroll in what most appealed to him, namely English, history, elocution, history of English language, and American literature. Later he confessed that he spent much of his time browsing in the library.[10] In March, 1887, he dropped out of school.[11]

Before entering the University of Kansas as a subfreshman, he tried teaching at the Wabash one-room country school in Rice County, Kansas, during the term of 1884-1885.[12] In preparation, he attended the Rice County Normal Institute.[13] What happened at the Wabash school during that four month term is unknown, but years later Borah admitted that his teaching suffered because of his reading of history and law.[14] Twice that year he delivered what the local paper called "orations"[15] before the monthly meetings of the Rice County Teachers' Association.

What are the facts concerning his formal training in public speaking? The Idahoan had one course in elocution at the University of Kansas, a class which met only fortnightly.[16] However from the days at Tom's Prairie he worked to perfect his speechmaking. His "maiden speech," he reported facetiously, was made between two rows of corn to a mule.[17] No doubt he first read the speeches of Patrick Henry, Wendell Phillips, Henry Ward Beecher, and Daniel Webster in a *McGuffey's Reader*.

Like many others, he profited from the activities of literary and debating clubs. In later years he remembered with pleasure the "debates of the common school."[18] At Enfield along with Wesley

Jones, later senator from Washington, he debated in the literary society.[19] When he moved to Lyons, Kansas, he joined the Young People's Band of the Presbyterian Church, a group to which he gave many addresses. At the University of Kansas, as an active Orophilian, he engaged in debate and oratory.[20]

From boyhood, Borah cherished a desire to study law. He was stimulated by hearing discussions of the local cases and by attending court,[21] but he could not persuade his father of the desirability of a legal career. Fortunately when he was seventeen, young Borah was invited to live with a sister whose husband, A. M. Lasley, was a practicing attorney in Kansas. During vacations and the year of teaching Borah read law under the guidance of his brother-in-law. Upon leaving college, he completed his legal studies, and on September 23, 1887, he was admitted to the Kansas bar "as a full fledged lawyer to practice in the district courts of the state." Thereupon the Lasley shingle was changed to read "Lasley and Borah" and a similar professional notice appeared in the local paper.[22]

THE LAWYER

For three years Borah practiced in partnership with his brother-in-law and served as the city attorney.[23] Clark Conkling, the Lyons editor and one of the first to comment on Borah's promise as a lawyer, said in reporting on one of his early cases, "W. E. Borah, one of the youngest attorneys at the Rice County bar, made a strong, logical speech before the jury Saturday in the case of the State *vs.* Weston. His speech gave great promise of a brilliant future."[24]

In the fall of 1890 Borah relocated in Boise, Idaho.[25] For two years, he experienced the usual difficulties of the young lawyer and subsisted upon work which the more prosperous attorneys refused.[26] The spring following his arrival he was appointed assistant district attorney,[27] a position in which he first attracted attention as a court room lawyer. The local paper thought him "an energetic and able young lawyer," who merited "success in his profession."[28]

Borah built a successful general practice, specializing in neither criminal nor corporation law. However, as his fame grew he was retained more and more to represent large corporate lumbering and mining interests of the Northwest.[29] On occasion he tried cases before the Idaho State Supreme Court, the Federal District Court, and the Federal Circuit Court of Appeals in San Francisco. During the later years of his practice he reputedly earned as much as $30,000 a year.[30]

Many who have written about Borah have stressed his participation in three widely publicized, sensational murder trials: the Diamondfield Jack Davis case of 1897, the Coeur d'Alene case of 1899,[31] and the Haywood case of 1907. In all these cases, Borah assisted district attorneys. The last named case involved the prosecution of William D. Haywood, official of the Western Federation of Miners, accused of being implicated in the bombing and brutal murder of former Governor Steunenberg. Borah was pitted against Clarence Darrow, famous Chicago criminal lawyer, who served on the defense. Over fifty special newspaper correspondents covered the battle of these two famous advocates.[32] Years later Darrow stated, "Few men that I have ever met in a court room contribute so much industry, learning and natural ability to a cause as Mr. Borah."[33] Although Darrow freed Haywood, Borah enhanced his reputation immensely throughout the nation. This case marked the peak of Borah's legal career as well as its close; for after his entry into the Senate he never again tried a case and never again accepted a retainer.[34]

READING AND SPEECH PREPARATION

According to William Hard, Borah "read books almost excessively."[35] After filling his book cases, he piled books and magazines on his desk, the floor, his lounge, the mantle of the fireplace, and the tops of the filing cabinets. Daily he read the Bible. He found stimulating Emerson, Swift, Carlyle, Hawthorne, Balzac, Dickens, Thackeray, Milton, Dante, and Shakespeare.[36] Seldom did he miss a Shakespearean performance that came to town.

He devoted much of his reading to history, biography, politics, and constitutional law, making a special study of the Constitutional Convention, the *Federalist Papers*, and writings of the Founding Fathers. He was wont to quote them as well as his favorite orators: Burke on free speech, Fox on the French Revolution, Pitt on public opinion, Bright on slavery, Webster on the Constitution, and Lincoln on the Union. In 1912, much to the amazement of his Democratic colleagues, he demonstrated that he had studied the writings of Woodrow Wilson.[37]

His study habits were thorough and systematic. Cora Rubin, his private secretary from 1907 to 1940, emphasizes that he employed a definite method in gathering material. When he became interested in a subject, he slipped into his file a large envelope or folder labeled with the appropriate title.[38] Letters, pamphlets, petitions, newspaper clippings, articles torn from magazines, and notes taken on his reading were filed for future reference. He underlined important passages, scribbling often a note of identification or simply "reread" on the margin. He might read and reread aloud a vivid passage to test its oral quality. Sometimes he memorized choice sentences.[39]

Nor did he hesitate to write for information from prominent authorities or persons actively associated with an activity. If he did not receive a sufficiently clear or definitive reply, he followed with a second letter, asking more specific questions. Among his correspondents for the League debate, for example, were Albert J. Beveridge, former senator from Indiana; Edward C. Stokes, ex-governor of New Jersey; James M. Beck, New York attorney; George Harvey, editor of the *North American Review*; Frank A. Munsey, editor of the *New York Sun*; and Daniel F. Cohalan, Irish-American leader.

When he contemplated speaking either before a popular audience or the Senate he reported that he made "a skeleton outline of the line of argument." He continued, "I do not undertake to reduce such speeches to manuscript form. Sometimes I dictate a paragraph or two or three paragraphs upon a particular phase, not with the idea of following such dictation textually, but rather to get the matter fixed in my mind."[40] The writing which he did for magazines and newspapers aided in crystallizing his ideas.[41] Among his private papers are some of his outlines written on half sheets of typing paper or Senate stationery. The topics listed are only suggestive, such as "our foreign policy for 150 years," "policy of Washington, etc.," "issue presented 1920—people settled it." The items are well spaced in order to facilitate reading them at a glance. Important words are underlined.

In refusing to supply advance copies of some speeches, he stated that he had not prepared anything in advance but expected to speak, "as I find it always necessary to do in public audiences, almost entirely from notes and very meager notes at that."[42] Attempts to write a political speech, he complained, generally resulted in "being stiff and inappropriate to the particular spirit of the occasion."[43]

Borah suggested that a speaker should let the occasion and the audience guide his presentation. He said: "The effectiveness of a speech is determined largely by the inspiration, or assistance which a speaker received from listeners. If he has his subject thoroughly in hand, he must depend in a very large measure upon the audience to determine what course he is to pursue in presenting it. No man was ever persuasive in his study room. If he is effective, it is because his audience helps him."[44]

His private secretary quotes him as saying jokingly that "a man can tell all he knows in forty minutes." In the League debate of 1919-1920, although he did not limit himself that rigidly, he probably spoke less than an hour and a half on most occasions. Many of his colleagues frequently used twice that much time. Although he opposed attempts to limit debate, he never participated in a filibuster nor did he hold the floor for long periods.

The Political Campaigner

For over fifty years the rough and tumble of the political arena delighted Borah. He thrived on hard travel, numerous appearances, and difficult audiences. In the West where he won his political spurs he learned how to meet the miner, the lumberjack, the sheep owner, the cattleman, the beet farmer, and the Mormon. These Westerners wanted a robust and energetic personality—one who could handle a horse, carry a gun, ride the top of a freight car down a canyon,[45] and match wits with the rowdy.

In 1888, a year after he was admitted to the bar, the Idahoan spoke to fourteen rallies in Rice County, Kansas, in his first political campaign.[46] No sooner did he relocate in Boise, Idaho, than he affiliated with the Idaho Republicans. In less than a year he addressed the Abraham Lincoln Club on "Young Republicanism," spoke at a Fourth of July celebration, and campaigned unsuccessfully for the city attorneyship.[47] In 1892 he was elected chairman of the Republican State Central Committee and talked to a state convention at Pocatello.[48] That same year he first stumped Idaho. From that time he filled his life with speech making, rallies, and campaigns.

Since he refused to let "blind partisanship" dictate his course of action, Borah seldom was in complete harmony with the regulars within or, for that matter, outside of Idaho. He first demonstrated his independence in his campaign for the Senate, which extended over ten years. Dissatisfied with the regulars' stand on the silver issue, he bolted in 1896 to run for the first time as a silver Republican.[49] After returning to the fold in 1900, he was defeated a second time at the hands of the regulars in 1902.

Much like Cummins in Iowa and La Follette in Wisconsin, Borah won election to the Senate in spite of opposition from within his party. In 1906 he called upon his friends to elect county delegates, instructed to demand a resolution favoring his election at the state convention; consequently he was nominated by acclamation.[50] In the ensuing campaign Borah addressed more than thirty-five rallies between September 12 and November 5, 1906, a real accomplishment before the days of modern automobiles and hard surfaced roads.[51]

Three factors partially explained his popularity: his extensive personal correspondence with key men in the state, his excellent relations with prominent newspapers, and his speaking throughout Idaho. When possible he spent July and August and sometimes part of the fall in the West. On these so-called vacations he spoke before churches, granges, Old Settlers' celebrations, miners' picnics, and dedications. Through the years, Idaho voters listened to him with increasing admiration and pleasure. They were equally proud of the publicity which he brought to the state; perhaps some even regarded it as a sufficient reason to vote for him time after time.

Entry into the Senate broadened Borah's political vistas and the scope of his speaking. During his first term, he won wide acclaim for his advocacy of direct election of United States senators. His *Scrapbook* contains more than 250 editorials from twenty-five states, commenting on his vigorous utterances.[52] Leading Republican clubs like the Hamilton Club of Chicago, the Marion Club of Indianapolis, the Union League Club of Baltimore, the National Republican League of Washington, D.C., and the Republican Club of New York proffered the new western senator invitations. His speech to New York Republicans on lawlessness, delivered December 20, 1911, evoked much editorial comment.[53] In every subsequent election Borah was in demand as a campaign speaker. As a result he was motivated to exert greater effort in order to reach a wider circle of listeners. It is difficult to deny that at times he directed his energies toward keeping his name in the limelight and his ideas in the press. In this respect he was eminently successful.

Borah believed that party affiliation did not require him to speak in behalf of a candidate with whom he did not agree; consequently on occasion he withheld his indorsement. In 1912 he confined his speaking to Idaho because he was reluctant to follow Roosevelt out of the party or to support Taft as a standard bearer. Again in 1920 he demonstrated his independence. After speaking for Hiram Johnson in the primaries of Michigan and the East, he remained aloof until Harding clarified his stand on the League. In 1924 he showed no enthusiasm for Coolidge. Likewise he refused to support Hoover in 1932 and Landon, four years later. By his independence he indeed irritated the party managers and campaign strategists.

The 1928 campaign proved to be one of the greatest in Borah's entire career. When other politicians were eager to side-step the prohibition issue because of the sharp division of opinion and the trend toward repeal, Borah came out forcefully for rigid enforcement of the Eighteenth Amendment. On May 30, 1926, he made what proved to be an important speech to the Presbyterian General Assembly at Baltimore, Maryland. In addition to condemning the liquor traffic as morally wrong, he argued that the real issue was whether the Constitution should be nullified.[54] Lauding him for defining and clarifying the issue,[55] the newspapers hailed the speech as the opening of the Borah-boom for president.[56]

From that moment until the election the Idaho senator strove to make prohibition a foremost issue. Perhaps his most dramatic effort was a two hour debate with Nicholas Murray Butler before a Boston audience, April 8, 1927, on the proposition "Should the Republican national platform of 1928 advocate repeal of the Eighteenth Amendment." Borah won a decision from the judges by a vote of six to three.[57] This appearance was only one of many that he made in behalf of prohibition.[58]

At the National Republican Convention in Kansas City, Borah demonstrated his adroitness and his power. He was successful in putting his planks on prohibition, on farm relief, and on campaign expenditures into the platform. He was influential in the nominations of Herbert Hoover and Charles Curtis. After long hours of debate on the platform in committee Borah made two significant speeches on the floor of the convention: one urging adoption of the majority report on the farm plank, and the other nominating Curtis.

In the actual campaign, Hoover, well aware of his own limitations as a speaker, was content to rely on the help of others. In two months Borah traveled ten thousand miles and addressed twenty rallies in fourteen states.[59] Many times he crossed the paths of Alfred E. Smith and Joseph Robinson. His speeches were broadcast over networks and were widely circulated in printed form.

Since Reconstruction he was the first Republican of major importance to invade Dixie in a presidential year. Much to the amazement of many he encountered no serious heckling nor disorder but considerable enthusiasm wherever he went. His vigorous advocacy of states' rights, his sympathy for the South, and his opposition to anti-lynching bills had won for him many southern friends. He concentrated about three-fourths of his speaking in the Democratic strongholds of Kentucky, Tennessee, Virginia, North Carolina, and Texas. His strategy was to hammer on issues over which northern and southern Democrats seriously disagreed, namely prohibition, farm relief, immigration, and Smith's connection with Tammany Hall; but he refused to be drawn into the controversy over Smith's religion.

As a speaker, what was Borah's contribution to the Hoover victory? The exact causal relations in the realm of human affairs are difficult to determine. In the election Hoover won forty states including Virginia, North Carolina, Tennessee, and Texas, and the border states of Kentucky, Missouri, and Oklahoma. Certainly an important factor in the victory was the speaking of the Idaho senator.

Second only to the 1928 campaign was Borah's attempt in 1936 to win the Republican nomination. Although after 1912 Borah was a perennial favorite, it was not until this time that he permitted a boom to develop in his favor. Realistically he recognized his handicaps. As early as 1914 he wrote his brother that he was at a disadvantage because he refused to let "expediency," which, he said, "always plays a prominent part in securing a presidential nomination," determine his course of action. Furthermore, he doubted his chances because he did not have the money necessary to launch a campaign and because he came from "the wrong section."[60]

Why then did the Idaho senator at age seventy-one decide to run? The answer is found perhaps in his fear that the Democratic landslide of 1932 endangered the important check inherent in the two party system. He is quoted as saying that "opposition only makes a strong measure stronger; it is only the worthless ones that are killed by it."[61] In 1934, after some months of neutrality, he took the lead in attempting to stir up effective opposition to the New Deal. As a Republican independent, he was able to draw considerable support from other independents, disgruntled Democrats, and the remaining Republican regulars.[62]

Remembering his responsibility as a tribune of the people, Borah did not confine his efforts to the Senate.[63] Said Turner Catledge, "armed with eloquence, the persuasiveness, the charm and sincerity which he is able to command in such abundance he has started out to 'save' the country from much of the New Deal."[64] Hence through four major radio addresses over the network of the National Broadcasting Company he warned the citizenry of what he considered unwise in the Roosevelt program.[65] Upon his return to Idaho he continued with twenty-five additional speeches in the late summer and fall. He demanded a return to the Constitution (an old theme with him), restraint in granting powers to the President, revision of the AAA, restoration of the antitrust laws, elimination of waste in the administration of relief, and a more liberal monetary policy.

Late that year Borah chided the leaders of his party for their lethargy. Under the auspices of the New York County Republican Committee, he spoke, December 13, 1934, on the subject, "The Reorganization of the Republican Party,"[66] a theme that he had discussed at some length after the Republican defeat in 1912.[67] He charged the Old Guard with the responsibility for the Democratic victory in 1932, and he predicted further disaster if liberal leadership was not found. Although popular with the voters, this line of attack was distasteful to Hoover's supporters who immediately angrily vocalized their resentment.

Enjoying this attention, Borah intensified his campaign by giving four more important addresses over national networks in 1935.[68]

His stirring utterances and the denunciations of the Old Guard won wide attention in the press and further increased his popularity. In fact in August, 1935, a presidential poll showed him leading all other aspirants.[69] He came out openly for the Republican nomination in December, 1935.

What did Borah hope to accomplish by entering the campaign? William K. Hutchinson suggests that he ran "without desire to gain the White House but solely to force both the Republican and Democratic Parties to declare themselves against entangling alliances abroad and monopolies at home."[70] In a campaign speech, delivered March 21, 1936, he told a Chicago rally as well as a radio audience that he came into the contest to put the issue of the leadership of the party before the people. "In this State [Illinois] the primary would have gone by default had it not been for the fact that I had the temerity to come in here and file, and I am going to give you an opportunity to exercise the blessed privilege of helping to select the nominee for the Presidency upon the Republican ticket."[71]

Borah seemingly reasoned that because his financial resources were limited his strength could best be tested in the preferential primaries of ten key states where he permitted his name to be entered on the ballots.[72] He personally addressed over twenty rallies scattered in six or seven of these states. He broadcast at least five of his speeches over national networks.

During the primaries Borah changed little his line of argument of the past two years. Much of it stemmed from his fear that the New Deal threatened the Constitution. He said: "I am one of those who believe that our Government is sufficient and efficient to render all service necessary to the American people. I believe that the powers which we have, if properly used, are sufficient and ample to enable us to remove the evils and the errors both economic and political, of which we complain."[73]

He bitterly attacked the Old Guard as well as the Democrats. Accusing big business of dominating the party, he said:

> The question of monopoly is purely a question of courage, but so long as these political organizations and political machines get their money from these corporations for the purpose of running their primary campaign and for the purpose of run-

ning their election, you will never have the courage after the
election is over to turn upon your friends who furnished you
the money.[74]

As many political analysts pointed out, these attacks could not
win a Republican nomination, especially when the Old Guard was
in control. A shrewder politician with less ethical sense and with
a greater desire for the nomination would have let expediency determine his course and would certainly have attempted to curry
the favor of those in control. But Borah, the moralist in politics,
was more interested in arousing the voters than he was in winning
the nomination.

What was the outcome? In the primary Borah won outright
control of only the delegates from Wisconsin. In Illinois, he carried
thirteen of the fifteen downstate congressional districts, but he lost
to Knox because of the Chicago vote. He carried Nebraska and
polled almost as many popular votes as Landon in South Dakota.
Landon's sweep of the National Convention at Cleveland did not
indicate an outright defeat of the Idahoan, for into the platform
went Borah's antitrust plank (taken from the 1912 Democratic platform) and his foreign policy plank. The backers of Landon thought
Borah important enough to make repeated attempts to enlist his
active support. But with little hope for a party victory and with
little faith in Republican promises, Borah returned to Idaho without endorsing the Kansas governor. In contrast to Landon, who
went down in defeat, Borah returned to the Senate for the sixth time.

Summary and Appraisal

Running throughout the political and popular speaking of William E. Borah were several oft-repeated themes: adherence to the
Constitution, pride in our national existence, strict respect for states'
rights, avoidance of entangling foreign alliances, destruction of
monopolies, economy in government, and reform of the Republican
party. These were favorite topics with millions of Americans, especially those who liked to be associated with the word "progressive."
As an independent, more or less free from troublesome pressure
groups and loyally supported by a small constituency far from
Washington, Borah was free to shape these themes to the changing
times.

His independence of thought and action partially explained his wide following. Washington correspondents, among whom he had many warm friends, found him stimulating as a conversationalist, refreshing in his frankness, and intriguing as a subject for feature articles. Editors discovered that his utterances made good editorials. Newspaper readers were familiar with his name and his pronouncements. As a "lone rider" he was in demand as a speaker.

The "lone rider" reputation was one which Borah was pleased to cultivate. Associated with it was his reputation for scholarship, earnestness, and fearlessness. The stories concerning his spartan living, his frugality, his horseback riding, his refusal to participate in Washington social life, and his outspokenness typified what many Americans thought a senator should be. His mail was filled with letters from his admirers who sought to call his attention to injustices or who merely wanted to express confidence in him.[75] As a speaker he had excellent personal appeal and drawing power. He was the type that the people wanted to hear.

Among his friends and even among his enemies there was general agreement concerning Borah's intellectual integrity. He was intensely sincere in what he said. He disliked compromise and expediency as a basis for action. He gave his speeches a moral fervor that made them persuasive.

Another important asset of Borah was his oratorical prowess. Whether in the Senate, before a radio microphone, or at a political rally, the Idahoan seemingly had a dynamic sense of communication. For himself, he set high standards of rhetorical excellence, based upon a careful study of Burke, Webster, Pitt, Fox, Bright, Lincoln, and others. From his active and alert mind he could draw endless sets of apt historical examples, pertinent quotations, and striking comparisons. On the platform his stocky figure, his "ruggedly sculptured" face, his earnest eyes, and sober dress pleased his auditors. Says a contemporary: "Even his mass of long brown hair [at age forty-four] and burly eyebrows fail to overcome the impression of cordial frank good nature, emphasized in the rest of his face—a peculiar face, usually dominated by a smile instigated by characteristic friendliness."[76]

He had an unusual ability to extemporize and to meet unexpected situations, a pleasant conversational voice capable of stirring his listeners emotionally, and a rich vocabulary in which he clothed his thoughts.

For over thirty years Borah wielded significant political power—without the backing of a populous state, without financial resources, and without party support. Perhaps a shrewder politician might have gained greater distinction; a more ambitious man might have accepted the vice-presidency or a cabinet post; a lesser personality might have been more consistent; and a more statesman-like individual might have directed his energies into more constructive legislation; but Borah cherished his independence.

As a tribune of the people, he refused to be silent; he looked beyond the Senate for his audience. In his popular campaigns he applied his youthful energy, his penetrating analysis, and his persuasive eloquence. Into his speaking he poured a moral fervor that lifted it above the common harangue of the stump. Perhaps others may outdistance him in a claim for greatness, but there is much to be admired in the political career of the Lone Rider of Idaho.

Footnotes

1. "Shall the Constitution of the United States Be Nullified," delivered October 15, 1923, before Citizens Conference on Law Enforcement, Washington, D. C., *American Problems*, ed. Horace Green (New York, 1924), pp. 307-329.
2. Found in "Lincoln the Orator," an address delivered at Lincoln's birthplace, November 9, 1911, *American Problems*, pp. 31-42.
3. Quoted by Beverly Smith, "The Lone Rider from Idaho," *The American Magazine*, CXIII (March, 1932), 38-40.
4. Henry F. Pringle, "The Real Senator Borah," *World's Work*, LVII (December, 1928), 133-144.
5. Walter Lippmann, *Men of Destiny* (New York, 1927), p. 146.
6. Oswald Garrison Villard, "Presidential Possibilities—William E. Borah," *The Nation*, CXXVI (March 14, 1928), 290-292.
7. The writer has a file, by no means complete, of 783 occasions at which Borah spoke. Of these 236 were appearances before the Senate.
8. Jonathan Mitchell, "Borah Knows Best," *The New Republic*, LXXXV (January 29, 1936), 333-334.
9. University of Kansas, *The Register*, 1885, deposited in the Office of the Registrar.
10. Claudius O. Johnson, *Borah of Idaho* (New York, 1936), p. 17.
11. *The Weekly University Courier* (University of Kansas), March 11, 1887.
12. For this undertaking Borah earned $35 a month or a total of $140. *Annual Report of District No. 22* for the year ending July 31st, 1885. This record is filed in the office of the County Superintendent of Rice County at Lyons, Kansas.

13. *Lyons* (Kansas) *Republican*, July 17, 1884, p. 5.

14. Johnson, p. 16.

15. *Lyons Republican*, October 9, 1884, p. 5; January 8, 1885, p. 4.

16. *Nineteenth Annual Catalogue of the Officers and Students of the University of Kansas*, p. 62.

17. Borah to G. Douglas Wardrop, November 3, 1914, *Borah Papers*, deposited in the Library of Congress.

18. *Ibid.*

19. Letter to the author from Mrs. Nettie Gowdy Montgomery, Los Angeles, California, September 28, 1940.

20. *The Weekly University Courier*, October 17, 1885, p. 1; November 13, 1885, p. 1.

21. Smith, p. 40.

22. *Lyons Republican*, September 29, 1887, pp. 1, 10.

23. He served from April 18 until May 18, 1888, and from April 15, 1889, until September 15, 1890. *Minutes of the Council*, City of Lyons, Kansas, 1888, p. 34; 1889, pp. 136, 185, 240; *Lyons Republican*, October 9, 1890, p. 5.

24. *Lyons Republican*, May 10, 1888, p. 5.

25. Borah's first professional advertisement appeared in *The Idaho Daily Statesman*, November 12, 1890.

26. C. P. Connolly, "Presidential Possibilities—Borah of Idaho," *Colliers*, LV (July 31, 1915), 5-6. Borah verified the facts in this article before it was published. Borah to C. P. Connolly, May 22, 1915, *Borah Papers*.

27. *Statesman*, March 17, 1891, p. 8.

28. *Ibid.*, April 28, 1891, p. 8.

29. Bartlett Sinclair, *New York Times*, February 8, 1925, Sec. 2, p. 6; F. W. Ellis, "Character Sketch of Honorable W. E. Borah," *The Idaho Magazine*, I (March, 1904), pp. 6-8; A. H. Ulm, "Mr. Borah Goes to the Country," *New York Times*, August 15, 1926, Sec. 4, p. 1.

30. Connolly, pp. 5-6.

31. For Borah's closing argument, see Frederick C. Hicks, *Famous American Jury Speeches* (St. Paul, Minnesota, 1925), pp. 354-407.

32. *Current Literature*, XLII (June, 1907), 587.

33. Clarence Darrow, *The Story of My Life* (New York, 1932), p. 153.

34. *Congressional Record*, LVIII, pt. 6, 6718.

35. William Hard, "Friendly Enemies," *Liberty Magazine*, II (March 27, 1926), pp. 20-21.

36. *Christian Science Monitor*, November 10, 1926, p. 1, "Senator Borah in Daily Chats Endears Himself to Reporters"; Jessie Fant Evans, "East and West Blend in Apartment of Borahs," *The Washington* (D. C.) *Star*, June 6, 1931, p. B4; S. J. Woolf, "Borah Looks to Emerson As a Guide," *New York Times*, November 13, 1927, sec. 5, p. 3.

37. *Congressional Record*, XLVIII, pt. 9, p. 9126; pt. 11, pp. 11261-11262.

38. Among his private papers are several of these envelopes or folders. One, which is labeled "League Court Documents Read and Analyzed," still contains the material he collected in the twenties.

39. Interview of Miss Cora Rubin, Washington, D. C., June 4, 1941.

40. Borah to Lionel Crocker, November 5, 1935, published in *The Speaker*, XXIV (March, 1940), 3.

41. The writer has a list of more than fifty articles which Borah wrote during his sojourn in the Senate and which appeared in over twenty different magazines. Among the magazines are *Forum, Colliers, Scribners, Christian Century, Outlook, Independent, Current History,* and the *North American Review.* He wrote numerous articles for the *New York Times* and other newspapers.
42. Borah to James T. Williams, Jr., September 9, 1919, *Borah Papers.*
43. Borah to Will Hays, August 31, 1914, *Borah Papers.*
44. Borah to Jean DeHaven, August 4, 1937, found in "An Investigation of William E. Borah's Use of Argumentation is Congressional Debate" (Master's thesis, University of South Dakota, 1939).
45. Borah performed this feat during the Coeur d'Alene case. Johnson, p. 75.
46. *Lyons Republican,* September, October, November, 1888.
47. *Statesman,* July 1, 1891, p. 8; July 14, 1891, p. 8.
48. *Statesman,* February 16, 1892, p. 8; May 6, 1892, p. 1.
49. Borah led his ticket and polled 6659 votes. That year McKinley won 5031 and Bryan, 15745 in Idaho. *Statesman,* November 10, 1896, p. 6.
50. Johnson, pp. 67-70.
51. *Statesman,* September 1–November 6, 1906.
52. Borah *Scrapbook,* Vol. XIV, December 19, 1910–March, 1911. Deposited at the University of Idaho, Moscow.
53. On this speech there are more than fifty editorials, which appeared in newspapers from Maine to Alabama, pasted in the Borah *Scrapbook,* Vol. XV, August 8, 1911–February 27, 1912.
54. Given in full, *Congressional Record,* LXVII, pt. 10, pp. 10752-10753.
55. "Borah Out to Fight the Dry Referendums," *Literary Digest,* LXXXIX (June 12, 1926), 5-8.
56. *New York Times,* May 31, 1926, p. 1.
57. *New York Times,* April 8, 1927, p. 3; April 9, 1927, p. 1.
58. At the commencement of the National Law School, Washington, D. C., June 12, 1926. Before the Protestant Ministers' Association, Augusta, Georgia, July 18, 1926. At the University of Minnesota, September 30, 1926. Before New York Women's Committee for Law Enforcement, Carnegie Hall, New York City, November 12, 1927. Before the National Grange Convention, Cleveland, Ohio, November 18, 1927. At Yale University, November 28, 1927. A radio address from Washington, D. C., to the Women's Law Enforcement League of Columbus, Ohio, March 28, 1928.
59. In the campaign Borah made three tours. The first was as follows: Detroit, Mich. (Sept. 19); Bowling Green, Ky. (Sept. 21); Nashville, Tenn. (Sept. 22); Tulsa, Okla. (Sept. 24); Mitchell, S. D. (Sept. 28); Lincoln, Nebr. (Sept. 29); Minneapolis, Minn. (Oct. 1).

The second tour opened at Richmond, Va. (Oct. 15); followed by rallies at Salisbury, N. C. (Oct. 16); Charlotte, N. C. (Oct. 17); Chattanooga, Tenn. (Oct. 18); Louisville, Ky. (Oct. 19); Dallas, Tex. (Oct. 22); Joplin, Mo. (Oct. 24).

The third tour was as follows: Charleston, W. Va. (Oct. 29); Norfolk, Va. (Oct. 30); Baltimore, Md. (Oct. 31); Boston, Mass. (Nov. 2); Utica, N. Y. (Nov. 3).
60. Borah to C. F. Borah, November 19, 1914, *Borah Papers.*
61. Woolf, p. 3.

62. Arthur Krock has an excellent discussion of his strategy. *New York Times,* November 15, 1934, p. 20.

63. An attack on the NRA codes, January 18, 1934. *Congressional Record,* LXXVIII, pt. 1, 871-877. On the gold reserve bill, January 26, 1934. *Congressional Record,* LXXVIII, pt. 2, 1400-1404. A criticism of the NRA codes on iron and steel, March 21, 1934. *Congressional Record,* LXXVIII, pt. 5, 4999-5003. Opposition to delegation of power to the president, May 17, 1934. *Congressional Record,* LXXVIII, pt. 8, 9006-9012.

64. *New York Times,* August 26, 1934, sec. 6, p. 3.

65. On the Anti-Trust Laws, February 7, 1934. *New York Times,* February 8, 1934, p. 13. "America Must Choose," an address on production curbs, March 22, 1934. *New York Times,* March 23, 1934, p. 7. In opposition to the New Deal, July 4, 1934. *New York Times,* July 5, 1934, pp. 1, 13. On relief, November 19, 1934, *New York Times,* November 20, 1934, pp. 1, 13.

66. Quoted in full. *New York Times,* December 14, 1934, pp. 1, 2.

67. "The Republican Party," February 12, 1914, before the Republican Club of New York City. *New York Times,* February 13, 1914, p. 3. Speech before a Republican Get-Together Meeting, Memorial Hall, Columbus, Ohio, February 26, 1914, published by Ohio State Republican Central and Executive Committee. A copy of this address is contained in collection of speeches entitled *Speeches of Hon. Wm. E. Borah on Noted Men and Before Prominent Clubs, 1909-1918,* owned by Mrs. Mattie Borah Rinard, Fairfield, Illinois.

68. "The Supreme Court Decision," June 2, 1935, from Washington, D. C., over CBS. Given in full in *New York Times,* June 3, 1935, p. 1. "Our Foreign Policy," September 22, 1935, from Boise, Idaho, *New York Times,* September 23, 1935, p. 10. Assailing Roosevelt and Hoover, December 7, 1935, from Washington, D. C., over CBS. Given in full in *New York Times,* December 8, 1935, pp. 1, 25.

69. Lucas poll, *New York Times,* August 19, 1935, p. 1.

70. William K. Hutchinson, *News Articles on the Life and Works of Honorable William E. Borah* (U.S. Gov't. Printing Office, 1940), p. 21.

71. Speech quoted in full in *New York Times,* March 22, 1936, p. 40.

72. Illinois, Kansas, New York, New Jersey, Nebraska, Ohio, Oregon, Wisconsin, South Dakota, and West Virginia.

73. From "Issues Before the People," *New York Times,* March 22, 1936.

74. *Ibid.*

75. In 1919, for example, he received as many as 3000 letters daily during the League debate. Borah to Frank Young, March 24, 1919, *Borah Papers.*

76. "Men We are Watching," *The Independent,* LXVII (July 15, 1909), 132-133.

Franklin D. Roosevelt: A Study in
Leadership Through Persuasion

FRANKLIN DELANO ROOSEVELT (*January 30, 1882—April 12, 1945*). *Born at Hyde Park, Dutchess County, New York; only son of Sara and James Roosevelt, cultured landed gentry; privately tutored by parents and French and German governesses until age of fourteen; at Groton, fashionable Episcopal preparatory school, 1897-1900; pursued classical curriculum; active as debater and as writer for* THE GROTONIAN; *at Harvard College, 1900-1904; majored in political science and history, completing requirements for the A.B. degree in three years; studied public speaking under George Pierce Baker; active in Signet and Political Club; president of Harvard* CRIMSON; *at Columbia Law School, 1904-1907; admitted to bar and practiced in New York, 1907-1910; New York state senator, 1911-1913; assistant secretary of the Navy, 1913-1920; Democratic nominee for vice-president, 1920; stricken with infantile paralysis, August, 1921; won national recognition for speeches nominating Alfred E. Smith for the presidency in 1924 and 1928; governor of New York, 1929-1933; elected president of the United States, 1932; began press conferences and fireside chats, and instituted vigorous action to combat depression, 1933; continued experimentation, 1934-1936; re-elected to presidency, 1936; lost Court fight and led in preparedness effort, 1936-1940; re-elected to presidency for third term, 1940; led nation into war against Japan and Germany, 1941; assumed leadership of Allies, 1942; negotiated for peace at Casablanca, Quebec, and Teheran, 1943; sponsored outline of world organization, 1944; re-elected to presidency for fourth term, 1944; conferred at Yalta, 1945; died suddenly at Warm Springs, Georgia, April 12, 1945. Author of* WHITHER BOUND, *1926;* LOOKING FORWARD, *1933;* ON OUR WAY, *1934;* THE AMERICAN WAY, *1944;* RENDEZVOUS WITH DESTINY, *1944; and* NOTHING TO FEAR, *1946.*

Franklin D. Roosevelt: A Study in Leadership Through Persuasion

Laura Crowell, L. LeRoy Cowperthwaite,
Earnest Brandenburg*

However history may judge the public career of Franklin Delano Roosevelt, his eminence as a speaker is not likely to be questioned. From the public rostrum, the well of the House of Representatives, the rear platform of his special trains, he talked with the people. By radio he reached the ears of greater numbers than had ever heard the voice of one man. During his early years as president, he exhorted his listeners to accept and support a new deal in American economic and political thought. Later, challenged by the crisis of a world in conflict, he spoke repeatedly to guide the nation and the democratic world to victory. Finally, he played a significant part in sketching the outlines for a peaceful world order. Always he informed the people and enlisted their support on the policies and actions of their government by talking to them. His was indeed leadership through persuasion.

The keys to Roosevelt's persuasive powers are revealed in a study of his education and training, his methods of speech composition

* Laura Crowell (A.B. University of South Dakota 1929, M.A. 1940, Ph.D. 1948, State University of Iowa) is associate professor of speech at the University of Washington.

L. LeRoy Cowperthwaite (B.A. Ottawa University 1939, M.A. 1946, Ph.D. 1950, State University of Iowa) is professor of speech and head of the School of Speech at Kent State University.

Earnest Brandenburg (B.A. Iowa Teachers College 1937, M.A. 1941, Ph.D. 1948, State University of Iowa) is associate professor of speech and dean of University College at Washington University in St. Louis.

and delivery, and in the weight and validity of his ideas, their arrangement, and the language in which they were clothed.

EDUCATION AND EARLY TRAINING

Early years

Until he reached the age of fourteen, Franklin Roosevelt's education was supervised by his parents, with the aid of German and French governesses and tutors. Under the guidance of his elderly father, James Roosevelt, young Franklin developed keen powers of observation and memory. In their frequent journeyings up and down the Hudson and numerous trips abroad, James pointed out to his son the well-known landmarks and explained their historic significance. Franklin received his earliest experience in reading, on the other hand, from his mother. At first Sara read to her son,[1] and later mother and son read aloud together. Sara observed that her son displayed at an early age considerable vocal fluency and talent as a conversationalist.[2] Although Franklin reputedly spent many hours browsing among the books that lined the walls of the large family library at Hyde Park, life itself was the greater influence in those formative years; he stated later: "I would dip into my father's good library, taking a book here and there; I studied the five-volume encyclopedia from end to end and even today I still find experience to be my best teacher."[3]

Groton

At fourteen Roosevelt was sent to Groton, fashionable Episcopal preparatory school for boys, characterized by its strict classical discipline and strongly religious atmosphere. Courses in Greek, Latin, ancient history, English composition and literature were a part of each semester's work. Spoken French and German, mathematics, physics, and the headmaster's required course in sacred studies rounded out the program for Roosevelt and others. Although "not brilliant," wrote Dr. Endicott Peabody, headmaster, of Roosevelt in 1932, "he was a quiet, satisfactory boy of more than ordinary intelligence, taking a good position in his form."[4] Franklin distinguished himself in the classics by winning the All-School Latin Prize upon graduation.

The Groton years produced Roosevelt's first attempts at formal writing. Besides the large number of required themes in English composition, Franklin in his third year began writing short articles for *The Grotonian*, the monthly school publication.

Roosevelt had considerable experience in speaking at Groton, where he participated in the debating societies, listened to the speeches of prominent visitors, and enjoyed the oral reading of great literature. Among the topics Franklin debated were the annexation of Hawaii, the Nicaraguan Canal Bill, and Philippine independence.[5]

Among the notables who appeared in the Groton chapel in Franklin Roosevelt's day was his distant cousin, Theodore, whom he greatly admired and whose vigorous speaking style and forthrightness must have impressed the boy.[6] The Rector, as well as the masters, made a regular practice of reading aloud to the boys. Franklin enjoyed especially the annual reading of Dickens' *Christmas Carol* by the Rector's father.[7]

School life at Groton in Roosevelt's day centered around the chapel, where each morning the inspiring passages of the *Book of Common Prayer* were read in unison and boys came to know long passages by heart. Roosevelt, like the other boys at Groton, read the Bible through once every two years.[8]

Thus, at Groton, Roosevelt heard the effective oral use of language in the speeches of noted visitors and in the readings from good literature. He grew acquainted with rhythmical, figurative language in the Bible and discussed word usage in his classical studies. He participated in the daily oral readings from the prayerbook and tried his own powers of expression in the debating societies. His Groton years gave him good training indeed for later speechmaking.

Harvard

Franklin Roosevelt graduated from Groton in June, 1900, and "went up" to Harvard in the fall under President Eliot's anticipation plan.[9] In the courses offered and in the men who taught them the Harvard of 1900 was brilliant and liberal.[10] Here Roosevelt, majoring in political science and history, studied also in English literature with such authorities as Dean L. B. R. Briggs, then Boylston Professor of Rhetoric and Oratory, George Lyman Kittredge, George Pierce Baker, and Charles Townsend Copeland. In later years Roosevelt often spoke of the enthusiasm with which he and his classmates gathered to hear "Copey," the beloved teacher of English composition, read in his inimitable style from the works of English and American authors and, above all, from the Bible.[11] Again Roosevelt was quickened by the power and glory of good literature read aloud and impressed by the use of voice and presence to make words and thoughts take life.

While at Harvard, Roosevelt received his first formal classroom instruction in speaking. It is noteworthy that the first speech course for which he enrolled was entitled "Public Speaking," a course described in the *Catalog* for 1901-1902 as "intended for students somewhat advanced in platform speaking." He also spent a year with George Pierce Baker in "The Forms of Public Address," where he learned through extensive practice in argumentative briefing, speech composition and delivery, and the study of models of the world's greatest speeches that "ideal public address means . . . significant thought presented with all the clearness that perfect structure can give, all the force that skillful sifting of the material can produce, all the persuasiveness that perfect understanding of the relation of the audience to speaker and subject can give, with vivid narration and description, a graceful style, and an attractive personality."[12]

Franklin Roosevelt's popularity as a student leader, his active participation in many societies and organizations, notably Signet and the Political Club, served to enhance his already well-developed conversational abilities as well as his platform speaking prowess. Pursuing with enthusiasm his interest in journalism developed at Groton, Roosevelt advanced to the presidency of the *Crimson*, whose editorial columns afforded him an outlet for expressing forthright views on campus problems and politics. With the lessons of his classroom training in oral expression and his observation of superb lecturers and platform readers sharpened by the test of these vigorous experiences in writing and speaking, Roosevelt's years at Harvard were significant in his development as a speaker.

Legal training

Roosevelt left Harvard in the spring of 1904 and entered Columbia Law School that fall. There, under some of the greatest legal minds of the day, he learned that logical discipline must underlie the thinking of the persuasive speaker.[13]

When Roosevelt was admitted to the New York bar in the spring of 1907, he left Columbia Law School without taking his degree, and was employed immediately by one of the foremost law firms in general practice and litigation, Carter, Ledyard, and Milburn. In 1910 he left that firm for a better position as junior partner in the new firm of Marvin, Hooker, and Roosevelt.

His desire for public service, however, had a stronger appeal than the enviable legal position he had reached so early. Spurred on by the constantly enunciated encouragement and example of his illustrious cousin, T. R.,[14] he went in 1910 to Rochester, New York, as a delegate to the Democratic state convention, taking the first step in a long public career closed only by his death.

Early public career

For Franklin Roosevelt, the quarter century of public life beginning in 1910, interrupted temporarily by a sobering personal tragedy, proved to be a period of apprenticeship and maturation. In the roles of state senator, assistant secretary of the Navy, invalid, governor of New York, and finally, candidate for the highest office in the land, Roosevelt, the public speaker, grew in force and stature.

In 1910, after a whirlwind campaign of four weeks and ten to twenty speeches plus many conversations over farm fences per day, Roosevelt took his seat in the New York State Senate.[15] There he rapidly won distinction as a skillful parliamentary debater.

After leading the floor fight for Woodrow Wilson's nomination at the Democratic national convention of 1912 and stumping his home state for his successful candidate in the fall elections, Roosevelt was appointed assistant secretary of the Navy in March, 1913. His seven ensuing years of work in the Navy department afforded him abundant opportunities for development as a skilled speaker and writer. With war in the offing, he conducted a relentless speaking and writing campaign in favor of a larger navy. After the Armistice and Wilson's tragic collapse in September, 1919, Roosevelt pleaded the League of Nations cause with vigor, delivering numerous addresses in all parts of the country in its support.

Nominated by acclamation in 1920 as the Democratic candidate for vice-president, Roosevelt campaigned by train, automobile, and plane back and forth across the nation, making nearly a thousand speeches in forty-two states. Though he lost this first fight for national office, he gained valuable experience in campaign speaking.

In August, 1921, this active and promising public career was summarily interrupted when Roosevelt, at the age of thirty-nine, was stricken with infantile paralysis. Nevertheless, after three years of virtual seclusion, on June 26, 1924, Roosevelt resumed the role of political spokesman when, with the aid of crutches, he mounted the speaker's rostrum in Madison Square Garden and placed in nomination before the Democratic national convention the name of Alfred E. Smith, then governor of New York. Known widely as the "Happy Warrior" speech, this classic in nominating speeches reintroduced Franklin Roosevelt to the nation as a highly persuasive political speaker.[16]

His early years of invalidism did not prevent Roosevelt from speaking on important political occasions: he campaigned for John W. Davis in the fall of 1924, keynoted the New York State Democratic convention in 1926, and campaigned for the re-election of Governor Smith. Inevitably selected to renominate Smith at the Democratic national convention of 1928, he appeared on the platform, this time free of crutches, to extol again the virtues of the Happy Warrior, and won another tremendous personal ovation and further recognition as a powerful political orator.

On numerous occasions during his years of recuperation, Roosevelt obeyed his journalistic urge and wrote magazine articles which revealed a maturing political philosophy. He also read widely his favorite subject, naval history, as well as American political history, books of travel, farm journals, and American literature. He greatly increased his knowledge of geography, already wide from his travels and his interest in stamp-collecting, by becoming what Perkins called "an avid atlas reader."[17]

The confining nature of Roosevelt's illness prevented his keeping in immediate touch with government and politics; hence, Mrs. Roosevelt, who had become active in New York political circles, and Louis McHenry Howe, journalist and Roosevelt's devoted companion, brought him reports. In frequent and lengthy conferences, with Roosevelt ever the questioner, these three discussed vital issues of the day. Howe also introduced his friend to many leaders in politics, industry, labor, and social work. In such meetings Roosevelt came to rely more and more upon his ability as a conversation-alist to gain an understanding of major problems.[18] Thus, through reading, writing, and conversing, Roosevelt used his seven years of semi-retirement to further his development as a political speaker.

At the urging of Alfred E. Smith and others, Roosevelt became the Democratic nominee for governor of New York in 1928. During the campaign he delivered six major addresses for Smith, the presidential candidate, plus more than thirty in his own behalf. Winning the governorship, although Smith lost the presidency, Roosevelt plunged into his duties with vigor; he "moved about more, traveled more miles, made more public appearances and delivered more speeches than any other chief executive . . . had done in any similar period."[19] He was re-elected in 1930 by the largest majority ever given a candidate for governor of New York. Throughout his administration as governor he used the radio extensively to win the understanding and support of the people of his state. Lindley observed that by 1931 Roosevelt had "probably better than any public man in New York . . . mastered the technique of speaking over the radio."[20]

In January, 1932, Roosevelt consented to have his name entered in the North Dakota primaries as a candidate for the Democratic nomination for the presidency. Between that date and the national convention in June, he delivered three major political addresses, each setting forth in decisive language what was to become a major premise in the thinking and speaking of Roosevelt the President. In Albany on April 7 he charged that the Republican administration had neglected "the infantry of our economic army . . . the forgotten man at the bottom of the economic pyramid."[21] At a Jefferson Day dinner in St. Paul on April 18, Roosevelt called for national economic planning, which he termed "a concert of action, based on a fair and just concert of interests." Finally, at Oglethorpe University on May 22, he advocated "bold, persistent experimentation" in solving the economic problems facing the nation.

On July 2, 1932, Roosevelt took the dramatic and unprecedented step of flying to the scene of the Democratic national convention in Chicago to accept his party's nomination for the presidency. In a ringing address that closed with the speaker's pledge of a "new deal for the American people," Roosevelt launched upon a nationwide, stump-speaking tour rivaling the earlier exploits of William Jennings Bryan. Probably of greatest significance among his campaign efforts was the address to the Commonwealth Club of San Francisco on September 23, which spelled out a concept of governmental function and declared the necessity for developing closer ties between the government and the people. He was addressing a nation three years deep in depression, disheartened by closed banks and factories, withering farmlands, and lengthening breadlines. In friendly, heart-warming fashion Roosevelt asked the people to elect him their president. At the polls in November he won the electoral votes of forty-two of the forty-eight states.

Thus introduced as a mature political orator of great persuasive power, Franklin Roosevelt assumed the role of national and world leader which he was to play, both in peace and war, for almost thirteen years.

IDEAS ON INTERNAL AFFAIRS

What stand did Roosevelt the President take upon internal issues in the half dozen years during which fortune permitted him to concentrate upon them? Basically, he stood for two things. First, he believed firmly in the development of "social justice." Holding paramount this aim of a constantly better and more meaningful life for all, he felt that the interdependence of the nation made its achievement a problem of importance to the whole country. Secondly, he urged that the needs of the country be continually discovered by the close relationship between people and government, and that government should find means, by experimentation where necessary, to fulfill those needs.[22]

Social justice

Roosevelt saw the achievement of social justice as a duty of government.[23] He believed that government must seek to make possible better jobs, better homes, recreation, and help in time of need for all citizens. These improvements in the quality of national life found their motivation, by Roosevelt's thinking, in the fact of "interdependence"; he described it as "our mutual dependence one upon the other—of individuals, of businesses, of industries, of towns, of villages, of cities, of states, of nations."[24] That he saw this interdependence as international was substantiated in 1941 when he alerted American laborers and farmers to their certain loss of social gains by an Axis victory;[25] and that he envisioned social justice in world terms was made triumphantly clear in his proclamation that same year of the "four essential human freedoms"—of speech and religion, from want and fear.[26]

But his concepts of social justice began with his countrymen. Speaking at Gettysburg in 1934, when the Administration was bending its efforts to combat the depression, he declared: "All of us, among all the States, share in whatever of good comes to the average man. We know that we all have a stake—a partnership in this Government of this, our country."[27] Indeed, he saw the economic life of the United States as "a seamless web."[28] Both Theodore Roosevelt and Woodrow Wilson had urged the desirability of serving the welfare of all groups, but neither had stressed the conviction that the interrelation of elements meant that no interest could be advanced unless all interests were advanced, the crux of Franklin Roosevelt's contention. The rhetorical strength of this position was utilized persuasively in numerous speeches throughout his presidency.

This firm belief that citizens are interdependent caused Roosevelt to reject the characterization of his efforts as "humanitarian": he saw aid to farmers, to factory workers, to the injured, to children, as the rightful relationship of interdependent citizens and fittingly termed it social justice. Interdependence was thus the basis for his repeated assertion that the drive toward these goals was a crusade,[29] for his reiterated description of the economic readjustments in the country as a war,[30] and for his labeling of his social objectives as an "Economic Bill of Rights."[31] Thus it was this essential fact of interdependence that underlay Roosevelt's keen perception of the need for the steadying power of government—representing the totality of citizens—behind the individual citizen, his welfare and his hopes.

Direct relationships with the people

In addition to the development of social justice, Roosevelt named the restoration of the democratic process as a major problem of the time. He interpreted the latter problem as the need for more vigorous use of public discussion and the voting privilege, but especially a more direct relationship between the people and the president. In 1932 he declared that "we are coming to a time when more of our citizens must exercise their rights if government is to be as useful as the citizen has the right to demand."[32] Hence, he urged citizens to write to him about their problems;[33] he suggested that local people watch federal relief projects and report to him on their progress and efficiency; he listened to advice and ideas from all manner of men; he plead for full participation in voting; and reported joyfully a wider interest in public issues.[34] Thus he invited a constant inpouring of information and opinion from citizens throughout the land, and quickened them by the invitation. But he also went out to them, to see conditions with his "own eyes." Through his visits, his heart-warming words and his bounteous governmental hand, he related himself—their president—to the common people of the country; and in 1940 he said in a campaign address in Cleveland: "I think that, in the years to come, that word 'President' will be a word to cheer the hearts of common men and women everywhere."

This direct relationship of the president with the people was consistent with his governmental concept: "Government includes the art of formulating a policy and using the political technique to attain so much of that policy as will receive general support; persuading, leading, sacrificing, teaching always, because the greatest duty of a statesman is to educate."[35] His tireless endeavors to perform this duty must not be underestimated in any appraisal of his conduct of government. Indeed, he treated his press conferences, almost a thousand in number, as seminars.[36] Robert E. Sherwood explained his relationship with the people thus: "He saw this country whole—not in terms of precincts but in terms of people."[37] And this close bond with the people injected a personal note into the fireside chats with which he lifted the hearts of the people in the depression days and later engaged their best efforts in the problems of war and peace. It produced a warmth which rang through his political utterances in a myriad of forms: the declaration that he was translating governmental problems into "human terms";[38] the exultation that there was "a constantly growing sense of human decency, human decency throughout our nation."[39] It gave rise to the idea of all people as neighbors, a concept repeatedly voiced in utterances to audiences small and large.

Experimentation

Roosevelt held that within a "consistency and continuity of broad purpose" in serving the needs of the people, as he explained in the noteworthy Commonwealth Club address, the president should search for workable methods. He did not consider this an easy assignment; in his second fireside chat of 1933, in the midst of the Hundred Days of swift action to combat the depression, he said to the people, "I have no expectation of making a hit every time I come to bat. What I seek is the highest possible batting average, not only for myself but for the team."

That these efforts were pioneering in nature he declared frequently, explaining that the frontiers now were economic and social rather than geographic. He described recovery in terms of the pioneer spirit: "As we have recaptured and rekindled our pioneering spirit, we have insisted that it shall always be a spirit of justice, a spirit of teamwork, a spirit of sacrifice, and, above all, a spirit of neighborliness."[40] As America faced the possibility of war, he relied upon this pioneer spirit: "We believe that, in the face of danger, the old spirit of the frontiersmen that is in our blood will give us the courage and unity that we must have."[41] Speaking in Chicago in his final campaign, he took pride in the fact that "America has always been a land of action—a land of adventurous pioneering—a land of growing and building." This persistent idea of a government busied in the search for new methods of meeting new problems or, on the other hand, old problems long unsolved was basic to all of Roosevelt's approaches to the internal problems of the country.

Theodore Roosevelt had urged the social importance of the individual; Woodrow Wilson had impressed the public with the citizen's importance in government, calling for dynamic usage of the democratic processes; Theodore Roosevelt had explained the praiseworthiness of experimentation; both had built their policies upon the interrelatedness of national life. In what lay the greater power of these ideas, then, when urged by Franklin Roosevelt? Consideration of his addresses may yield an answer.

Problems in internal affairs

During Roosevelt's first two administrations and again at the end of the war, when his attention centered principally on internal affairs, he devoted much of his speaking to explaining his basic objectives in terms of such problems as those of needy citizens, of agricultural workers, and of small businessmen.

Through Roosevelt's years as president, giving aid to needy persons took a host of tangible forms, such as minimum wage and hour legislation, unemployment relief, public works projects, the Civilian Conservation Corps and the National Youth Administration, and, particularly, the Social Security Act. And Roosevelt's bold assertion in the First Inaugural that "the only thing we have to fear is fear itself" and his strong, clear explanation of the plan for closing the banks given in the fireside chat a week later—these were the country's first and strongest weapons in routing the paralyzing depression. In the years to follow he recaptured the impact of the nation's dark moment through vivid picturization of sheriffs' sales and hungry families, of smokeless, silent factories, contrasting these widespread distresses with the busy prosperity won through his administrations.

In 1933 the need for self-preservation—strongest of human drives —was powerfully felt throughout the nation. That Roosevelt spoke to the people's need with timely, courageous, warm words was an event of historical importance. He further insisted that this aid to the needy be rendered through social action since the causes of their distress lay beyond the control of individuals. Thus, whether condemning the Federal Farm Board or urging reciprocal trade treaties or talking directly with the farmers in the drought areas, he was in all cases predicating his arguments and his actions upon the fact of interdependence and its effects on national welfare. Moreover he asserted that these governmental actions should be performed in a personal way, explaining as he accepted renomination to the presidency in 1936, "We seek not merely to make Government a mechanical implement, but to give it the vibrant personal character that is the very embodiment of human charity."

In his second inaugural address, although pointing to the great gains of the four years just ended, Roosevelt painted the picture of a nation yet distant from its "happy valley," and concluded his sketch with the trenchant declaration: "I see one-third of a nation ill-housed, ill-clad, ill-nourished." Hard upon the stormy reassessment of governmental power that marked his second term came war. And Roosevelt, although he realized earlier and perhaps more fully than most others the gigantic national effort which the nation's defense would require, yet urged that "we must make sure, in all that we do, that there be no breakdown or cancellation of any of the great social gains we have made in these past years."[42] In 1944, Roosevelt, returning from the conference at Teheran and knowing the full seriousness of the war, reminded the Congress in his State of the Union address of the necessity of laying plans for an even higher standard of living in America: "We cannot be content, no matter how high that general standard of living may be, if some fraction of our people—whether it be one-third or one-fifth or one-tenth—is ill-fed, ill-clothed, ill-housed, and insecure." He delineated these social objectives again and again, perhaps never more carefully than in his address to the Congress on January 6, 1941:

> Equality of opportunity for youth and for others.
> Jobs for those who can work.
> Security for those who need it.
> The ending of special privilege for the few.
> The preservation of civil liberties for all.
> The enjoyment of the fruits of scientific progress in a wider
> and constantly rising standard of living.

And when the war was over, he again gave these objectives his major attention, describing them repeatedly as a second, an economic, Bill of Rights, thus using the analogy of our founding fathers' fight against political autocracy for strong motivative appeal.

Among the legislative acts passed in quick succession in the spring of 1933 by the Congress in order to establish Roosevelt's pledged New Deal was the National Recovery Act, which embodied his concept of the government as a partner in business and industry. But the operation of its codes failed to yield the expected increase in employment, and, furthermore, the Act was declared unconstitutional by the Supreme Court in 1935. But now Roosevelt was moving to a position of attack upon big business, and in his second presidential campaign launched a particularly strong verbal attack on these "economic royalists." And he made this attack in the name of the ordinary citizen, who "must have equal opportunity in the market place."

Truly, Roosevelt succeeded so dramatically in personalizing the efforts of government in assistance to citizens in distress that many recipients thought of him as the personal source of their benefits. In addition, his emphasis upon the spiritual forces of government tied his efforts to the highest motives of mankind. In his annual message to the Congress on January 4, 1935, he declared: "Beyond the material recovery, I sense a spiritual recovery as well." Several years later he spoke again of "a growing devotion to the teachings of the Scriptures, to the quickening of religion, to a greater willingness on the part of the individual to help his neighbor and to live less unto and for himself alone," and claimed that it was in such a spirit that the government itself was seeking to perform its duties.[43]

Campaigning in Brooklyn in 1940, Roosevelt declared that "we have pushed ahead with social and economic reforms, determined that this period in American life should be written down as an heroic era—an era in which men fought not merely to preserve a past, but to build a future." Thus Roosevelt held out his social objectives, urging that the interdependence of the nation makes Americans partners in the movement toward a better life for all, showing himself the warm-hearted President interested in the welfare of each citizen and daring to pioneer with new methods in his behalf. He brought vitality, personification, drama to themes which in the discourse of others had remained impersonal and abstract. His crowning achievement lay in his invention of arguments for political communication about the functioning of government.

Use of governmental power

To those in distress Roosevelt extended the hand of government; his swelling use of governmental power, however, became the major issue of the 1936 campaign. Pointing to his failure to keep his promise of 1932 to cut expenditures as a step toward balancing the budget, his critics neglected the condition which he had appended to the promise, that if need among the citizens rendered additional expenditures necessary the need would be met.[44] When emergency struck, the announced policy gave way before the general objective, as ever with Roosevelt, and expenditures for relief and public works pyramided to serve his highest aim, a decent life for all American citizens. Here he revealed vividly his belief that the people would understand if explanations were made carefully to them. And his authoritative majority in the election of 1936 revealed that the public approved both the extensiveness of his programs and the experimental nature of his approach.

Another struggle over governmental function occurred over Roosevelt's plan to increase the number of Supreme Court justices through presidential appointment. He answered the resulting widespread and vigorous attacks with the charge in his Victory Dinner radio address on March 4, 1937, that the Court was out of step with the country's wishes, and five days later tried in a fireside chat to convince the public that his plan would not violate sacred traditions. But the strong adverse reaction was not swept away by these two rhetorical efforts. The public would not agree that tampering with the Supreme Court was essential to national welfare; indeed, many felt an element of trickery in the proposal.[45] He employed the same graphic language and resonant voice which had repeatedly during dark days of depression won the people's faith in his stalwart leadership. But his characteristic subtle timing of proposal to public temper (either present or elicited) was absent here, and one of his closest advisers, Samuel I. Rosenman, commented that he spoke without his usual depth of conviction.[46] It is certain that in these Court addresses he did not plead the grand experiment so cogently but took rather an almost punitive approach. And they did not win public support for his proposal to reform the Supreme Court.

Summary

It is clear that, whatever domestic issue Roosevelt was discussing, he was viewing it in the light of progress toward the development of social justice; he was basing his interpretation of problems and his proposal of solutions upon his concept of interdependence in the United States; and he was attempting to guide the nation forward through dynamic, bold experimentation and a warm, vibrant relationship between executive and citizenry.

Why then were the ideas of interdependence and experimentation stronger when urged by Roosevelt than by others? Because he tied them consistently to basic human motivation: he made the people a part of a noble undertaking in which they had fellowship with a sympathetic, invincible leader who held out a great future for them all, and for their children. The rhetorical critic will point out the warm voice, the well-timed pauses, the homely examples as elements in Roosevelt's particular effectiveness in public address, but will emphasize most strongly this superbly created identification of speaker and listeners.

That Roosevelt's ideas on internal affairs have left permanent marks upon the American scene is unquestionable. Their impact was due to the unique suitability of Roosevelt's pioneering spirit—its courage and daring, its good-fellowship, its zest for the goal—suitability to the need of the time, but even more was it due to his masterly use of rostrum and radio to enlist his countrymen in a common crusade. And his opponents, filled with bitterness and hatred at seeing a man use public office so boldly and face its tasks so buoyantly, feared most of all this power of oral persuasion.

IDEAS ON INTERNATIONAL AFFAIRS

While Franklin D. Roosevelt was president of the United States, the nation moved from apathy toward world political issues to ardent sponsorship of cooperation among the states of the world. Through the 1930's the overwhelming majority of Americans agreed that it had been a mistake for the United States to enter the first World War, that if another war broke out in Europe this country should not become involved, and that the United States could, if it desired, stay out of wars on other continents.[47] By January, 1945, the attitude of Americans had so changed that general approval greeted Roosevelt's adoption of universal responsibility for the United States when he told Congress, "It is our purpose to help the peace-loving peoples of Europe to live together as good neighbors. . . ."

To determine the exact contribution of Roosevelt in changing these attitudes is obviously impossible. But that he did play a part few will deny. Both those who praise and those who condemn him[48] agree that he advocated policies which made the United States a powerful factor among the nations.

Hemispheric solidarity

Roosevelt's speeches and actions were unusually successful in promoting for the Western Hemisphere the unity and good will he advocated. His concern in 1928 for the unfortunate state of inter-

American relations was more than campaign oratory. Roosevelt's realization that "the nineteen or twenty republics to the south of us . . . do not scorn us, they hate us" was not shared by the vast majority in this country. He explained that Latin Americans "have seen us in Haiti, Nicaragua, and Santo Domingo. They have seen what they call our imperialism."[49] Through the next six or seven years, he echoed this theme frequently with the plea that concrete action be taken to correct the distrust, even hatred, of Latin America for the United States. Gradually, he won supporters both in Congress and throughout the nation for his reiterated contention that the United States should deal with the other nations of the hemisphere as with equals, that armed intervention or financial domination was never justified.

The phrase, "good neighbor," which came to be applied to relations among nations of the Western Hemisphere, was used by Roosevelt in his First Inaugural Address. It aroused citizens, as they had not been previously aroused, to the objectionable features of attempts to dominate Latin America. The favorable responses evoked among citizens of the other nations concerned were strengthened by Roosevelt's further declaration that "the definite policy of the United States from now on is one opposed to armed intervention."[50] Reinterpreting the Monroe Doctrine, the President asserted that maintenance of orderly processes of government was not a responsibility of the United States alone, but that "only by sympathetic respect for the rights of others and a scrupulous fulfillment of the corresponding obligations of each member of the community can a true fraternity be maintained."[51] This declaration of a joint enterprise suggesting mutual respect and genuine friendliness provided strong emotional proof for these smaller countries.

Succeeding acts reinforced Roosevelt's assertion, for the Marines were withdrawn for the final time from Nicaragua in 1933, and in August of that year the United States refused to intervene in Cuba even when that country presented a "classical opportunity."[52] In 1934, at Roosevelt's insistence, the Platt Amendment, which gave the United States the right to intervene at its own judgment for the preservation of order in Cuba, was abrogated—and Cuba staged a three-day celebration. That same year, a treaty with Panama eliminated clauses of the treaty of 1903 by which that republic was made a semi-protectorate of the United States.

This good neighbor policy, frequently enunciated by Roosevelt and followed by the State Department, brought improvement in relations and received widespread praise.[53] Such phrases as "Yankee imperialism," "Colossus of the North," and "dollar diplomacy" were no longer used to characterize the policy of the United States in this hemisphere. As far as Latin Americans were concerned, the good neighbor policy was due almost entirely to Franklin D. Roosevelt.

With the beginning of World War II, Roosevelt advocated that all the Americas should be kept free from European influence. As Hitler swept over Western Europe, Roosevelt introduced into his addresses frequent appeals to self-preservation and fear. Quoting the exact flying times and distances from possible Axis bases to strategic Western Hemisphere positions, he drew analogies showing that the task of a European aggressor who might attack the Americas was simpler than many of the well-known conquests of history.

During the months just prior to December 7, 1941, Roosevelt's emotional appeals concerning the safety of the Western Hemisphere made use of specific plans which he claimed the Nazis possessed. The President told of a "secret Nazi map" which revealed German plans to abolish existing Latin American boundary lines and to create five German vassal states, one of which would include the Panama Canal. These appeals to fear and to self-preservation were augmented by reviews of Nazi treatment of the Balkans. The profit motive was invoked in his charges that the Fascists "would fasten an economic strangle-hold upon our several nations."

Such arguments and proofs, coming from a leader recognized as having the best interests of all the Americas at heart, were highly effective.[54]

Internationalism

In the thousand speeches delivered in his vice-presidential campaign of 1920, Roosevelt constantly repeated the thought that America must participate in the League if there were to be any hope of abolishing war. During the next decade, although less specific about the desirability of the League, he continued to advocate greater unity among nations with such statements as: "More and more we become interdependent. Communities merge into states, states into nations, nations into families of peoples."[55] Thus, when he declared his opposition in 1932 to the United States joining the League of Nations, he was called a political opportunist by many.[56] Clearly his attitude was politically expedient, but clearly also his arguments were both persuasive and justified as he contended that the League had not developed along the lines intended by Woodrow Wilson.

In his speeches of the 1930's Roosevelt invariably identified himself with those wanting peace,[57] but he did not support the widely accepted isolationist philosophy then current in the United States. When Congress passed the Neutrality Act of 1935, the President declared that the Act's inflexible arms embargo "might drag us into war instead of keeping us out." His State of the Union address on January 3, 1936, warned that the world situation "has in it many of the elements that lead to the tragedy of war."

Germany, Italy, and Japan began openly to defy world opinion. Hitler cast aside the Versailles Treaty; Mussolini overran Ethiopia; Japan's military launched full-scale war against the Chinese. Then, on October 5, 1937, Roosevelt made his one significant attempt to avert the approaching world catastrophe. His "quarantine" speech in Chicago called on the peace-loving nations to unite in opposing "international anarchy" against which "mere isolation or neutrality" stood helpless. His apt analogy has been frequently quoted: "When an epidemic of physical disease starts to spread, the community approves and joins in a quarantine of the patients in order to protect the health of the community against the spread of the disease." When the American public deplored these remarks as warmongering, Roosevelt realized that his customary rhetorical method of setting forth the goal and enlisting the people in the concerted attack to gain it had been prematurely used;[58] thereafter he neglected to reiterate his strong sentiment. Although he sent appeals to the leaders of other states for peaceful solutions to problems, he did not propose concrete policies to throw the might of the United States against aggressors.

Franklin Roosevelt led his fellow Americans through three distinct public attitudes from September, 1939, to December 7, 1941—

neutrality, non-belligerency, and active-defense.[59] Gradually, his fundamental thesis became more clear in his speeches and more obviously valid to his audience. Examination of his specific arguments through the months before Pearl Harbor reveal that they stemmed from his basic conviction that the United States and the Western Hemisphere would be imperiled by a Nazi victory. He also believed that keeping the Allies in the war would speed the eventual defeat of the Axis.

Striking changes, however, took place in his specific arguments between 1939 and 1941. Although he reasoned in September, 1939, that repeal of the embargo provisions would make the United States "neutral," he declared openly on March 15, 1941, that the embargo had been repealed to "aid the democracies." Again, on September 21, 1939, he advocated that "American merchant vessels . . . be restricted from entering war zones" as a preventive of war; on October 27, 1941, he argued, "American merchant ships must be free to carry our American goods into the harbors of our friends." At the outbreak of the war, Roosevelt had led in advocating that American ships should stay at home to prevent any possibility of warlike incidents; on September 11, 1941, however, the President went to great lengths to show that the United States' policy "from time immemorial" had demanded "freedom of the seas." In each instance he took that view concerning the specific issue which in the current political climate would best win adherents for his basic purpose. Moreover, Roosevelt's supporting arguments were not always accurate. For example, his definitions and historical interpretations of neutrality were not accepted by experts in international law.[60] He was clearly inconsistent and opportunistic in his handling of the "freedom of the seas" issue.

With the defeat of France and the Low Countries in 1940, Roosevelt moved from neutrality to a non-belligerent stand which put the United States unquestionably on the side of the Allies. By the following summer Roosevelt believed that defeating the Axis was more important than preserving peace, and took the attitude of active-defense. That this evolution was the most rapid possible for the Chief Executive of the United States, desiring to retain his leadership of the American people, is generally accepted.[61] Moreover, public opinion polls give evidence that Roosevelt's addresses did at times influence, modify or change the beliefs and attitudes of his listeners as, for example, on the issues of lifting the embargo and of arming merchant ships.[62]

The President's opponents declared again and again that he was leading the United States into war. Roosevelt persuasively and successfully met those charges, by reviewing both his official acts as president to preserve world peace and his activities following World War I to improve international relations. He repeated many times his desire for peace and his hatred of war. Although the American people consistently "opposed" getting into war, with similar consistency they "favored" the President in public opinion polls.

As the rhetorical critic might expect, Roosevelt developed his specific arguments for "aid to the Allies," "increases in American military strength," "freedom of the seas," "national unity," "neutrality," and "peace" with many appeals to the emotions of his listeners. An analysis of seventeen of his speeches on international affairs delivered between September, 1939, and December, 1941, reveals that in sixteen he appealed to the motive of self-preservation.

Whenever the President used logical proofs, he customarily appealed to the emotions of his listeners at the same time. He quoted exact flying times and distances to strategic points the Axis might attack; he proposed tremendous increases in America's military might and gave details as to what was needed; he revealed Hitler's plans for South America and for the religions of the world from captured Nazi documents. These uses of specific instances and of authority were convincing, and they had the added value of emotional impact.

The attack on Pearl Harbor ended disputes in this country about the desirability or necessity for American participation in World War II. The President's speeches became reports to the people—of trips, of conferences, of the state of the war—and appeals for still greater unanimity and effort among Americans. Winning the war and winning the peace were the two all-important issues. The bitter realities of war brought increasing determination to prevent another conflict through some system of world order. Roosevelt devoted portions of his World War II addresses to forwarding the conviction, which had been vigorously rejected following the first World

War, that the United States should agree to use force in the maintenance of peace abroad.[63] The important fact here is not that he was
peculiarly persuasive with such arguments, for only an insignificant
minority then disagreed, and no responsible spokesmen for influential groups took a contrary view. But the President's call at these
early dates for continued cooperation of the United Nations and
for a peaceful world—upheld by force, if necessary—clearly demonstrated his ardent internationalism.

In February, 1945, President Roosevelt, Prime Minister Churchill,
and Marshal Stalin discussed their war plans and peace aims at
Yalta. This conference completed Roosevelt's work on American
foreign policy, for two months later he died. At Yalta, however,
the three allies agreed that a conference of the United Nations
would meet in San Francisco on April 25 to draw up a charter for a
world organization. Thus, Roosevelt was a key figure in establishing a new organization dedicated to the unity of all the nations.
His fervent but unfulfilled hopes for the League of Nations, his
determination not to repeat the League's weaknesses, his unwavering belief in the desirability of international cooperation—all these
deep-seated convictions Roosevelt expressed forcefully to the American people. He made the establishment of a world order seem not
only possible and desirable, but absolutely essential.[64] Yet he approached the problem realistically, anticipating to some extent the
problems which have beset the United Nations organization in the
following years.[65]

Summary

Franklin Roosevelt devoted much time in his speeches to Western
Hemispheric solidarity and to internationalism. During his entire
career he advocated, and, as president, he successfully promoted,
unity among the nations of the Western Hemisphere. Both his
speeches and his actions were important in inspiring new confidence
and good will among North and South Americans.

By means of his public speeches, Roosevelt worked for an entire
world of mutually responsible and cooperating nations. Although
his exact contribution to awakening America to dangers from the
Axis powers and to readying her to meet them cannot be determined, unquestionably President Roosevelt's speeches were one of

the important factors in winning World War II and setting up the peace. His specific arguments were not always consistent with each other, but the end results he sought and helped to bring about are almost universally accepted today as for the best interests of this nation and the world. By means of speeches to his countrymen and to the world, Franklin D. Roosevelt exercised significant leadership in international affairs.

SPEECH COMPOSITION AND DELIVERY

Speech preparation

Preparation of the major addresses by which Roosevelt sought his goals nationally and internationally developed during his years as governor of New York and president of the United States into a complex yet highly systematic procedure. Roosevelt himself described the procedure as follows:

> In the preparation of campaign speeches as well as speeches on other occasions I have called on many different people for advice and assistance. . . . On various subjects I have received drafts and memoranda from different people, varying from short suggestions as to a sentence here and there, to long memoranda of factual material and, in some cases, complete addresses.
>
> . . . .
>
> In preparing a speech, I usually take the various drafts and suggestions which have been submitted to me and also the material which has been accumulated in the speech file on various subjects, read them carefully, lay them aside, and then dictate my own draft. . . .[66]

The final "reading copy," that manuscript used during delivery, was usually the result of a succession of revisions and redrafts, numbering from five or six to as many as twelve. Careful attention was given to the inclusion or exclusion of specific ideas, and to the tone and phraseology of the whole speech. For these detailed tasks of reworking, sifting of ideas, and rephrasing, Roosevelt relied upon the advice and assistance of a small group of technical and political advisers. Although the question of authorship of Roosevelt's speeches remains necessarily a moot one, Samuel I. Rosenman, who assisted with the preparation of speeches throughout Roosevelt's career as

governor and president, reported that "the speeches as finally delivered were his [Roosevelt's]—and his alone—no matter who the
collaborators were. He had gone over every point, every word,
time and again. He had studied, reviewed, and read aloud each draft,
and had changed it again and again, either in his own handwriting,
by dictating inserts, or making deletions. Because of the many hours
he spent in its preparation, by the time he delivered a speech he
knew it almost by heart."[67] During actual delivery from this familiar
manuscript, Roosevelt demonstrated versatility in platform authorship by frequent impromptu interpolations and alterations. Critics
may conclude that since Roosevelt made the final choice of ideas
expounded, supporting details presented, and phraseology used, the
speeches as delivered were indeed his own.

In view of the care with which ideas and phraseology were
adapted to the audience and occasion, it is not surprising to discover
that Roosevelt's speeches display no characteristic organizational
patterns. Whatever the speech or the occasion, his veteran skill as
an organizer plus his keen sense of listener response resulted in the
shaping of each unit and each paragraph to suit the mood of the
audience and theme. Baird has observed that Roosevelt's speech
structure "employed a high degree of organic movement and illustrated the 'natural procedure' in persuasion."[68]

Language

Roosevelt was acutely conscious of the power of words, their
tone, their oral quality, their accuracy and connotation. He and his
assistants exercised considerable care in finding the words most suit-
able for securing the effect desired.

The President enhanced the effectiveness of his ideas through
well-used rhetorical devices. With metaphor he struck vigorously
at the heart of his arguments: "As long as it remains within my
power to prevent, there will be no black-out of peace in the United
States,"[69] and "We must be the great arsenal of democracy."[70] He
often achieved vivid contrast by setting strong metaphors in opposition: "There are men who believe . . . that, for some unexplained
reason, tyranny and slavery have become the surging wave of the
future—and that freedom is an ebbing tide."[71] His similes were often
warmly human: "A Nation, like a person, has a body—a body that

must be fed and clothed and housed, invigorated and rested. . . . A Nation, like a person, has a mind—a mind that must be kept informed and alert, that must know itself, that understands the hopes and the needs of its neighbors. . . . A Nation, like a person, has something deeper, something more permanent, something larger than the sum of all its parts . . . the spirit—the faith."[72] Ideas were brought swiftly into focus through personification: "Many voices are heard as we face a great decision. Comfort says, 'Tarry a while.' Opportunism says, 'This is a good spot.' Timidity asks, 'How difficult is the road ahead?' "[73]

Roosevelt quoted Dante, Franklin, Lincoln, and many others whose prestige added force to his own ideas. He favored biblical allusion to clothe his ideas with the respect and veneration accorded scriptural concepts: ". . . the path that our children must tread and their children must tread, the path of faith, the path of hope and the path of love toward our fellow men";[74] "As men do not live by bread alone, they do not fight by armaments alone";[75] "We must always be wary of those who with sounding brass and a tinkling cymbal preach the 'ism' of appeasement."[76]

The speeches of Roosevelt were characterized by concreteness and simplicity. Abundant use of specific names, places, and dates brought the events vividly to mind: "In July, 1937, Japan invaded China. On January 3, 1938, I called the attention of the nation to the danger of the whole world situation."[77] Graphic picturization emerged through detail: "I saw the workmen in the mills, the mines, the factories; the girl behind the counter; the small shopkeeper; the farmer doing his spring plowing; the widows and the old men wondering about their life's savings."[78] The words were simple and vigorous, and the phrases read well; these characteristics typified Roosevelt's platform language.

Colloquialisms gave the ideas in which they appeared a familiar and acceptable ring: ". . . have asked for it—and they are going to get it," and "climb back into an American hole and pull the hole in after them."[79] The combination of vivid detail and colloquialism often presented compelling word pictures:

> And I cannot help but think of the families in other lands—
> millions of families—living in homes like ours. On some of these

homes, bombs of destruction may be dropping even as I speak to you.

Across the seas life has gone underground. I think I speak the minds of all of you when I say that we thank God that we live in the sunlight and in the starlight of peace . . . that we propose and expect to continue to live our lives in peace—under the peaceful light of Heaven.[80]

Dialogue and direct quotation heightened the interest of his materials: "But when you and I step into the voting booth, we can proudly say: 'I am an American, and this vote I am casting is the exercise of my highest privilege and my most solemn duty to my country' ";[81] "The gist of that telegram was: 'Please, Mr. President, don't frighten us by telling us the facts.' "[82] In one 1932 campaign speech Roosevelt quoted his opponent, Herbert Hoover, twenty-two times.[83]

Roosevelt's speeches were distinguished by their frequent use of climactic thought structure, with parallel, repeated, and contrasted elements: "The proposed 'new order' is the very opposite of a United States of Europe or a United States of Asia. It is not a Government based on consent of the governed. It is not a union of ordinary, self-respecting men and women to protect themselves and their freedom and their dignity from oppression. It is an unholy alliance of power and pelf to dominate and enslave the human race."[84]

Short, terse, and even fragmentary sentences, as well as numerous rhetorical questions suggested the conversational mode of discourse so characteristic of most of Roosevelt's forensic efforts: "I say that the delivery of needed supplies to Britain is imperative. I say that this can be done; it must be done; and it will be done"; "Farm income? What happens to all farm surpluses without any foreign trade?"[85]

Roosevelt, the phrase-maker,[86] will long be remembered for his contributions to the American political vocabulary through his aphorisms, notably "new deal," "forgotten man," "policy of the good neighbor," and "arsenal of democracy"; and for his many quotable passages such as "the only thing we have to fear is fear itself," and "this generation of Americans has a rendezvous with destiny." The inevitable salutation, "My friends," served well its intended function of achieving rapport with his listeners and came to be inextricably linked with Franklin D. Roosevelt, speaker.

Words and phrases of strength and warmth, of simplicity and graphic power—these were characteristic of Roosevelt's language.

Delivery

Roosevelt typically delivered his major addresses from manuscript. His intense involvement in the task of preparing the text as well as his superior ability as a reader were notable factors in his vivid presentation. When the occasion called for extemporizing, he demonstrated his facility in reaching his audience by this method.

The Roosevelt personality emerged as a highly significant factor in his speaking effectiveness. Characterized by observers as "magnetic," "winning," and "charming," his speaking personality was one which inspired admiration and respect in his hearers. People everywhere received a powerful impression of buoyant confidence, sincere friendliness, broad human sympathy, and boundless energy. His hearty, infectious laugh—he reputedly laughed more than any man then in politics—rarely failed to get the desired response. Upon his speeches was, according to one observer, "the stamp of deep sincerity which the audience did not miss."[87] Not the least effective of his personality traits was his keen mind, manifested to his audiences by what Flynn has referred to as his "prodigious memory for facts" and his "faculty of perception."[88]

To his visible audiences, Roosevelt's physical bearing, in spite of his severe handicap, appeared powerfully athletic. Audiences saw a physical giant six feet in height, weighing 180 pounds, deep-chested, with an imposing width of shoulders, large hands and muscular arms. They were usually unaware of the protruding steel braces clamped to the spindly legs which supported his powerful torso. The Roosevelt physiognomy became a favorite subject for cartoonists, whose profile sketches caught the ever-present broad grin, darkly circled eyes, and patrician nose.

Made a prisoner of the rostrum by his infirmity, Roosevelt seldom used hand gestures. In apparent compensation, he employed quick, expressive head movements to emphasize his points. He was a master of facial expression, and, to the close observer, his "lively countenance ran the gamut of expressions."[89]

The Roosevelt voice came to be readily identified by millions of radio listeners through its tenor pitch and pleasingly clear quality. Enriched by his cultivated up-state New York dialect, his impeccable articulation and pronunciation, in the opinion of speech experts, approached the standard for Eastern speech. His keen sense of rhythm, deliberation, and pause, revealed strikingly in such phrases as the much-relished trilogy, "Martin, Barton and Fish," was noteworthy. Roosevelt's vocal flexibility, responsive to widely differing emotions—the sarcasm of his Fala story,[90] the bitterness of his epithet, "economic royalists," the satire of the "nice old gentleman wearing a silk hat,"[91] the comradeliness of his greeting, "my friends," the high purposefulness of his charge to his generation to meet "a rendezvous with destiny"[92]—gave his ideas a maximum of power. Thus, through his own strong responsiveness to his ideas as he spoke them, through his vocal excellence and his exquisite sense of timing, and through his conversational intimacy with his listeners, Roosevelt achieved at the pinnacle of his speaking career a fullness of communication not attained by any other contemporary radio speaker.

Conclusion

The keys to Roosevelt's persuasive power seem, then, to have been three: (1) *The peculiar fitness of the principles he espoused to the time of his leadership.* Social justice appealed strongly to a people shaken by depression and to a world tormented by Nazi tyranny. Neighborliness smoothed hemispheric relations. Vigorous, personal government gave a vivid sense of movement toward a goal. (2) *The peculiar fitness of Roosevelt's temperament for the application of these principles to the tasks at hand.* His willingness to lead, his love of action, his comradeliness, his personal courage, his laughter, his spiritual bent, his pioneering spirit—these traits were superbly suited to marshalling a nation's force to fight a depression or a war, or to build a peace. (3) *The surpassing excellence of his oral presentation of these principles.* His words had tremendous impact upon his hearers through his physical impressiveness and his conversational directness, but especially through the excellence of the words which clothed his ideas with vividness and vigor, and through the flexibility and responsiveness of the voice with which he uttered them.

Truly, the history written by Franklin Delano Roosevelt took form in the lives of his countrymen and of people around the world through the power of his spoken words.

Footnotes

1. Rita Halle Kleeman, *Gracious Lady: The Life of Sara Roosevelt* (New York, 1955), p. 154.
2. Sara Delano Roosevelt, *My Boy Franklin* (New York, 1933), p. 35.
3. Emil Ludwig, *Roosevelt, A Study in Fortune and Power* (New York, 1938), p. 338.
4. Frank D. Ashburn, *Peabody of Groton: A Portrait* (New York, 1944), p. 341.
5. *F. D. R., His Personal Letters, Early Years,* ed. Elliott Roosevelt (New York, 1947), *passim.*
6. In later years Franklin named the elder Roosevelt as one of the five "versatile" men in history who had "always attracted" him most. The other four were Thomas Jefferson; Benjamin Franklin; Napoleon Bonaparte (as a social and legal reformer); and Benjamin Thompson, better known as Count Rumford, a Tory genius of Revolutionary days.—Ernest K. Lindley, *Franklin D. Roosevelt: A Career in Progressive Democracy* (Indianapolis, 1931), p. 337.
7. *F. D. R., His Personal Letters, Early Years,* p. 247.
8. Mrs. Franklin Roosevelt observed that her husband was a "student of the Bible," and believed it to be the "main literary influence" in his life.—Personal interview with Mrs. Roosevelt, Hyde Park, N. Y., August 17, 1947.
9. Roosevelt, at the top of his form at Groton, was permitted to "anticipate" fifteen hours during the sixth form, thus enabling him to complete his undergraduate work in Harvard College in three years and to spend the fourth in graduate study.—*F. D. R., His Personal Letters, Early Years,* pp. 324, 333.
10. For a description of Harvard at the turn of the century, see Rollo W. Brown's *Harvard Yard in the Golden Age* (New York, 1948).
11. Personal interview with Mrs. Roosevelt, Hyde Park, N. Y., August 17, 1947.
12. *The Forms of Public Address,* ed. George Pierce Baker (New York, 1904), p. xix.
13. Employing the recently developed case method, Roosevelt learned to analyze precedent-setting cases, from which, by analogy, he could build his own arguments. Charles Thaddeus Terry, instructor in contracts and a master logician, taught that cases in law are resolved within certain well-defined logical confines from which the student's mind must not stray. William C. Dennis taught how to evaluate evidence, to test the competency of witnesses, to use the art of cross-examination, and to fix the burden of proof. Harlan Fiske Stone, master of the art of analysis, described the method of discovering the pertinent issues in a mass of detailed evidence.—Personal interview with James P. Gifford, associate dean of the Columbia Law School, New York City, June 7, 1950.
14. Eleanor Roosevelt, *This is My Story* (New York, 1937), p. 166.
15. *News-Press* (Poughkeepsie), November 9, 1910.
16. Typical of listener reaction was this editorial comment: "The speech of Franklin Roosevelt naming Governor Smith was a noble utterance. It will rank as the

high point of the present convention, and it belongs with the small list of really great convention speeches."—*New York Herald Tribune*, June 27, 1924.

17. Frances Perkins, *The Roosevelt I Knew* (New York, 1946), p. 33.

18. See Howe's "As His Closest Friend Sees Roosevelt," *New York Times Magazine*, November 27, 1932; Eleanor Roosevelt's "This I Remember," *McCall's*, LXXVI (June, 1949), 122-124.

19. Estimates are between 550 and 600, an average of one for each working day.— Lindley, pp. 31-32.

20. *Ibid.*, p. 308.

21. The "Forgotten Man" speech, April 7, 1932. This address and the ones referred to in the pages that follow, unless otherwise noted, appear in one of the thirteen volumes of *The Public Papers and Addresses of Franklin D. Roosevelt*, ed. Samuel I. Rosenman (New York, 1938, 1941, 1950).

22. Roosevelt explained thus in his General Introduction, written January 14, 1938, to *The Public Papers*, I, ix, xiii.

23. Address at Marietta, Ohio, July 8, 1938.

24. Franklin D. Roosevelt, *Looking Forward* (New York, 1953), p. 250.

25. Fireside chat, May 27, 1941.

26. Address to Congress, January 6, 1941.

27. Address, May 30, 1934.

28. Address at Chicago, December 9, 1935.

29. "Give me your help, not to win votes alone, but to win in this crusade to restore America to its own people."—Acceptance of nomination for the presidency, July 2, 1932.

30. Roosevelt accepted his first nomination on July 2, 1932, with a "call to arms," and accepted his second on June 27, 1936, with the declaration that this was "a war for the survival of democracy. We are fighting to save a great and precious form of government for ourselves and for the world."

31. Campaign address at Chicago, October 28, 1944; also radio address, January 6, 1945.

32. *Government—Not Politics* (New York, 1932), p. 25.

33. Some 7,000 per day wrote, their letters implying "a simple, straightforward belief in him as the man to set things right."—Morris Markey, "F. D. R.'s Mail," *McCall's*, LXI (May, 1934), 4, 48.

34. Speech at Vassar College, August 26, 1933.

35. Commonwealth Club Address, San Francisco, September 23, 1932.

36. John Gunther, *Roosevelt in Retrospect* (New York, 1950), pp. 135-136.

37. "He was a Political Genius," *New Republic*, CXIV (April 15, 1946), 537.

38. Acceptance of nomination address, July 2, 1932.

39. Acceptance of nomination for third term address, July 19, 1940.

40. Address before the National Conference of Catholic Charities, October 4, 1933.

41. Address at the dedication of the Great Smoky Mountains National Park, September 2, 1940.

42. Fireside chat on national defense, May 26, 1940.

43. Address at Oklahoma City, July 9, 1938.

44. Address at Pittsburgh, October 19, 1932.

45. John Gunther reasoned: "If Roosevelt had been more candid, if he had explored opinion more subtly and taken Congress into his confidence, the result might have been different. But people could not get over the feeling that the

proposal had been cooked up in an underhanded way."—*Roosevelt in Retrospect,* p. 296.

46. *Working With Roosevelt* (New York, 1952), pp. 154-160.

47. Seventy per cent of those questioned in April, 1937, held the first view; 95 per cent in November, 1936, the second; 62 per cent in January, 1937, the third.— George Gallup and Claude Robinson, "American Institute of Public Opinion Surveys, 1935-38," *Public Opinion Quarterly,* II (July, 1938), 388.

48. For example, Charles A. Beard believed that Roosevelt deliberately deceived and led the United States into World War II by making secret commitments to Great Britain and by misrepresenting to Congress and the people the actions of Japan and Germany.—*President Roosevelt and the Coming of the War: 1941* (New Haven, 1948), pp. 582-583. Winston Churchill, however, told the House of Commons that "in Franklin Roosevelt there died the greatest American friend we [the British] have ever known and the greatest champion of freedom who has ever brought help and comfort from the New World to the Old."— "A Bitter Loss to Humanity," *Vital Speeches,* XI (May 1, 1945), 422.

49. Address at Manchester, Georgia, October 2, 1928, *New York Times,* October 3, 1928.

50. Address before the Woodrow Wilson Foundation, December 28, 1933.

51. Address to the governing board of the Pan-American Union, April 12, 1933.

52. Basil Rauch, *The History of the New Deal, 1933-1938* (New York, 1944), p. 141.

53. Deposited at the Franklin D. Roosevelt Library in Hyde Park, New York, is a White House file (O.F.F. 87) containing hundreds of letters, written between 1933 and 1940, from United States' citizens traveling in Latin America who commented on the increased friendliness for the United States because of Roosevelt's good neighbor policy. Clippings from newspapers of those countries were frequently enclosed.

54. At the same time, isolationists stated on their own authority or quoted Hitler to show that the Nazis had no intentions or were incapable of attacking the Western Hemisphere. Obviously, Roosevelt was but one of many influences upon public opinion. Of some significance as a measure of his effectiveness, however, is the fact that almost three-fourths of those questioned in late summer, 1941, were convinced that Hitler would not be satisfied until he had "tried to conquer everything including the Americas."—"The Fortune Survey," *Fortune,* XXIV (August, 1941), 77.

55. Franklin D. Roosevelt, *Whither Bound?* (Boston, 1926), p. 32.

56. See, for example: "The Governor and the League," *New York Times,* February 4, 1932, and "Tumulty Criticizes Roosevelt, Baker," *Ibid.,* February 5, 1932.

57. See his appeal in May, 1933, to the heads of fifty-four governments "for peace by disarmament and for the end of economic chaos" (*The Public Papers,* II, 185); and his declaration in June, 1937, of readiness "at all times to cooperate with all nations and peoples."—*Ibid.,* p. 284.

58. Samuel I. Rosenman judged that Roosevelt had made the mistake of "trying to lead the people of the United States too quickly, and before they had been adequately informed of the facts or spiritually prepared for the event." Rosenman quoted Roosevelt: " 'It's a terrible thing,' he once said to me, having in mind, I am sure, this occasion, 'to look over your shoulder when you are trying to lead— and to find no one there.' "—*Working With Roosevelt,* p. 167.

59. Approximate dates: neutrality, September, 1939, to June, 1940; non-belligerency, June, 1940, to June, 1941; active-defense, June, 1941, to December 7, 1941.

60. Edwin Borchard and William Potter Lage, *Neutrality for the United States* (New Haven, 1940), p. vi; Charles G. Fenwick, *International Law* (New York, 1948), pp. 611-659.

61. Ralph Volney Harlow, *The Growth of the United States* (New York, 1943), II, 586-588; Ray Allen Billington, Bert James Loewenberg, and Samuel Hugh Brockunier, *The United States: American Democracy in World Perspective* (New York, 1947), pp. 713-715.

62. Gallup polls show that affirmative sentiment before Roosevelt's speech of September 21, 1939, on lifting the embargo was 57 per cent of those having opinions, and became 62 per cent afterward.—George Gallup, "The Gallup Poll," *Washington Post*, October 4, 1939. After the President sent a message to be read in Congress on October 9, 1941, urging the arming of merchant ships, Gallup Polls showed an immediate affirmative shift of opinion of 8 per cent and for the first time a majority of Americans believed that the measure was desirable. When he reiterated his belief on October 27, 1941, an additional 7 per cent immediately shifted to an affirmative opinion.—"Gallup and Fortune Polls," *Public Opinion Quarterly*, VI (Spring, 1942), 162.

63. ". . . we are agreed that if force is necessary to keep international peace, international force will be applied—for as long as it may be necessary."—Report to the American people on the Teheran Conference, December 24, 1943; "The American people now know that all Nations of the world—large and small—will have to play their appropriate part in keeping the peace by force, and in deciding peacefully the disputes which might lead to war."—Acceptance of fourth term nomination, July 20, 1944.

64. See two excerpts from the State of the Union Address, January 7, 1943: "After the first World War we tried to achieve a formula for permanent peace, based on a magnificent idealism. We failed. But, by our failure, we have learned that we cannot maintain peace at this stage of human development by good intentions alone" and "There are cynics, there are skeptics who say it cannot be done. The American people and all the freedom-loving peoples of this earth are now demanding that it must be done. And the will of these people shall prevail."

65. "No plan is perfect. Whatever is adopted at San Francisco will doubtless have to be amended time and again over the years, just as our own Constitution has been.

"No one can say exactly how long any plan will last. Peace can endure only so long as humanity really insists upon it, and is willing to work for—and sacrifice for it. . . . We cannot fail . . . and expect the world . . . to survive."—Report to Congress on the Crimean Conference, March 1, 1945.

66. *The Public Papers*, V, 391.

67. *Working With Roosevelt*, p. 11. See also Robert Sherwood, *Roosevelt and Hopkins* (New York, 1948), pp. 213 ff. Others who assisted with speech preparation over the years were Harry Hopkins, Stanley High, Benjamin Cohen, Thomas Corcoran, and Adolph Berle, Jr.

68. A. Craig Baird, *Representative American Speeches, 1946-1947*, *The Reference Shelf* (New York, 1947), p. 9.

69. Fireside chat on the war in Europe, September 3, 1939.

70. Fireside chat on national security, December 29, 1940.
71. The third inaugural address, January 20, 1941.
72. *Ibid.*
73. The second inaugural address, January 20, 1937.
74. Campaign address at Detroit, October 2, 1932.
75. Annual message to Congress, January 6, 1941.
76. *Ibid.*
77. Campaign address at Madison Square Garden, October 28, 1940.
78. Fireside chat on national security, December 29, 1940.
79. Address on the state of the Union, January 7, 1943.
80. Final radio speech of 1940 presidential campaign, November 4, 1940.
81. *Ibid.*
82. Fireside chat on national security, December 29, 1940.
83. Campaign address at Columbus, Ohio, August 20, 1932.
84. Fireside chat on national security, December 29, 1940.
85. Radio address announcing the proclamation of an unlimited national emergency, May 27, 1941.
86. "Franklin Roosevelt," observed Charles Michelson, "is a better phrase maker than anybody he ever had around him."—*The Ghost Talks* (New York, 1944), p. 13.
87. Claude G. Bowers, *New York Journal*, November 9, 1932.
88. Edward J. Flynn, *You're the Boss* (New York, 1947), pp. 212-213.
89. K. Monohan, *Pittsburgh Press*, October 20, 1932.
90. Teamsters' Union address, September 23, 1944.
91. Campaign address, Syracuse, New York, September 29, 1936.
92. Acceptance of renomination address, Philadelphia, June 27, 1936.

Thomas E. Dewey: The Great Oregon Debate of 1948

THOMAS E. DEWEY (*March 24, 1902–   *). *Born in Owosso, Michigan, son of George Martin Dewey and Annie Thomas Dewey; educated in the public schools of Owosso; A.B. University of Michigan, 1923; LL.B. Columbia University, 1925; became associated with Larkin, Rathbone, and Perry, 1925; admitted to New York bar, 1926; in 1927 became associated with McNamara and Seymour; 1931 to 1933, served as chief assistant to the United States attorney for the Southern District of New York; 1933, United States attorney; 1934 and 1935, while in private practice, he served as unpaid counsel to the Association of the Bar of New York in removal proceedings against Municipal Justice Harold L. Kernstler; appointed special prosecutor to conduct an investigation of organized crime in New York City in 1935 and served until elected district attorney of New York County in 1937; Republican party nominated him for governor, 1938; in 1942 he was again nominated and was elected; re-elected in 1946 and 1950; Republican party nominated him for president of the United States in 1944 and 1948; defeated by the incumbents, Franklin D. Roosevelt and Harry S. Truman respectively; sixteen institutions of higher learning have conferred honorary degrees upon him; upon completion of his third term as governor of New York, in 1955, became a member of the firm of Dewey, Ballantine, Bushby, Palmer, and Wood in New York City.*

Thomas E. Dewey: The Great Oregon Debate of 1948

ROBERT F. RAY*

EVERY four years American democracy sets into motion great electoral machinery to select national leadership. From the time of the New England town meeting, public address and debate have played a part in choosing candidates.

Prior to the June meeting of the Republican national convention in 1948, New Hampshire, Wisconsin, Nebraska, Ohio, and Oregon conducted presidential preference primary elections. No candidate could be assured of nomination even if he won all the presidential primaries, but it was clearly to his advantage to do well in these contests.

The final Republican primary in Oregon was climaxed on May 17, 1948, by a debate between Governor Thomas E. Dewey of New York and former Governor Harold E. Stassen of Minnesota. The question for debate was "Should the Communist party in the United States be outlawed?" Stassen took the affirmative position and Dewey the negative. This study seeks to determine the effectiveness of Governor Dewey as a speaker in this debate.

THE CANDIDATES, THE AUDIENCE, AND THE ISSUE

As 1947 came to a close and 1948 began, the American people were becoming concerned about Communism and were beginning to demonstrate an interest in the forthcoming presidential election. Stassen opened headquarters in New York City and supporters of General Dwight D. Eisenhower, soon to become president of

* Robert F. Ray (B.A. Coe College, 1944, M.A. 1945, Ph.D. 1947, State University of Iowa) is professor and dean of the Division of Special Services at the State University of Iowa.

Columbia University, announced they would enter his name in the New Hampshire presidential primary election to be held March 3. By mid-January Dewey had announced he was "too busy" with the New York legislative session actively to seek the Republican nomination, but would accept if nominated. On January 23, Eisenhower declared himself out of the race. Three days later Stassen announced he would enter the Ohio primary against Senator Robert A. Taft— the election to be held on May 4.

Meanwhile national concern about the dangers of Communism found expression as the Loyalty Review Board, with an eleven million dollar appropriation, embarked upon the business of screening two million government employees to determine if there existed any "reasonable basis for questioning the employee's loyalty."[1] In February the House Subcommittee on Legislation of the Committee on Un-American Activities began hearings on legislation designed to control Communist activities in the United States. Concern about control of domestic Communism was matched by anxiety about the growing influence of the Soviets abroad. As devices to meet the threat, Congress was studying the Marshall Plan, measures to re-establish the draft and universal military training proposals.

General Douglas MacArthur joined the slate of Republican presidential hopefuls by announcing on March 8, "While . . . I do not covet any office . . . I would be recreant in my duty were I to shrink [from the nomination]."[2]

On March 9 the people of New Hampshire pledged six convention delegates to Dewey and two to Stassen.

On March 14, James Reston of the *New York Times* posed the key question of foreign policy which disturbed the nation: "Now, finally, we are talking about a system of alliances, but are they going to be the old-fashioned if-you-march-across-the-frontier-we'll-fight commitment, or are we going to deal with the real aggression, the real fear, which is Communist fifth column aggression by infiltration?"[3] This "real fear" was further aggravated the same week as Czechoslovakia fell in a Communist *coup d'état* and Jan Masaryk was reported by the new government as a "suicide."

Poland, Yugoslavia, Bulgaria, and Rumania had already fallen and there was growing anxiety about the forthcoming Italian elections. On March 31 Congress passed the six billion dollar European Recovery Plan with hope that the plan devised by Secretary of State Marshall would mark a turning of the tide in the international battle against Communist aggrandizement. The next day Russia jolted the free world with its answer—the first blockade of Berlin.

In this atmosphere of extreme tension Dewey left Albany for a forty-eight hour campaign in Wisconsin against Stassen, a former governor of a neighboring state, and a favorite son, MacArthur.

THE ISSUE FIRST JOINED

In the Wisconsin primary the issue of outlawing the Communist party was first directly joined by the governors. At Milwaukee on April 1 Dewey said he liked to keep the Communists "out in the open where we can beat them." In the same city the following day Stassen declared: "I think the Communist party organization has been clearly shown to be a subversive arm of the foreign policy of the Soviet Union and as such I think it should be outlawed in the United States and all freedom loving countries. . . . We should not permit a treasonable form of organization to murder world freedom."[4] He said further that an Act of Congress should outlaw all organizations, regardless of name, that operate as subversive arms of a foreign power; and he repeated these assertions that day at Racine and Milwaukee.[4] On election eve, Senator Joseph McCarthy, head of the Stassen slate of Wisconsin delegates, announced: "I don't think the presidential hopes of any of the candidates could survive running a bad third." Stassen won nineteen of the twenty-seven delegates—the remainder were pledged to General MacArthur.

Having returned to Albany from Wisconsin, Dewey left again on April 7 for Nebraska where he made ten appearances in two days. The Nebraska primary election, held April 13, was a seven man contest. The results gave Stassen 80,000 votes, Dewey 64,000, Taft 21,000, Vandenberg 9,000, MacArthur 7,000, Warren 2,000, and Martin 900. Dewey had been the victor in the Wisconsin primary elections of 1940 and 1944 and had carried the Nebraska contest in 1940. The Stassen victories were unquestionably important in strengthening his drive for convention delegates. The Dewey showing in Nebraska was generally regarded as respectable; Taft forces were thought to have received a severe set-back.

Meanwhile, the international scene provided cause for ever-increasing anxiety. On April 9 rioting began in Bogota, Colombia, the city which two weeks later was to be the site of a conference of twenty-two Inter-American nations. Unrest was reported in Costa Rica; civil war was raging in Greece; revolt in Ecuador was reported at hand; skirmishes were taking place in Hunan Province in China; tempers were flaring between Communists and anti-Communists in Korea. At these tension points around the globe the disturbances were attributed to Communist infiltration. On April 22 the conference of twenty-two inter-American countries adopted unanimously a resolution calling for urgent measures to keep "agents of international Communism" from tampering with the "true will" of the people of the Western Hemisphere.[5]

As April came to a close the American audience shifted its attention to Ohio as the focal point in the domestic political scene. Ordinarily candidates had avoided seeking delegates in the home states of their opponents, but Stassen had determined to do battle with Taft in the Senator's own bailiwick. Fifty-three delegates were at stake. Stassen, contesting for twenty-three, declared he was confident of winning twelve; Taft announced he would be unhappy to lose more than six.

In a speech at Akron, April 23, Stassen again proposed that the Communist party be outlawed. At a press conference before the speech the Minnesotan had said: "The peace loving nations of the world should first outlaw the Communist parties within their borders. . . . This would involve removal of the Communist party from the ballot both in the United States and abroad."[6]

The May 4 Ohio election gave Stassen only nine delegates of the twenty-three he sought. Taft had lost more than six. The results were generally regarded as a stand-off in which neither candidate could claim the kind of victory he anticipated.

THE OREGON CAMPAIGN

The last day of April, Dewey departed from Albany for Portland, Oregon, and Stassen announced he would be in the state May 17 to 20. Stassen was the five-to-three choice of professional gamblers.[7] An informal poll conducted by a Portland newspaper showed Stassen 70 per cent, Dewey 30 per cent. Senator Taft was not entered in the Oregon contest, but it was now clear the Republican convention would probably select one of the three, Stassen, Dewey, or Taft; a deadlock would have to occur if any other aspirant were to receive the nomination.

From the outset of the Oregon contest it was apparent that the major issue was to be whether or not the Communist party should be outlawed (even though both Dewey and Stassen proposed programs concerning irrigation, forestry regulation, public power, and foreign policy).

Appearing before the Oregon State Junior Chamber of Commerce convention in Portland, May 1, Dewey described the suggestion to outlaw the Communist party as hysterical. He declared the question to be a "major issue of our time"—one that "goes to the very root of the qualifications of men to hold high public office." He argued that outlawing the Communist party would drive it underground. He drew attention to his New York record in combatting crime and the underworld in "11 years as a public prosecutor and 6 years as governor." He said the Communists had fought him "every time [he] ran for office" and declared: "We have diminished their influence, discredited them, exposed them and defeated them because at all times we kept a spotlight on them."[8]

On May 3 he devoted an entire radio speech from Portland to the subject, "Communism and How to Deal With It." He said:

> I want the people of Oregon and of the United States to know exactly where I stand on this proposal because it goes to the very heart of the qualification of any candidate for office and to the inner nature of the kind of country we want to live in. I am unalterably, whole-heartedly and unswervingly against any scheme to write laws outlawing people because of their religious, political, social or economic ideas. I am against it, because it is a violation of the Constitution of the United States and of the Bill of Rights. I am against it because it is immoral and nothing but totalitarianism itself. I am against it because I know from many years experience in enforcement of the law that the proposal would not work and instead would advance the cause of Communism rapidly both in this country and all over the world.[9]

The next morning found Dewey ready to travel the vote-seeking trail. A bus carrying him, two assistants, including the writer, and representatives from the press wire services and major New York and Oregon newspapers left Portland at 6:30 A.M. By the end of the week the party had stopped in more than forty places. The Communist issue was discussed in every speech: at breakfasts, luncheons and dinners, from town squares, courthouse steps, schools and colleges. The campaign was waged with great vigor. Probably more Oregonians were personally to see Dewey and hear him speak than were to see and hear their own candidates for governor or even sheriff. In one week he faced small audiences aggregating more than 25,000 persons, and delivered three formal addresses to audiences of 3,000 at Corvallis, 4,000 at Eugene, and at least a thousand at Medford. Some of the smaller audiences had stood in Oregon showers for more than an hour awaiting his appearance.

The Governor was, indeed, campaigning in earnest. With his own blood, drawn by a physician, he signed a permit to enter the city of Coos Bay as demanded by the Coos Bay Pirates, a chamber of commerce publicity group. He posed with the Grant's Pass cavemen supposedly eating raw meat from a large red bone. He was made an honorary Indian chief, complete with feathered bonnet.

By the time he and his staff arrived at Bend, Oregon, at the end of the first week's itinerary, the strain of so many speeches and public appearances became apparent. Dewey had a severe case of laryngitis. A Bend physician ordered him to rest his voice, so he wrote everything he wished to say, or spoke only in a whisper, for forty-eight hours. By May 11 he had not yet recovered the full use of his voice, and he told an Ontario, Oregon, audience he would become "Whispering Tom" if the condition did not improve rapidly. From Ontario he had to work his way through another vigorous week of campaigning to Portland via Baker, Pendleton, The Dalles, and Hood River, with about the same number of intermediate appearances. By mid-week the voice problem had disappeared.

The Agreement to Debate

While Dewey was campaigning in Oregon, Stassen was busy seeking convention votes on the other side of the continent. May 7 he appeared on a Mutual Broadcasting network radio program, "Meet the Press." One of the reporters asked him if he had heard a rumor that Dewey had challenged him to debate. Dewey had issued no such challenge. Stassen replied: "Of course I want to debate with Governor Dewey in Oregon. I am making arrangements to fly to Oregon to do so." Dewey released a press statement May 8 from Bend saying he had "issued no challenge to anybody for a debate" and charged Stassen with seeking an excuse to return to Oregon prior to May 17. The statement was released by James Hagerty.[10]

Peter H. Odegard, president of Reed College, sent identical telegrams May 10 to Dewey and Stassen. The telegram to Dewey at Bend said: "The people of Oregon, cognizant of the heavy responsibility placed on them, are eager to hear you and Mr. Stassen discuss election issues. Reed College would be honored to sponsor public meeting this purpose at Portland Auditorium at time agreeable to both candidates. Identical invitation being extended Mr. Stassen." The telegram did not specifically propose a debate; it proposed a "discussion," but specified no topics beyond "election issues." Stassen replied immediately, accepting the invitation. Whatever interpretation one might place on the meaning of the Odegard telegram, it was clear Stassen had agreed to be present on the same platform with Dewey. The press representatives clamored for Dewey's reply. Issued the same day, it was as follows:

> I usually disapprove of personal debates between Republicans, because they tend to weaken and divide our party. However, I consider the proposal to outlaw the Communist party as so dangerous to our freedom and the security of this country that I think a full discussion of it under the auspices of the Multnomah County Republican Committee, using every modern facility of communication, is essential, so that every citizen of the United States may know just what is at stake. The whole future of our free institutions is involved. Accordingly, I have authorized Mr. John C. Higgins to arrange with Mr. Stassen or his representatives a full hour of debate on the radio, on the subject, "Shall the Communist Party be Outlawed?"

Governor Dewey thus rejected the Odegard invitation while responding to the challenge inherent in it. Neither candidate had directly challenged the other, unless one assumes Stassen's acceptance of the Odegard proposal constituted such a challenge. The Dewey reply, however, forced Stassen to accept a whole new set of conditions for the meeting: a debate about a single issue. Stassen was to learn of additional conditions when his representative, Robert Elliott, met Higgins.

On May 11, Elliott proposed a public meeting be held at the Ice Arena in Portland on the day Stassen was to return (apparently May 15 on the revised Stassen schedule). Dewey decided to make no comment on this proposal or on any other aspect of the debate until Higgins could meet with Elliott. Stassen arrived at Portland on May 12, five days earlier than he had originally planned. At the Higgins-Elliott meeting next day, according to the Higgins report, it was obvious that Stassen wanted a free-for-all discussion of issues before a large audience. Higgins argued the Communist party issue was of such grave importance that it alone should be debated and that the debate should be conducted in a radio studio, in an atmosphere free of audience interruption. He insisted upon the following additional conditions: (1) each speaker was to be in his studio; (2) no pictures were to be taken during the debate; (3) opening speeches were to be twenty minutes in length, Stassen speaking first; (4) rebuttal speeches were to be eight and a half minutes in length, Stassen opening; (5) the moderator was to be the chairman of the Multnomah County Republican Committee, Donald R. Von Boskirk.

Stassen later held a press conference in which he held out for a public meeting as the debate setting. He declared "the people should have a chance to participate, to see, hear, and participate. There will be applause, there may be some heckling, but that's the American way."[11] Higgins accused Stassen of a "campaign trick designed to cover Mr. Stassen's contemplated refusal to debate jointly with Governor Dewey before the people of the country the issue raised by his proposal to outlaw the Communist party." He said he expected Stassen to debate Dewey the following Monday, May 17 on the radio.[12]

At Bonneville Dam May 14, Stassen told the press: "We've now reached the point where we will let Dewey write his own ticket. And we will meet his terms—reluctantly."[13] The debate was now certain to be held, and held on Dewey's terms.

Dewey's Debate Strategy

May 16 was a Sunday—the day before the debate. Neither candidate campaigned. The sitting room of Dewey's suite at the Multnomah Hotel in Portland was the scene of the final strategy meeting before the debate. Assembled there shortly after dinner were Governor Dewey, Elliott V. Bell, and the writer. Bell, a principal policy adviser and chief among the candidate's speech architects, had come especially for the debate. Ordinarily a Dewey speech evolved only after a long process. The Governor usually first discussed the main ideas in conference with staff members, and then a preliminary draft would be prepared by Bell or someone designated by him. Next Bell and then the Governor would edit the draft and possibly offer further suggestions for research or drafting. Several drafts would follow the same process until the speech satisfied the Governor. In the course of preparation, the speech, usually after five or six drafts, ultimately reflected not only what Dewey wanted to say—it also became "his" in the sense that it suited his manner of delivery.

Preparing for the debate required a great deal of deviation from this process. The staff could not know exactly what Stassen would say in his opening speech, but agreed that Dewey should lead off with sharp rebuttal for three to four minutes. In the jargon of debate, since Dewey was to "grab a rope," he and his aides spent about two hours reviewing Stassen's earlier speeches in an effort to determine what were his weakest arguments—the arguments upon which the most devastating attack could be made. The staff was also concerned that Stassen might not follow the same course he had in his prior speeches on the subject. What if, for example, Stassen espoused the Mundt bill as the device to outlaw the party? Since Mundt was clearly on the record to the effect that his bill would not outlaw the party, it did not seem likely Stassen would take such a course. Nonetheless the possibility was carefully reviewed, and quotations from Mundt were on cards ready for use.

A vast amount of research data on Communism had been prepared in Albany under the direction of John Burton, director of the New York State Budget and chief of Dewey's research staff, and Charles D. Breitel, counsel to the Governor. A large volume of material was at hand, including a summary of the congressional hearings on the

Mundt bill, the substance of twenty-seven federal laws concerning conspiracy, subversion, treason, etc., an analysis of the Alien and Sedition Acts, and quotations from historians, lawyers, and other authorities. The substance of much of this material was reduced to cards so that it could be ordered easily by Dewey and arranged prior to use in delivery of his rebuttals. The Dewey advisers engaged in lengthy discussion of the sub-issues and ways of answering possible arguments. They were urged by the candidate to pose questions and to comment on the answers, adding suggestions for use of evidence or additional arguments for strength when and if possible. This "debate before the debate" constituted the immediate preparation for the event.

THE DEBATE

The clock in the studio of radio station KEX, Portland, indicated 5:34 P.M. Pacific Standard Time as Dewey and his advisers entered, twenty-six minutes before the debate was to get under way. At 5:38 Stassen entered the studio. The contestants met in the middle of the room. Stassen said, "Good evening, Tom. We've certainly stirred up a lot of interest." "We surely did," replied Dewey. They shook hands and smiled at one another as the photographers took pictures. Stassen commented, "We've seen a lot of Oregon." "I'll say we have," replied Dewey. The two candidates then shook hands with Von Boskirk, who showed them the material he would use by way of introduction. They posed for further pictures with the county chairman and then each man went to his own table. Dewey's table was to the left of Von Boskirk's, and Stassen's to the right. Each candidate spoke from his own metal speaking stand located between his table and that of the moderator. Each spoke into four microphones which relayed the debate to 870 radio stations across the nation via Mutual, National, and American networks. Cancelled for the evening were the popular Carnation Milk program and General Motors' Fred Waring program.

The studio audience consisted of the Multnomah County Republican Committee and the press. Seated in the studio were twenty-eight members of the committee and twenty-four non-working newsmen. In an adjoining room were sixty-two more newspapermen, separated from the debate studio by a large triple-plate glass window, sitting in three bleacher-like tiers with typewriters on planks before them in the front rows. The working photographers, newsreel and still, were in the rear. At 5:55 a station official announced that there would be no applause during the debate and that no more pictures were to be taken until the debate was over.

About twenty minutes before the debate began, Stassen and Dewey were seated at their tables engaged in discussion with their aides. Seated with Stassen were Senator Joseph McCarthy of Wisconsin; Fred Seaton, his Nebraska campaign manager; and Theodore Gamble, who had been in charge of War Bond sales in World War II. Seated with Dewey were Paul Lockwood, his Oregon campaign manager, Bell, and the writer.

A tape recording made by station KEX, Portland, has been used to establish the authenticity of the text of the debate.[14]

Stassen's First Affirmative Speech

Upon being presented by Von Boskirk, Stassen began to speak in a slow and deliberate manner. In the first two minutes he uttered fewer than two hundred words, and only 450 words by the end of the first four minutes of his presentation. His manner of speaking was precise and heavy. These first four minutes of speaking were consumed with a recital of his war experiences and his wartime resolution to "do everything within my power after V. J. Day to keep America free and avoid a third world war." He next declared himself in favor of control of inflation, preventing depressions, developing natural resources, improving housing, bettering labor-management relations, advancing civil rights, and strengthening military power and the United Nations.

Because Stassen had been reluctant to debate the single issue as he had finally agreed, those at the Dewey table were concerned at this point. Would Stassen debate only incidentally the question of outlawing the Communist party? Relief came with the answer as he began the fifth minute of his twenty minute presentation; from then on he stayed with the question at hand.

First among his contentions was that the Communist party was directed from Moscow. He alluded to a trip he had taken through Europe which had satisfied him the premise was true. He next argued that the objective of the Russian dominated movement was designed to infiltrate other nations and conquer them by subversion. He cited as evidence the recent fall of Czechoslovakia.

The third premise of his presentation was that America was vulnerable to such subversion. He declared that there was no law to prevent secret organizations from promoting strikes and racial and religious dissension on direction from Russia.

His fourth contention was that a law was needed to meet these problems—to outlaw these Communist organizations. Such a law, he argued, should be constitutional, consistent with the Bill of Rights, and make it illegal to carry on any "organization . . . directed by the rulers of a foreign power for the purpose of overthrowing the government of the United States."

Stassen's first four contentions came as no surprise to Dewey. Sunday night the staff had gone over each of them as Stassen had presented them in earlier speeches. He next declared the Mundt bill then before Congress would meet the requirements and would outlaw the Communist party in the United States. Dewey reached for the cards containing the Mundt quotes. Stassen then declared the secretary and chairman of the party had said the bill would outlaw the party.

At this point, he injected an *ad hominem* argument linking by implication Henry Wallace, who had opposed the Mundt bill, and Governor Dewey. He said the Governor's policy in the matter coddled Communism with legality.

Reverting to his first premise, he cited Russia, Poland, Czechoslovakia, Hungary, Yugoslavia, Rumania, Bulgaria, Albania, Estonia, Latvia, and Lithuania where, he contended, the legal overground organization had organized an underground movement. He contended the Communist Bolshevik party was legal in Russia "right up to the first war with Germany." Having so supported his first premise, he apparently sought next to anticipate the Dewey claim that to outlaw the party would be to endanger the rights of the people. He declared the party had been outlawed in Canada for years and "the people lost none of their liberties."

Next he asked Governor Dewey four questions:

> 1. Do you agree that the Communist organizations throughout the world are directed from Moscow?
> 2. Do you agree that the objective of the Communist or-

ganizations throughout the world is to overthrow free governments, destroy liberties, and bring the countries under the domination of the Kremlin?

3. Do you agree that Communist organizations throughout the world are a menace to future peace?

4. Do you agree that because of this menace to world peace it is necessary that we require American young men to serve in our armed forces and to take military training?

In a final appeal to his listeners he argued that the United States should not have to draft young men while allowing "Communist" organizations to flourish under the cloak of constitutional protection. There was, he said, "no such thing as a freedom to destroy freedom."

DEWEY'S FIRST NEGATIVE SPEECH

As Chairman Von Boskirk introduced him, Dewey carried to the rostrum a sheet of yellow note paper on which he had jotted Stassen's questions and the prepared text based largely on his May 3 speech at Portland. Roscoe Drummond of the *Christian Science Monitor* described the manner in which Dewey dismissed the first four minutes of the Stassen speech as "a light left jab."[15] The "jab" was in the form of these words "I have listened with great interest to his [Stassen's] eloquent discussion of the subject and of all the other matters which he brought up." No further mention was to be made of these "other matters" by either candidate.

The Governor's manner of speaking was reminiscent of his courtroom style. He paused to look over his notes between sections of his presentation, then spoke in an even flow of words at about 120 words per minute. He employed volume for emphasis, as opposed to increased rate.

In accordance with the planned strategy, the New York governor at once offered a rebuttal to the Stassen speech. Saying, "He has asked me four questions," he then repeated in paraphrase the first three from his notes answering each one with a single word, "Certainly." Thus, the candidates agreed to the first two of the Stassen premises and to the answers to the first three of Stassen's questions. In response to the fourth question concerning the Communist menace as the cause for drafting American youth into the armed services, Dewey declared it begged the question. He declared he was opposed to outlawing the party lest it flourish underground and give cause to "drafting all the young men in the nation."

Dewey next attacked the Stassen assertion that the Mundt bill would outlaw the Communist party. Employing the same *ad hominem* kind of appeal that Stassen had employed, Dewey now linked Stassen with the head of the Communist party and declared Stassen's only authorities for stating the bill would outlaw the party was the party chairman and Stassen himself. Stassen had been correct in his assertion that William Z. Foster, head of the Communist party, had opposed the Mundt bill on the ground that it would make the party illegal.[16]

Dewey then quoted Mundt's words before the House Subcommittee on Legislation of the Committee on Un-American Activities. On February 5, 1948, Mundt had said: "I have been one of those who have not looked with favor upon proposals to outlaw the Communist party or to declare its activities illegal, because I fear such action on the part of Congress would only tend to drive further underground the forces which are already largely concealed from public view. What I want to do is to drive the Communist functionaries out of the ground into the open, where patriotic Americans of every walk of life can come to learn their identity and understand their objectives."[17]

Having quoted Mundt, Dewey again declared Stassen and Foster to be the only authorities Stassen had presented for the opposite view. Dewey then went on to quote the House subcommittee report to the effect that the bill would not outlaw the party. Thus he followed to the letter his predetermined plan to quote these authorities in opposition should Stassen take the position he did.

The Governor next offered his own definition of outlawing. Insisting that Stassen had repeatedly urged outlawing the party, Dewey said the only way it could be done would be a law to deny Communists the right to be named on ballots, and after the passage of the law to try persons who were Communists and, if proved guilty, to convict them and sentence them to prison. Having given his definition to the term, the speaker moved into his prepared remarks.

His first contention was that outlawing the Communist party would encourage its underground growth and power and would not defeat its purposes. As evidence he cited Russia, where, he said, Trotsky and Lenin had been exiled in 1917. He further offered the example of Italy where Mussolini had outlawed the party for twenty-five years and where the party had polled 30 per cent of the vote one month prior to the debate. He named Germany under Hitler as a nation in which the Communist party was outlawed as it was outlawed in Czechoslovakia for seven years under German domination. At this point he thanked Stassen for bringing up the Czechoslovakian question, and said the country gave further evidence of the futility of making the party illegal.

His second premise was that outlawing the party would mean the employment of a totalitarian method in an effort to defeat totalitarianism. He described it as the method of Hitler and Stalin. In support of his premise he appealed to the patriotism of his hearers, declaring the struggle for world leadership to be between those who would destroy freedom and those who believed in it. He called for a reaffirmation of the nation's fundamental beliefs in freedom of religion, speech, assembly, and the press. To outlaw the party would be to surrender these beliefs, he said. To this argument he added a strong appeal from his own experience. A popular concept of Dewey was that he was the man who had cleaned up the racketeers of New York as a special prosecutor and as District Attorney. It was, indeed, in such a role that he first came to attract great public attention. Against this background he now declared there were twenty-seven federal laws to combat the kind of activity Stassen wanted to combat. He alluded to his eleven years as a prosecutor in New York. He said people then urged him to use "the methods of dictators" to attack the underworld, but these methods were rejected and the task was accomplished in accordance with constitutional means.

He next cited Canada since Stassen had said Canada had outlawed the party without loss of civil rights. Dewey now alluded to the same law and indicated that while it was in effect the Communists "developed the greatest atomic spy ring in history," and that Canada had to repeal the law in 1943.

STASSEN'S REBUTTAL

Neither candidate could, of course, prepare his rebuttal. Both spoke extempore in their final presentations.

At this point in the debate it was clear the two men could not agree on a definition of the term "outlaw." Stassen's case had been based on the assumption that the Communist party was ordered to do whatever it did from Moscow. He obviously believed the Mundt bill would make it illegal for the party in the United States to continue to operate as a puppet force. He opened his rebuttal with a quotation from the Mundt bill: "It shall be unlawful for any person to attempt in any manner to establish in the United States a totalitarian dictatorship, the direction and control of which is to be vested in or exercised by or under the domination or control of any foreign government, foreign organization, or foreign individual, or to perform or attempt to perform any act with the intent to facilitate such end." Because this would apply, in his opinion, to the Communist party, it would therefore make the party illegal—it would "outlaw" the party.

Stassen then argued that if Dewey would support the Mundt bill, he would be satisfied they had reached agreement on the question of outlawing the party.

Stassen then attacked Dewey's premises. If adequate laws were on the statute books, he asked, why had the Communist organization been growing so strong in New York? With 9 per cent of the national population, he charged 40 per cent of the Communists were in New York. He further cited as evidence for the need for new legislation the fact that only one Communist had been convicted in the prior eight years—and the conviction was for libel. He asked if the Governor had called upon the federal government to enforce the federal laws in New York. He said that ten years before in Minnesota he had worked as Governor in close cooperation with the federal government and weeded out Communists who had infiltrated labor movements, but had been handicapped because there was no law such as the Mundt bill proposed.

He argued there would be no way to stop subversion under existing laws until an act of violence had occurred. Appealing to the fears of his listeners he suggested secret Communist organizations, on

orders from Moscow, could conceivably promote strikes and violence and endanger the Panama Canal and Alaska.

In conclusion he repeated his assertion that he would be satisfied
that the party would be outlawed if the Mundt bill were passed and
urged Dewey to agree with him.

DEWEY'S REBUTTAL

During Stassen's rebuttal, Dewey whispered to those seated with
him at his table, "He has surrendered." At the top of the sheet of
notes he had made during the Stassen speech was the single word
"Surrendered," underlined. His notes further contained the following entries:

American Bar Ass'n quotes
N. Y. Socialists—Hughes
Italy—⅓ of people in prison
Red Flag statutes
deJonge v Oregon (1936) 299 U.S. 353
American history—Federalist memo
Lincoln—disloyal press—Burnside
Commies in New York—marches—most irresponsible, disagree-
able, noisy, subversive, lying group of *worms*. Prosper under-
ground. But don't drive underground, leave out in open where
we can lick 'em
7 per cent of earth—Bill of Rights
Wallace, etc.
Don't impair it for party—World praying for leadership—
Commies hoping we'll surrender our freedom

With the above notes before him, Dewey opened his rebuttal
speech with this assertion: "I gather from Mr. Stassen's statement
that he has completely surrendered."

He next turned his attention to the Mundt bill. Clearly this was
now the key issue in the debate. Again he reminded his hearers that
Stassen and the head of the Communist party were the only authorities presented by Stassen to support his claim the bill would outlaw
the party. Again he declared Mundt and the committee report on the
bill had specifically stated the bill would not outlaw the party.

Three more times in his rebuttal he was to say that Stassen had
"surrendered." If all Stassen wanted was the Mundt bill, he said,
"then he admits he didn't mean it when he has been demanding from

one end of this country to the other that the Communist party be outlawed."

Picking up the memorandum prepared by Brietel concerning federal statutes, the candidate next read from the list of activities then illegal. He cited titles and crimes covered by the list of twenty-seven laws before him. He then said these laws were adequate to meet all of the dangers cited by Stassen. He added: "The Mundt bill is perfectly harmless, probably. I have some doubts about its constitutionality. It doesn't outlaw the Communist party. It may have the virtue of helping to keep them out in the open, because its main provisions are that the Communists must register, must register all their members and keep them everlastingly out in the open. That is a very good provision of law. The other parts of it, if they are constitutional, they're swell."

The remainder of Dewey's rebuttal was devoted to an attack on the concept of outlawing the party in terms of his own definition. He cited the Alien and Sedition laws as an example of an effort to "shoot an idea with a law." Next, he cited Lincoln's Civil War action in stopping General Burnside's suppression of the anti-Union press. He quoted Lincoln: "It is better that the people hear what they have to say than fear what they might say if they were suppressed."

In response to Stassen's assertion that New York was the Communist center of the United States, Dewey concluded his rebuttal by agreeing that "we have a lot of Communists in New York . . . and they cause us great troubles. But we lick them." Citing a then recent F.B.I. report on the number of Communists in the United States, he stated the number nationally had declined from "100,000 two years ago to 70,000 last year to 68,000 this year." He said in New York the Communists had "ganged up with the Democrats, the American Labor Party, the 'miscalled' Liberal Party and the P.A.C. [Political Action Committee of the Congress of Industrial Organizations], . . . labeled him as their Public Enemy Number 1 . . . and we licked them by the biggest majority in history." This result was due, he said, "because we kept them out in the open." He concluded by declaring the Communist party, if kept out in the open, would "never get any place in the United States."

The debate ended amidst more picture-taking by the press photographers. The candidates shook hands and returned to their headquarters. Both issued statements claiming victory.

APPRAISAL AND CONCLUSION

Would the Mundt bill have outlawed the Communist party? This became the central issue. Dewey accurately quoted Mundt's statement that it would not do so.[17]

Because neither candidate would accept the other's definition of the term "outlaw" and because of their divergence of views as to the effect of the Mundt bill, the debate was lacking in direct clash on the issue. If the listener felt the Mundt bill "outlawed" the party he would surely have to conclude Stassen "won" the debate. If he felt the bill did not "outlaw" the party he would most certainly believe Dewey the victor.

Confusion on this score was reflected in two Portland, Oregon newspaper editorials the following day.

The *Oregon Journal* called it a debate of "Tweedledum and Tweedledee." The editorialist added in reference to Stassen's espousal of the Mundt bill: "Dewey who has had the best of the legal argument all along, employs a prosecutor's trick to call this 'surrender.' It might with equal accuracy and more forebearance be called 'redefinition.' "

The *Portland Oregonian* declared: "The subject of the debate could have been more clearly stated. We are not sure that both were arguing the same question. If any votes were won by either debater, we fancy they were won by their respective debate conduct, rather than by what they said."[18]

On May 19, 1948, the House of Representatives by a vote of 319 to 58 passed the Mundt bill. Sponsors of the bill declared it would outlaw only the party's subversive activities, while Representative Vito Marcantonio of the American Labor Party declared it would "wipe out" the party itself.[19] In the Senate the bill was sent to the Committee on Judiciary. It was not reported out of that committee during the rest of the session of the Eightieth Congress.

Who was the more effective debater in terms of speaking and technique? Dewey employed proofs of a personal nature not available to Stassen in describing his work against the underworld as a prosecutor and District Attorney. He refused to accept Stassen's premise concerning the Mundt bill and offered authority more likely to be accepted by his audience than that offered by Stassen. He adamantly refused to agree that outlawing the party could mean less than forbidding it the use of the ballot, and Stassen was on the public record in demands that the right of the ballot be denied the Communist party. Stassen offered no rebuttal to the argument that flowed from Dewey's definition. At least 25 per cent of Dewey's speaking time was thus devoted to subject matter not refuted by Stassen, and a fifth of Stassen's opening speech was not germane to the topic for debate. For these reasons Dewey must be adjudged the more effective of the two debaters.

On election day the voters of Oregon cast 111,657 votes for Dewey and 102,419 votes for Stassen.[20] In the June national convention of the Republican party, Dewey was nominated on the third ballot. Whether or not he may be said to have won the debate on outlawing the Communist party, there can be little doubt the Oregon victory (in the face of great odds at the outset of the Oregon campaign) greatly enhanced his prestige and did serious damage to Stassen's bid for the nomination.

The question for the debate was not a key issue in the 1948 presidential campaign, but the nation was to hear much of it in the next decade. Perhaps, indeed, the Dewey-Stassen meeting was most significant as the prelude to the then forthcoming necessity of reaching important national decisions on the enormous issues beneath the rhetorical surface of the debate.

Footnotes

1. Jay Walz, *New York Times*, January 4, 1948, p. E7.
2. *New York Times*, March 14, 1948, p. E2.
3. James Reston, *New York Times*, March 14, 1948, p. E3.
4. Clayton Knowles, *New York Times*, April 3, 1948, p. 13.
5. *New York Times*, April 23, 1948, p. 1.
6. Warren Moscow, *New York Times*, April 24, 1948, p. 1.
7. Richard L. Neuberger, *New York Times*, May 2, 1948, pp. E7 and 65.
8. Thomas E. Dewey, *Public Papers of Governor Thomas E. Dewey* (Albany, 1948), pp. 602-605.
9. *Ibid.*, p. 606.
10. Hagerty had been unable to participate in the first week of campaigning in Oregon because of a throat infection.

11. *New York Times,* May 12, 1948, p. 24.
12. *Ibid.,* May 14, 1948, p. 19.
13. Knowles, May 15, 1948, p. 1.
14. Dewey-Stassen debate, State University of Iowa Record Library, Iowa City. *Cf.* also Dewey, pp. 620-632.
15. Roscoe Drummond, "State of the Nation," *Christian Science Monitor,* May 18, 1948.
16. Alexander Feinberg, *New York Times,* April 30, 1948, p. 1.
17. *Hearings,* Committee on Judiciary, U.S. Senate, 80th Cong. 2nd Sess. (H.R. 5852), 489-498. In this same testimony Mundt also declared:

> My bill as amended, provides that the Communist party and all organizations controlled by it or originating from it must register as agents of a foreign principal. It provides, secondly, that all printed matter distributed by such organizations or any members thereof shall be clearly labeled in bold face type as being published in compliance with the laws of the United States governing the activities of agents of foreign principals.
>
> In the third place, my bill provides that such publications shall be conspicuously marked to show that the persons transmitting such propaganda through the mails or through other interstate channels are agents of a foreign principal and that the name and address of both the agent and the foreign principal be included on the propaganda. In the fourth place, my bill provides that violation of the terms of this act is punishable by a fine of not less than $1,000 and a prison sentence of not less than 12 months in one of the federal penitentiaries. . . . It does not deny to Communists or crypto-Communists the right to participate in a political campaign or to have their candidate listed on a political ballot.

18. *New York Times,* May 19, 1948, p. 23.
19. John D. Morris, *New York Times,* May 20, 1948, p. 1.
20. *Time,* LI (May 31, 1948), 23.

SOCIAL AND POLITICAL ISSUES

Eugene Victor Debs
Spokesman for Socialism

EUGENE VICTOR DEBS (*November 5, 1855–October 12, 1926*). *Born of a French emigrant father who taught him the philosophy of Eugene Sue and Victor Hugo; self-educated after the eighth grade in school; influenced by Robert G. Ingersoll in both writing and speaking; became nationally prominent as an organizer of railroad unions; imprisoned for contempt of court during the Pullman strike of 1894; became convinced that the interests of labor could only be served by socialism and thereafter spoke and wrote ceaselessly for this cause; nominated in 1900, 1904, and 1908 as the Socialist candidate for the presidency; convicted, because of a speech delivered in Canton, Ohio, in 1918, of violating the Espionage Act and obstructing the war effort; nominated for the presidency by the Socialist party in 1920 while still in the Federal Penitentiary in Atlanta; polled 900,000 votes in the election; released from prison in 1921; attempted to resume strenuous speaking and writing program but hampered by broken health; died October 12, 1926.*

Eugene Victor Debs
Spokesman for Socialism

THE historian John Clark Ridpath declared in 1907 that Eugene Victor Debs was "one of the most masterful orators ever reared on American soil" and that "he had already a secure place in American history."[1] Later historians may disagree, passing him by with scant mention as a champion of lost causes and a dangerous radical in times of national peril. Most would accept him, however, as the first spokesman of national stature to expound the principles of American socialism.

Eugene Debs first learned of socialism from his father, who had been educated in France at a time when the influence of Eugene Sue and Victor Hugo was strong. The father not only named his son after these writers, but he taught him their social philosophies. This instruction was fortunate, for the boy was to abandon formal schooling after the eighth grade and depend thereafter on his own individual efforts. Remembering these early struggles, Debs wrote:

> In my own case the power of expression is not due to education or to training. I had no time for either and have often felt the lack of both. The schools I attended were primitive and when I left them at fourteen to go to work I could hardly write a grammatical sentence; and to be frank I am not quite sure that I can do so now. But I had a retentive memory and was fond of committing and declaiming such orations and poems as appealed to me. Patrick Henry's revolutionary speech had first place. Robert Emmet's immortal oration was a great favorite and moved me deeply. Drake's "American Flag" stirred my

* Herold Truslow Ross (B.A. DePauw University 1918, M.A. Columbia University 1924, Ph.D. State University of Iowa 1932) is head of the Department of Speech, DePauw University.

273

blood as did also Schiller's "Burgschaft." Often I felt myself
thrilled under the spell of these, recited to myself, inaudibly
at times, and at others declaimed boldly and dramatically, when
no one else was listening.[2]

Les Miserables was also a book he read and reread as the inspiration for his thinking about the social problems of contemporary life.

Young Debs went to work in a railroad paint shop but soon became a locomotive fireman on the Terre Haute and Indianapolis
Railroad (1871-74). These years as an active railroader became the
background for his subsequent career although he later became an
office clerk in a grocery concern (1874-79). Railroading was in
his blood and his association with the workers was so close that
he joined the Brotherhood of Locomotive Firemen when a local
lodge was established in Terre Haute in 1875.[3] His organizing
ability soon became so evident that in 1878 he was elected an associate editor of their publication, *The Locomotive Fireman's Magazine*. Two years later he was elected national secretary and treas-
urer. In the next twelve years he increased the union from sixty
lodges, in debt for $6,000, to 286, financially sound and healthy.

In the meantime Debs had entered politics. He was elected city
clerk of Terre Haute on the Democratic ticket in 1879 and again
in 1881. As his term expired he ran for a seat in the Indiana Assembly and was elected. Early in the session he was proud to nominate
Daniel Voorhees for the Senate of the United States and see him
elected by the Assembly. At this time Debs hoped that the problems
of railroad management and labor could be settled by the passing
of laws. As measure after measure was defeated, however, he lost
his faith in legislation; it was too slow and involved too much political pressure and compromise. He decided against further office
seeking but remained an active Democratic speaker until 1896 when
he joined Bryan, Darrow, and Altgeld in the struggle for Illinois.
He spoke more than twenty times in opposition to the foremost
Republican campaigners who had been rushed into the area.

Through this activity Eugene Debs was now rapidly gaining
recognition as a speaker of national stature, a goal which perhaps
unconsciously he had set out to achieve many years before. While
still an office clerk he had realized the handicap of his meager
schooling and had resolved to overcome it. He began to buy books

and joined with others in forming a literary and debating society. In his first public appearance before the society Debs attempted to render Patrick Henry's famous oration but he suffered badly from stage fright and was bitterly disappointed with his performance. As a consequence, he began a vigorous program for self-improvement in public speaking. He was enthusiastic, therefore, when the society proposed to bring Robert G. Ingersoll to Terre Haute to deliver his lecture on "The Liberty of Man, Woman, and Child." Debs immediately chose Ingersoll as his model with the result that much of his early speaking was imitative. He was also impressed with Wendell Phillips when he was brought before the society.

Debs was now constantly engaged in writing articles and editorials for *The Locomotive Fireman's Magazine*, giving him increasing facility with language. His sincerity, vigor, and forthrightness, whether in print or on the platform, met with immediate and enthusiastic response from the railroad men. Although he was successful in organizing them, he was not happy because he soon realized that craft unions could not successfully cope with railroad management. The firemen could not win without the coordinated effort of the engineers, the conductors, and the other divisions of workers. Yet this cooperation was not only lacking but often was thwarted by the deliberate strikebreaking activities of rival unions. Eventually, Debs resigned his offices with the firemen and announced his intention of founding an American Railroad Union, an organization to include in its ranks all white railroad employees, except those in management.

The new union grew rapidly, with workers on railroad after railroad organizing solidly. The industrial crisis of 1893 brought a threat of wage cuts and unemployment; consequently hundreds enrolled for self protection. A first real test of the union's powers came too quickly for the officers striving to establish stable local lodges. Successive wage cuts on the Great Northern brought about a strike on April 13, 1894. Debs was soon in St. Paul directing the strike, which through bold leadership he brought to a substantial victory eighteen days later. The turning point was a speech he made to the St. Paul Chamber of Commerce. Although the business men had been distinctly hostile, Debs was adept in audience analysis. He made no pretense at conventional oratory on a lofty plane.

Instead he began to talk quietly and earnestly about the unhappy lot of the men who could barely provide for the needs of their families. As he strode back and forth before the crowd, pointing with his long finger to intolerable conditions, his overwhelming concern gradually changed the attitude of the listeners. At the end of his remarks, they were ready to support his cause. Debs's return to Terre Haute was a triumphal journey, railroad men lining the tracks to acclaim their champion.

A few months later the ARU was involved in another bitter strike. The workers in the Pullman Company, members of the union because they manufactured and operated Pullman cars on the railroads, struck against intolerable living conditions forced upon them by the corporation. Debs was reluctant to have the strike spread beyond Pullman, but the vast majority of the railroaders voted to refuse the movement of Pullman cars over the rails. Management insisted on carrying these cars on all trains and then assigned them mail to carry, thus involving the Federal government.

Fearing the consequences, Debs issued orders that strikers were to stay away from all railroad property, and not to engage in acts of violence. The situation steadily deteriorated as the railroads brought armed guards into the Chicago area. At this point the federal court issued a sweeping injunction prohibiting any act which would aid the boycott. Debs and his officers had but two choices: to violate the injunction or to terminate the strike, which would have meant that thousands of the workers would lose their jobs, since all of them had been blacklisted by the railroad managers. Debs secured Clarence Darrow as a legal adviser.

As tension grew, President Cleveland ordered in federal troops. Debs again appealed to his union members to be orderly and to keep away from railroad property. He could not, however, control the irresponsible crowds milling about the railroad yards. On July 5, rioting broke out; troops fired into the crowds and charged with bayonets. On July 6 more than three hundred forty thousand dollars worth of damage was done. The next day four rioters were killed and forty injured although not one of these was a member of the ARU.

The Federal Attorney, nevertheless, asked and received from a grand jury an indictment charging Debs and his union officers with conspiracy to interfere with interstate commerce. They were immediately arrested. Released on bail they attempted to save the ARU from disintegration but in doing so were held by Judge Grosscup to have violated his injunction. They were thrown into jail and refused bail. The strike was completely broken. For contempt of court Debs was sentenced to six months in the Woodstock, Illinois, jail, but he appealed to the Supreme Court. While awaiting the decision, Clarence Darrow conducted a successful defense against the conspiracy charge, but the Supreme Court refused the motions against the conviction for contempt. Debs served his sentence from May to November, 1895.

Debs and his friends were granted the greatest freedom in the McHenry County jail, and devoted many hours to the reading of books that were sent in by the score. Much of their study was socialistic, including the writings of Bellamy, Blatchford, Gronlund and Kautsky, the Fabian essays, the economic theories of Henry George, and Henry Demarest Lloyd's *Wealth Against Commonwealth*. Eventually Victor Berger, the Milwaukee socialist, visited Woodstock, and after long conversations, left Debs a copy of Karl Marx's *Das Kapital*. As a result of this reading, study, and discussion, Debs wrote that "it was here that Socialism gradually laid hold of me in its own irresistible fashion."[4]

In 1896 Eugene Debs was so popular with members of the Populist party that he probably could have had the nomination either for the governorship of Indiana or the presidency of the United States. He refused permission to have his name considered, first, because he had resolved to stay out of politics and second, because he felt that the Populists, a capitalist reform party, were not sufficiently identified with the true problems of labor. To him it seemed better to support William Jennings Bryan.

After the election, however, Debs began a vigorous campaign to unite the remnants of the American Railway Union with socialistic groups centered in various parts of the country. By March 6, 1900, he had achieved sufficient unity to call a national convention in Indianapolis under the name of the Social Democratic Party. The delegates came from 226 branches and represented 4,536 party members.[5] Eugene V. Debs was named their candidate for the presidency. His aggressive campaign brought him 94,864 votes in the election.[6]

After a short rest, Debs began a strenuous effort to build up his party, which adopted the name "Socialist" in 1901. Debs normally scheduled about seven two-hour speeches a week, traveling endlessly back and forth across the country. The admission charged for his meetings netted about a hundred dollars a week. He supplemented this income with the sale of books and pamphlets printed in Terre Haute. This exhausting activity brought substantial results. In 1904 Debs and the Socialist party polled 402,895 votes .

In the summer of that year Debs began his third campaign for the presidency, running eventually against William Jennings Bryan on the Democratic ticket and William Howard Taft, the Republican candidate. The Socialists, not to be outdone by their opponents, projected plans for a sweeping tour of the country by Debs in the Red Special—a locomotive pulling a single coach painted a bright red. This bold venture was financed by charging admission to all of Debs's principal speeches. The meetings in the larger cities were attended by thousands of partisans. On the western half of the tour, the Red Special traveled more than 9,000 miles, making 190 stops. Debs's managers estimated that in one month he had spoken to 275,000 people. The final month was spent in the East and Middle West. Debs enjoyed the campaign and threw himself recklessly into every speaking opportunity. He was at his best in the rough heckling sessions that characterized many of the meetings. When the Red Special came to its last stop he had spoken from five to twenty times a day for sixty-five days. Exhausted and ill he returned to Terre Haute on election day. The results were disappointing. Only 420,890 Socialist ballots were cast. Taft became President.[7]

Debs, now in his prime, was a man six feet two inches in height, slim but powerfully built, with a fine head, long, full neck, and broad shoulders. He was smooth shaven and later became bald. As he spoke he paced the platform, leaning far out toward his audience and gesturing with his right hand and forefinger. His voice was warm and friendly, but on occasion it became harsh with anger or denunciation.

Debs was again the Socialist candidate in 1912 but he headed a party full of dissension. Ernest Untermann voiced the right wing opposition to Debs when he said, "Comrade Debs is no doubt a great orator and fiery revolutionist . . . but he is also one of the poorest generals and tacticians our movement has."[8] On June 29, Debs began another strenuous campaign, speaking more frequently than in 1908. Again he charged admission for his formal public appearances and with striking success. Eighteen thousand listeners in Philadelphia paid in twenty-seven hundred dollars, while thirteen thousand in New York collected almost ten thousand dollars for the cause.

Inasmuch as both Wilson and Roosevelt were campaigning for changes included in the Socialist platform, Debs lost much of the reform vote. Nevertheless, he received 901,873 ballots, almost double that of 1908 and about 6 per cent of the total vote cast.

In 1916 Debs denied his name to the National Socialist convention but was drafted to run for Congress in the Fifth Congressional District in Indiana. Although he campaigned strenuously he was defeated. His opposition to military preparedness and his insistence that the United States stay out of the war in Europe were undoubtedly important factors in the contest. Now he took to the lecture platform to support his views. His opposition to America's entry into the war and to the military draft grew in violence as the nation entered World War I.

Meantime Congress had passed amendments to the Espionage Act which forbade abusive criticism of the government and its acts. Under its provisions, a number of Socialists were arrested as pro-German and un-American. For a time, however, Debs was threatened by individuals but ignored by the government, even though his public utterances were extreme in their criticism of the government and in opposition to the war. Debs became angrier and angrier. Why should he be free when those who believed as he did were thrust into jail? He resolved to state again his position in unequivocal language which the government could not ignore. He chose Canton, Ohio, as the place for this speech since three Socialists were in jail there. Debs began by saying:

> I have just returned from a visit over yonder where three of our most loyal comrades are paying the penalty for their devotion to the cause of the working class. They have come to

realize, as many of us have, that it is extremely dangerous to exercise the constitutional right of free speech in a country fighting to make democracy safe in the world.

I realize that, in speaking to you this afternoon, there are certain limitations placed upon the right of free speech. I must be exceedingly careful, prudent, as to what I say and even more careful and prudent as to how I say it. I may not be able to say all I think; but I am not going to say anything I do not think. I would rather a thousand times be a free soul in jail than be a sycophant and coward in the streets.[9]

He then began a sweeping indictment of the "misrepresentatives of the masses" in Congress, the lying capitalistic newspapers, and the Wall Street Junkers. He condemned the Supreme Court because by a vote of five to four it had declared the child labor law to be unconstitutional. He attacked the stupidity and short sightedness of the ruling class. He condemned war and shouted that the working class "who fight all the battles, the working class who make the supreme sacrifices, the working class who freely shed their blood and furnish corpses, have never yet had a voice in either declaring war or making peace. It is the ruling class that invariably does both. They alone declare war and they alone make peace.

> Yours not to reason why;
> Yours but to do and die."

He said little that had not been said before, some of it many times, but this time it brought forth a federal grand jury indictment on ten counts. On September 9, 1918, his trial began in Cleveland. He was ready to admit that he had made the Canton speech; his defense was that it was not criminal. Further it was to be argued that the Acts violated the first amendment of the Constitution, a question which could be settled only if Debs were found guilty and the matter appealed to a higher court.

The courtroom was packed with spectators, most of them Socialists. The jury was carefully picked but obviously not sympathetic to Debs. The judge was resolved to conduct a fair trial. The first three days were used by the government to establish the text of the speech and to hear testimony from those who had heard or talked with Debs about his views. When the government rested its case, the defense surprised everyone by doing likewise, asking only that Debs be allowed to make his own closing argument. This request was granted.

The courtroom was darkening from a summer storm as the tall gaunt form of the speaker approached the jury, a few notes in his left hand and the long bony forefinger of his right poised to emphasize what he had to say. This was a climactic moment for a veteran who had spoken to thousands of his fellow citizens under every conceivable circumstance. Fearless and unafraid he voiced his unshaken convictions.

"I do not fear to face you in this hour of accusation," he began, "nor do I shrink from the consequences of my utterances or my acts. Standing before you charged as I am with crime, I can yet look the court in the face. I can look you in the face. I can look the world in the face for in my conscience, in my soul there is festering no accusation of guilt."[10]

He continued: "I wish to admit the truth of all that has been testified to in this proceeding. I have no disposition to deny anything that is true . . . I would not retract a word that I have uttered that I believe to be true to save myself from going to the penitentiary for the rest of my days. Gentlemen, you have heard the report of my speech . . . and I submit that there is not a word in that speech to warrant the charges set out in the indictment."

He spoke of many things that afternoon before he concluded with the words:

> I cannot take back a word I have said. I cannot repudiate a sentence I have uttered. I stand before you guilty of having made this speech. I do not know, I cannot tell, what your verdict may be, nor does it matter much, so far as I am concerned.
>
> I am the smallest part of this trial. I have lived long enough to realize my own personal insignificance in relation to a great issue that involves the welfare of the whole people. . . . American institutions are on trial here before a court of American citizens. The future will render the final verdict.

Although visibly moved by his words, the jury found him guilty and on September 14th he was brought before the court for sentencing. Asked if he wished to speak he delivered perhaps the one **great oration** of his lifetime:

>Your Honor, years ago I recognized my kinship with all living beings, and I made up my mind that I was not one bit better than the meanest on earth. I said then and I say now, that while there is a lower class, I am in it, while there is a criminal element I am of it, and while there is a soul in prison, I am not free. . . .
>
>When the mariner, sailing over tropic seas, looks for relief from his weary watch, he turns his eyes toward the southern cross, burning luridly above the tempest-vexed ocean. As the midnight approaches, the southern cross begins to bend, the whirling worlds change their places, and with starry finger-points the Almighty marks the passage of time upon the dial of the universe, and though no bell may beat the glad tidings, the lookout knows that the midnight is passing and that relief and rest are close at hand.
>
>Let the people everywhere take heart of hope, for the cross is bending, the midnight is passing, and joy cometh with the morning.[11]

These words, eloquent in their simplicity, were the epitome of Debs's deep-rooted convictions so often worded and reworded, and now forever molded into the faultless flow of matchless rhetoric.

Heywood Broun was wrong in writing that "when his [Debs's] great moment came, a miracle occurred" unexplainable in that his previous speeches "seemed to be second rate utterances."[12] Norman Thomas has made the truer judgment. "I am inclined to think," he wrote, "that the greatest of his speeches were those when he was on trial. There was in them true eloquence; they were less florid—I think that is the word I want— than many of his speeches and freer from the clichés—in his case socialist clichés—all political campaigners, after some fashion, are forced to use."[13]

Debs entered the state prison at Moundsville, West Virginia, April 13, 1919, and was transferred to the federal prison in Atlanta, Georgia, two months later. "I enter the prison doors," he said, "a flaming revolutionist, my head erect, my spirit untamed and my soul unconquerable."[14]

In May, 1920, the Socialist party nominated him as its presidential candidate. Although he was not permitted to leave the prison, he was permitted party conferences and freedom to correspond and release campaign statements. In November he received 919,799 votes, double the number he had received in 1904 and 1908. After the election President Wilson refused to commute his sentence but on December 25, 1921, President Harding released him from prison.

Debs was resolved to resume his writing and speaking. He began an effort in defense of Sacco and Vanzetti, under sentence of death in Massachusetts. Debs, however, was a sick man; his broken health continually interfered with his plans. Active opposition to his platform appearances also necessitated last minute changes. He was particularly gratified, however, when the legislature of the State of Wisconsin urged its members by resolution to attend his lecture at the University in Madison. In September, 1926, he again entered a sanitarium in an attempt to regain his strength, but instead he rapidly became worse. He died October 26, 1926.

Eugene V. Debs will occupy a unique place in the history of American oratory. "No man in America has been more hated," wrote Max Ehrmann, "and few have been so much loved."[15] He identified himself so completely with labor that he early became an heroic figure in the eyes of working people everywhere. His innate and boundless humanity became almost legendary. "It is hard," wrote Norman Thomas, "to separate his effectiveness as a speaker from the total impact of his personality and romantic career as a leader and spokesman for the worker."[16] To many of his followers, Debs exemplified the Christian virtues, although as Heywood Broun wrote, Debs was "not a Christian by any precise standard."[17] Though he repudiated the Bible and churches,[18] he nevertheless often spoke and wrote in the Christian idiom, sometimes with almost stereotyped conventionality but on other occasions with a strange intermingling of irreverence and respect. Thus at one time he said in a eulogy of Martin Irons: "And thus it has been all along the highway of the centuries, from Jesus Christ to Martin Irons . . . Let it not be said that Irons was not crucified. For fourteen years he was nailed to the cross and no martyr to humanity ever bore his crucifixion with finer fortitude."[19] On another occasion he declared: "Had the carpenter of Nazareth been in Chicago at the time, He would have been on the side of the poor, the heavy-laden and the sore at heart. . . ." In contrast to this conformity was his statement that Jesus was "the great Divine Tramp who never had a dollar, but who understood and loved the common folk, the ordinary ruck of men, with an absorbing and abiding affection."[20] But regardless of what he said, those who knew him accepted him as he was. Mayor Lyons of Terre Haute recognized this fact when he wrote: "The overwhelming majority of the people here are opposed to the social and economic theories of Mr. Debs, but there is not perhaps a single man who enjoys to a greater degree than Mr. Debs the affection, love and profound respect of the entire community."[21]

Debs augmented his background by speaking with a compelling sincerity. Max Ehrmann stressed this characteristic as he made an interesting comparison of Debs with Albert J. Beveridge:

> This [Debs's] style is very different from that of such speakers as Senator Beveridge. Mr. Beveridge's orations on occasions and in the Senate are finished, modeled, filed and practiced. Intonation and gesture are carefully managed to fit the sentiment. It is a piece of good workmanship. But the whole effect lacks sincerity. You feel that Mr. Beveridge is secretly using you for his personal ends. None of these elements enter the oratory of Mr. Debs, and his sincerity is almost terrible in its reality. You feel that he will tell you what he thinks regardless of consequences. . . . He resorts to no tricks of rhetoric, no claptrap and stage effects, no empty pretense of deep emotion."[22]

August Claessens expresses the same thought in writing that "above all it was his sterling sincerity, his lack of any artificial mannerisms, his penetrating seriousness that struck sparks from the anvil of his themes."[23]

His appeals were directed, of course, toward social, political, and economic justice for all men. These elements far outweighed his logical arguments. "Debs talked in pictures and parables. . . . He described visions of a better day and left facts and figures to other speakers," wrote Louis Stark in *The New York Times*.[24] His primary aim was to move men to action; he was not accurate as to detail or careful in his reasoning. He disliked to read or hear heavy logic or abstract theory. Both his writings and speeches are disappointing to those seeking a brilliant exposition of Socialistic philosophy, but finding only a vague and impressionistic argument, strangely compelling but mentally disappointing. It must be remembered that many of Debs's audiences were composed of people not given to critical analysis.

Debs left a record of his own about public speaking:

> No man ever made a speech on a mean subject. . . . The highest there is in oratory is the highest there is in truth, in honesty, immortality. . . . Had Ingersoll and Phillips devoted their lives to the practice of law for pay, the divine fire within them would have burned to ashes and they would have died in mediocrity.[25]

Debs often acknowledged Ingersoll as his model, writing that, in his opinion, Ingersoll was "the perfect master of the art of human speech. He combined all the graces and powers of expression, and stood upon the pinnacle of oratorical achievement." Ingersoll and Wendell Phillips, he declared "were the two greatest orators of their time, and probably of all time."[26] But when Debs attempted to follow the sensuous style of Ingersoll be became overly sweet and sentimental, as for example, in these sentences about his ideal speakers: "Their power sprang from their passion for freedom, for truth, for justice, for a world filled with light and happy human beings. . . . The sacred fire burned within them and when they were aroused it flashed from their eyes and rolled from their inspired lips in torrents of eloquence."[27]

Coleman aptly described the "oratorical pattern which Gene was to follow to the end" as "socialistic generalities, couched in Ingersollian phrases, with talk of a new world, the emancipation of the workers, the happiness of the little children of the future."[28]

The editor of the *Springfield Union* was more critical still. He wrote: "Debs did not hesitate to employ all the stale shibboleths, all the outworn words and phrases, all the ready-made ideas of the common variety of the socialistic soap-box exhorter."[29] A sentimental sweetness also seemed inconsistent in a speaker intent on radical reform. Sentences such as the following recur time and again:

> Flowers blossom from his lips and you can hear the ripple of silver springs in the music of his voice.
> How good the touch of the hand of a comrade is, and a sip of water furnished by a comrade; as refreshing as if it were out of the desert of life.

> As a rosebud yields to the tender influence of a summer
> shower, so I now open my heart to receive your benediction.

Doubtless, on many occasions, such passages were effective because
they were infused with the charm and magnetic personality of
the speaker and given for audiences eager to respond to him.

Many of his sentences reflect his love of poetry. They may also
explain the reason for his close friendship with the poets James
Whitcomb Riley, Eugene Field, Edwin Markham, and Max Ehrmann. He used verses to point up passages in his speeches. His
quotations came from Mark Twain, Longfellow, Emerson, Tho-
reau, Alcott, Victor Hugo, Sardou, Phillips, Lombroso, Henley,
and Patrick Henry, among others. Typical is this:

> On that day Thoreau said: "Some eighteen hundred years ago
> Christ was crucified. This morning perchance Captain Brown
> was hung. These are the two ends of a chain which is not with-
> out its links. He is not Old Brown any longer; he is an Angel
> of Light."[30]

Debs was particularly successful in weaving musical alliteration
into his sentences, many instances of which could be included:
"our democratic domain," "whirled from point to point in his royal
carousal among the plebeians," "gorgeous glittering splendor,"
"dim as dirt," "prince and pauper, power and poverty, money
and misery." "This is the secret of their solidarity; the heart of
their hope, the inspiration that nerves them all with sinews of steel."
"The Red flag—to the plutocrat it is a peril; to the proletaire, a
promise."

But if Debs could quote from the poetry and prose of literature
he could also use the violent and vulgar language of the labor hall
and the saloon. As an agitator and revolutionary it was to be expected that he would use provocative phrases in talking of "Rockefeller's blood-stained dollars," of "capitalistic leeches . . . gouging
out profits," of "begowned corporation lawyers on the supreme
court," of "Wall Street gamblers and brigands cackling from their
piles of loot," of "the prostitute press of the robber regimes." At
times his invective became extremely personal as illustrated by his
reply to Billy Sunday's statement that "every woman in Russia is a
common prostitute under the Soviet system": "I wish I had the
strength to go to Charleston and meet that public vulture on a

public platform. I would strip him to his naked hide and demand that he eat that insult against a race of noble women, God damn him!"[31]

Remarks by Debs often brought laughter but his humor was close to irony and touched with sarcasm. Speaking of his political enemy, Theodore Roosevelt, he said: "You remember that at the close of Theodore Roosevelt's second term as president he went over to Africa to make war on some of his ancestors." Again he declared that "Chauncey M. Depew has 150 pairs of creased trousers; many of his sovereign constituents have patches on their only pair of pants." Describing the Civic Federation in 1905 he said: "The capitalists are represented by that great union labor champion, August Belmont. The working class by Samuel Gompers, the president of the American Federation of Labor, and the public by Grover Cleveland. Can you imagine a fox and goose peace convention? Just fancy such a meeting, the goose lifting its wings in benediction and the fox whispering, 'Let us prey.'" The passages cited reveal the chief characteristics of Debs's compositional style. In general it was short of true oratorical eloquence but it was nevertheless a powerful instrument for persuasion when delivered with the vigor of the veteran campaigner.

Debs was professionally an editorial writer, a pamphleteer, and a lecturer. He wrote and spoke throughout most of his life. As a speaker he traveled back and forth across the country teaching unionism and socialism, generating enthusiasm for his cause. These lectures were sometimes repeated, but more often they were rearrangements of stock arguments and passages put together either beforehand or extemporaneously to meet audience situations. The material had excellent vocal quality and was rhetorically smooth and polished, audience tested for maximum effectiveness. Yet it must have seemed original, for Max Eastman wrote: "His tongue dwells upon a 'the' or an 'and' with a kind of earnest affection for the humble that throws the whole accent of his sentences out of the conventional mold and makes each one seem a special creation of the moment."[32]

John Swinton, who had heard Lincoln speak in the Cooper Union in 1860 and Debs in 1894, felt that "there was a marked resemblance in appearance, manner, thought and speech."[33] Certain it was that these two tall, lanky midwesterners, self educated and naturally eloquent, were leaders of men. The burning sincerity of their convictions gave their simple words and homely illustrations the compelling powers of persuasion. They influenced those who crowded eagerly to hear them. Loved and revered by their followers but hated and mercilessly lampooned by their enemies, each in his own way and in his own time caught a vision of a nobler America to which he dedicated his life.

Footnotes

1. Max Ehrmann, "Eugene V. Debs as an Orator," *The Saturday Spectator*, VII (August, 1907), 9.
2. Eugene Debs, *Labor and Freedom* (St. Louis, 1916), p. 16.
3. Eugene V. Debs, "How I Became a Socialist," *Writings and Speeches* (New York, 1948), p. 43.
4. Eugene V. Debs, "How I Became a Socialist," *Writings and Speeches*, p. 43.
5. McAllister Coleman, *Eugene V. Debs, A Man Unafraid* (New York, 1930), p. 203.
6. Stefan Lorant, *The Presidency* (New York, 1951), p. 449. All subsequent election figures from the same source.
7. Coleman, p. 248.
8. Ray Ginger, *The Bending Cross* (New Brunswick, 1949), p. 309.
9. Canton, Ohio, Speech, *Writings and Speeches*, pp. 417-433.
10. Address to the jury, *Writings and Speeches*, pp. 433-437.
11. Address to the jury, *Writings and Speeches*, p. 437.
12. Heywood Broun, "The Miracle of Debs," *Collected Edition*, pp. 181-182.
13. Norman Thomas, letter to the author (November 10, 1950).
14. Coleman, p. 301.
15. Ehrmann, p. 9.
16. Norman Thomas, *loc. cit.*
17. "Eugene V. Debs, The Gentle Hoosier Socialist," *Literary Digest*, XCI (November 13, 1926), 46, quoting Broun's column, *New York World*.
18. Ginger, *The Bending Cross*, p. 309.
19. *Writings and Speeches*, p. 42.
20. Ginger, p. 309.
21. Mayor Lyons in a letter to John Cuthbertson, February 27, 1907. Quoted by Arthur Schlesinger, Jr., in his introduction to *Writings and Speeches*, p. ix.
22. Ehrmann, p. 9.
23. August Claessens, *Eugene Victor Debs* (New York, 1946), p. 7.
24. "Eugene V. Debs, The Gentle Hoosier Socialist," p. 44.
25. Eugene V. Debs, "The Secret of Efficient Expression," *Labor and Freedom* (St. Louis, 1916), pp. 15-16.
26. "The Secret of Efficient Expression," p. 15.

27. "The Secret of Efficient Expression," p. 16.
28. Coleman, p. 210.
29. "Eugene Debs, The Gentle Hoosier Socialist," p. 46.
30. *Writings and Speeches*, pp. 289, 280, 279.
31. H. M. Morias (with W. Cahn), *Eugene V. Debs, The Story of a Fighting American* (New York, 1948), p. 22.
32. Max Eastman, *Debs and the War*, p. 51.
33. Referred to by Claessens, p. 4, and Ginger, p. 183.

Ralph Bunche, Negro Spokesman

RALPH JOHNSON BUNCHE *(August 7, 1904–)*. *Born in Detroit, Michigan; son of Fred Bunche, a barber from Ohio, and Olive Johnson Bunche, housewife and amateur pianist from Kansas; elementary schooling in Detroit, Albuquerque; intermediate and secondary schooling in Los Angeles; A.B. degree from the University of California at Los Angeles; commencement speaker at graduation; M.A. and Ph.D. degrees, Harvard; postdoctoral work in anthropology and economics at Northwestern University, the London School of Economics, and the University of Cape Town (South Africa); married, 1930, to Ruth Ethel Harris; Ozias Goodwin Fellow, Harvard, 1929; Rosenwald fellowship in Europe and Africa, 1931-1932; Social Science Research Council postdoctoral fellowship in Europe, Africa, Malaya, and Netherlands Indies, 1936-1938; staff member, Carnegie Corporation's Survey of Negro in America, 1939; assistant in political science, UCLA, 1925-1927; instructor in political science, Howard University, 1928-1929; assistant professor, 1929-1933; assistant to president, 1930-1931; associate professor, 1933-1938; professor since 1938; head of department, 1929-1950; codirector, Institute of Race Relations, Swarthmore, 1936; senior social-science analyst in charge of research, Office of Strategic Services, 1941-1944; deputy chief, Near East-Africa Section, 1943; chief, Africa Section, 1943-1944; territorial specialist, Division of Dependent Area Affairs, Department of State, 1945-1947; adviser, U. S. delegation, International Labour Conference, Philadelphia, April, 1945; associate secretary, U. S. delegation, Dumbarton Oaks, 1944; adviser, U. S. delegation, UNCIO, San Francisco, 1945; member, U. S. delegation's executive committee at the UN, London, 1945; U. S. delegation, International Labour Conference, Paris, 1945; U. S. delegation, General Assembly, UN, London, 1946; director, Division of Trusteeship, UN, 1946-1948; principal secretary, UN Palestine Commission, 1948; personal representative of Secretary General of UN as mediator in Palestine, 1948-1949; professor of government, Harvard University; trustee of Oberlin College; Under-Secretary for Special Political Affairs, UN, 1958–; member, Lincoln Sesquicentennial Commission, 1957–; member, New York City Board of Higher Education, 1958–; member, Phi Beta Kappa; Nobel Peace Prize, 1950; Spingarn Medal, 1949; Four Freedoms Award, 1951; Peace Award of Third Order of St. Francis, 1954; member and past president of American Political Science Association; office: UN, New York City.*[1]

Ralph Bunche, Negro Spokesman

GREGG PHIFER*

I lay no claim to leadership and I have no right whatsoever to act as a spokesman for some 15,000,000 Negro citizens. I have always been a strong individualist, and since there are already literally millions of self-anointed Negro leaders and spokesmen, far be it from me to join the crowd.[2]

DESPITE his professed unwillingness to speak for his race, Ralph Bunche is, by virtue of prestige, position, and articulateness, inescapably and almost universally accepted as a foremost Negro American spokesman. From the quiet shores of Lake Chautauqua in upper New York state to bustling NAACP conventions in Atlanta and Dallas, he has carried the challenge of human relations to whites and Negroes alike.

"I have flown out here just for this occasion," Bunche told a Dallas convention of the NAACP, "not because I have anything new or of particular importance to say, but simply because I want to be a part of and want to do whatever I can to aid the great crusade which the NAACP leads. . . . Those are enough reasons to have induced me even to walk out here from New York if it were necessary."[3]

Few contemporary issues have caused more intense feeling than Negro-white relations, particularly the issue of segregation versus integration. Because, whether he wishes it or not, Bunche is regarded as a spokesman for the intelligent, educated Negro, it is appropriate to study his views on race relations in the United States.

Twelve complete speech texts,[4] three newspaper summaries from the *Chautauqua Daily*,[5] a brief statement reported verbatim in *Town Meeting*,[6] and a four-page dittoed set of excerpts[7] form the

---

* Gregg Phifer (A.B. College of the Pacific 1940; M.A. 1941, Ph.D. 1949, State University of Iowa) is associate professor of speech at Florida State University.

basis of this study. Several deal almost exclusively with the Negro and his role in America; others contain little or no reference to race.[8] Of his many other speeches during this ten-year period, 1949-59, he has only "rough notes, which would be of little use to anyone but me."[9]

It is not always easy to assess the authenticity of available texts. Bunche himself says that "most of my talks are based on notes only and are not available in manuscript form."[10] Even as he made this comment, however, he enclosed a *Christian Century* reprint of his speech before the Chicago Sunday Evening Club and a mimeographed copy of his speech to the NAACP in Dallas. The first was unmarked; the second, a mimeographed text, had been corrected in ink in seven places, and at the bottom of one page a carbon copy of a typewritten paragraph had been added. Interlineations and corrections had also been made on the carbon-copy manuscripts of his speeches at the University of Pittsburgh commencement exercises and before the Fellowship House dinner.

This paper discusses the way Bunche answers, in these speeches, four questions on race relations: (1) What are the bases of race prejudice? (2) Are race prejudice and segregation in the United States harmful? If so, how? (3) What should be done about segregation? (4) What are the future prospects for race relations in the United States?

THE BASES OF RACE PREJUDICE

Repeatedly during these speeches Ralph Bunche discussed the causes of race prejudice. He argued that prejudice is learned, not innate, behavior. For instance, he told his Chautauqua audience that "one has to learn to be prejudiced. Our children are not born with prejudice and do not manifest prejudices in their early years, not until they learn them from us, their elders."[11]

Prejudice is blind, unreasoned, said Bunche. At Morgan State College he attacked the "ridiculous lengths" to which segregation had been carried when local park-board police refused to permit a tennis match between two tennis clubs, one white and one Negro,

> because it was contrary to the board's policy to permit inter-
> racial matches. The members of the two clubs were prevented
> from playing the match under threat of arrest. Danger in a

tennis match! What utter nonsense! Can there be anyone in this community ingenious enough to explain what harm could possibly be done to the community if tennis players of the two races, voluntarily wishing to do so, should play tennis together? What a strange doctrine it is that requires Negro taxpayers of Baltimore to play tennis on public courts only with Negroes, even though others may wish to play with them![12]

Prejudices become habit patterns of which people are often unaware. In his last address in the Chautauqua lecture series, Bunche said that "prejudices become a part of society's cultural heritages, of people's practices and belief of the folk ways, and many people have them and are not really aware that they harbor and nurture in themselves such attitudes."[13] As an illustration of such uncritical acceptance of popular stereotypes Bunche cited his experience at a dinner given by Trygve Lie, then Secretary-General of the United Nations. When Lie proposed a toast to the President of the United States (Harry Truman), the lady on Bunche's left muttered under her breath, "I hope he chokes." Surprised, Bunche asked the lady, "Who, Mr. Lie?" Her reply was that she hoped Truman would choke. When Bunche asked "Why?" she replied by citing his humble origins and unsuccessful career as a haberdasher. Bunche replied that such experiences were much in the American log-cabin tradition. His neighbor looked at him sharply and said, "You speak like some of these people who believe that Negroes ought to be equal!" The story continues in Bunche's words:

Well, that sort of shocked me because it had never occurred to me that this lady was not aware of my racial identity. I don't know yet what she took me for, but obviously she did not mean to insult me. . . . And so we had quite a discussion about race, and I threw the book at her, all of the books—anthropology, biology, and psychology—right down the line. She listened politely, and after a while she said to me, "Why, Mr. Bunche, I've heard all of that before, but I don't believe it any more than you do. Tell me this, Mr. Bunche. A while ago you mentioned your family (and here she looked me straight in the eye). Tell me, would you wish your daughters to marry Negroes?"

Well, I've been a Negro all my life, you see, and have been in the struggle for equal treatment all of my adult life; and this was the first time, I think, that I had ever found myself even momentarily speechless on this particular question. I looked her straight in the eye and thought now I was going to deliver a shock to her; and I said, "My dear lady, I couldn't possibly object because, you see, I happen to be a Negro, and therefore my daughters are also!" It didn't faze her at bit. She fired right back, "In that case you're different."[14]

After long discussion Bunche's neighbor finally admitted that she did not know much about the problem and asked how she might learn. He "rather impishly" suggested that she join the NAACP. Almost all of Bunche's illustrations are, like this one, drawn from personal experience.

What justification exists for prejudice against the Negro? More than once Bunche defended the role of the Negro in American life. Despite segregated status, he told a 1954 NAACP audience in Dallas, "the Negro played the role of the good citizen—he paid his taxes, served his society in every capacity, gave his life for his country willingly and courageously on battlefields the world over even though he had died under the shadow of 'separate but equal' and usually while serving in segregated military units."

A few white Americans see a traitor beneath every black skin. This, thought Bunche,

> is mainly a reflection of bad conscience. They know the Negro has suffered much injustice and therefore assume that his resentment is directed against his country. They do not know the Negro and typically are unfamiliar with the Negro's magnificent record of toil, sweat, and sacrifice for his country. . . . They need to know that the Negro has fought valiantly for American liberty from Crispus Attucks to the foxholes of Korea. And he will always do so against any enemy of the country he has helped mightily to build.[15]

Before a NAACP banquet audience in New York City, Bunche described American Negroes as "good solid Americans. There are none better. They have given unstintingly to their country, through all its history, their sweat, their tears, their blood. They have never failed, never will, when their country calls."[16]

Is prejudice always an unpremeditated and unthinking phenomenon? Unfortunately it is not, Bunche believes. Sometimes it is the result of careful planning by unscrupulous dictators or demagogues. "Hitler developed the fearful strength of Naziism and the emotional appeal of anti-semitism," Bunche told his Chautauqua audience, "and went on to try to subdue and poison the entire world, and he came dangerously close to doing so. The Japanese militarists tried and succeeded to no little extent to win all of Asia through their effort toward world domination by appeal to anti-white, anti-Western emotions." The same pattern is all too prevalent in our own country, where "there is exploitation of race and religion by political demagogues, and racial and religious poisons are spread by professional bigots." Here we find that "prejudice and discrimination are often used by individuals and groups. Power arrangements in some societies and communities in fact rest largely upon such attitudes, and there is often in communities the tendency to look for scapegoats."[17]

A frequent theme is the cause of race prejudice and discrimination. Prejudice, Bunche said, is learned behavior taught by adults. It is unreasoned and unreasonable, without scientific basis in anthropology, biology, or psychology. It is deep-rooted in the attitudes of the individual and in the folk ways of the people. Dictators and demagogues cultivate prejudice as a base for power. Despite the diatribes of professional demagogues, the Negro has been a good citizen, ready to support and defend his country in all emergencies.

DANGER OF SEGREGATION

The fruit of prejudice is segregation. And what, according to Bunche, is wrong with segregation? To this question he devoted much time—more, perhaps, than to any other theme. Four problems were emphasized in these speeches:

Segregation contradicts democracy

A recurring argument in Bunche's speeches is that "segregation and democracy are utterly incompatible."[18] Once Bunche drew an analogy with Lincoln's attitude toward slavery as "contrary to human morality" and "inimical to the interests of the 'plain people' of America. By the same token," he continued, "present-day practices of racial segregation and discrimination should be outlawed as inimical to the interests of all who believe in and derive benefit from democracy, whatever their race or religion."[19]

In addressing the graduating class at Morgan State College, in Baltimore, Bunche pointed to

> the great irony of our nation—a nation firmly dedicated to a democratic way of life, that a substantial proportion of its citizens must still overcome unjust and undemocratic racial handicaps, must surmount arbitrary obstacles of racial bigotry, in running the race of life. And this is so not because of any misdeeds, of any shortcomings, of any lack of industry, ability, or loyalty on the part of those citizens so handicapped. It is so only because they are Negroes, because of their color or race.[20]

Can segregation be reconciled with our philosophy of life? No, said Bunche. "The Negro asks only that American democracy walk on its black as well as its white feet."[21]

Segregation undermines our international prestige

As a responsible official of the United Nations, Bunche frequently emphasized the damage segregation inflicts upon our international relations. In "The Challenge of Human Relations" he said: "Attitudes of bigotry, when widely prevalent in a society, involve staggering costs in terms of prestige and confidence throughout the rest of the world."[22] But his indictment in "Freedom Is a Blessing" was most prolonged:

> The practices and incidents of racial bigotry . . . are costly to the nation in these dangerous times. They are costly because they raise serious doubts, internally and externally, about the true nature of the American democratic way of life. Because they seriously question our sincerity in our democratic professions. Because they cannot fail to induce our friends abroad to doubt the genuineness of our democracy and to question our ability to treat nonwhite peoples anywhere as equals.

Segregation could, in the judgment of Ralph Bunche, prove an expensive luxury, handicapping us either in avoiding or in conducting wars. There is a "contradiction between the democratic ideals we proudly profess and the domestic practices of which we cannot boast. These contradictions have already cost us prestige, good will, and more lives than we have needed to lose on far-off battlefields. In the future, for the same reason, these costs in lives of fine American boys—white, black, brown, yellow, and red—could be far greater."[23]

Race relations in the United States are of crucial importance in her international relations because "the world's peoples are preponderantly nonwhite. The voices of darker peoples the world over are vigorously raised against racial prejudice in whatever guise and wherever it appears."[24] Colonial peoples, most of them nonwhite, are well aware of the apparent correlation between colonialism and racialism and highly critical of their practitioners. These same areas have been and are, moreover, the world's trouble spots. These places, where the prestige of the United States is most sorely tested by her racial practices, offer the gravest dangers of local wars or world-wide conflagrations.[25]

Segregationists aid communism

In recent years the charge of communism has been tossed into virtually every American conflict, including race relations. Bunche noticed charges "that any time a Negro demands equality he must be a Communist" and told his Dallas NAACP audience that if this were true, "that would make for an awful lot of Communists in this country." On the contrary, the Communist party has never been able to enlist more than a handful of Negroes.

Then Bunche took the offensive. Communists scoffed most loudly at the Supreme Court anti-segregation decision, arguing that as a propaganda gesture in the cold war it would never be implemented. "Now, could any good American support and join the Communists in that stand?" asked Bunche. "Here is a new kind of guilt by association, a new test of good Americanism and loyalty." Later in the same speech he asked, "Who would give aid and comfort to the Communists by denying the judgment of the highest court in the land? For clearly only the Communists could profit from the undermining of our institutions."

Essentially the same theme was expressed at Chautauqua, where Bunche pointed to the significance of the struggle of segregation versus integration "for the outcome of our titanic struggle against the tyranny and slavery of communism. Every time that any one of us finds his heart big enough to accept his neighbor of any color or creed as a brother, a blow is struck for freedom and against slavery."[26] Not satisfied with ridiculing the charges of those who equate the struggle for equal rights for Negroes with communism,

Bunche insisted on the contrary that those who oppose integration are doing the work of the Communists in weakening our national institutions and our national unity.

Segregation wastes human resources

Frequently in these speeches Bunche urged that racism prodigally wastes our human resources. In "The Challenge of Human Relations" Bunche told his Rochester, New York, audience:

> The most valuable resources of any country are its people. But in our country and in the South particularly our human resources, white and black alike, are being recklessly squandered. They are being squandered in interracial conflict, in prejudices and animosities among two groups of citizens—Americans all—which prevent that unity of purpose and that co-operative effort which alone could insure the full realization of the nation's potential in its human resources, and this at a time when it vitally requires its maximum strength.

In "Prospects for Peace" Bunche denounced race prejudice along with anti-Semitism and anti-Catholicism as "un-American attitudes . . . harmful to our national unity. These," he added, "are seriously divisive influences, which sap our national strength at the very moment in our history when we most urgently need our *maximum* strength." At the University of Pittsburgh commencement exercises he condemned the "shocking waste of human resources through denial of opportunity and growth to those discriminated against, thus reducing their productivity and their contribution to the progress of mankind."

What, then, in Bunche's view, is wrong with race prejudice and continued segregation? They contradict our democratic principles, undermine our international prestige, and serve the interests of communism by undermining our institutions, dividing our people, and squandering our human resources.

WHAT SHOULD BE DONE ABOUT SEGREGATION?

"What is wrong?" leads logically to "what to do." Bunche never dodged the second part of this obligation. Repeatedly, before audiences of Negroes or whites, he urged the elimination of race prejudice and the end of segregation. Four of the questions to which he addressed himself follow:

Is gradualism enough?

More than once Bunche expressed pleasure over the progress that has been and is being made. Insistently, however, he returned to the theme that gradual evolution is not enough. "But I must add that where birthrights are concerned, gradual progress can never be rapid enough for those deprived, since rights and birthrights can never be enjoyed posthumously."[27]

The same mild *reductio ad absurdum* appeared in "Freedom Is a Blessing," Bunche's address to the graduating class at Morgan State:

> These graduates, as you and I, must think of rights and privileges and opportunities as something to be enjoyed in one's life span or not at all. These benefits cannot be taken with one to the great beyond, nor can they be enjoyed in the hereafter. I will be happy, of course, to be assured that my children or my grandchildren or my great-grandchildren will enjoy their full right of American citizenship at some distant date. But I wish to enjoy them too—for the simple reason that as an American citizen I am fully entitled to do so and because I need the benefit of them to make my way in our highly competitive society.

What about the Supreme Court decision against segregation?

A "momentous forward step in the onward march of democracy"[28] was Bunche's salute to the decision of the Supreme Court of the United States outlawing segregation in the public schools. The old doctrine of "separate but equal" facilities he denounced as "a monstrous fiction, an unabashed lie. Every Negro knows this is so from his harsh experiences with separate schools for Negroes, separate residential areas for Negroes, separate railroad accommodations for Negroes, separate facilities of every kind." The entire concept of and motivation for segregation involves, said Bunche, "discrimination and inequality. Involuntary segregation means a status of inferiority for those segregated."[29]

So what did the Negroes do about the Supreme Court decision approving the "separate but equal" principle? Indirectly, Bunche criticized recent Southern actions when he said:

> Negroes, being good Americans, cherishing the American way of life, did not try to defy the court, did not threaten violence, did not claim the right to take the law into their own hands.

Rather, in the typical American and democratic way, the Negro set about, through his organizations and with the sympathetic assistance of an increasing number of fair and democratic white Americans, to convince the American public, the government, and the courts that this doctrine was wrong and fundamentally incompatible with the principles and ideals of our founding fathers and our Constitution.[30]

The implied contrast between Negro reactions to "separate but equal" and those of White Citizens Councils to recent Supreme Court decisions was clear.

The 1954 decision of the Supreme Court was, for Bunche, a momentous event. "I had never imagined," he said, "that legal phraseology could be so beautiful, that a court's decision could read like poetry." It was a milestone in the climb of the Negro in the United States toward first-class citizenship: ". . . the decision of the court in the school-segregation cases marked encouraging progress in democracy, advance in the removal of the racial stigma from the innocent children of a very large segment of the nation's population, and confidence in our ideals, our Constitution, and the good sense and decency of the American people."[31]

What should Negroes do?

At least five speeches included in this study were delivered to predominantly Negro audiences. Especially on these occasions Bunche offered suggestions to members of his own race:

1. Shun "Uncle Tomism." Before the NAACP in Dallas, Bunche criticized "Negroes . . . who . . . claim to prefer segregation to integration." Vested interests, he said, have developed in the Negro community "behind the walls of segregation," while some Negroes "have already begun the effort to safeguard their positions by reassuring their white superiors, in effect, that the Supreme Court decision did in fact go too far, since the Negro is very happy with separate schools and prefers not to be integrated." Such an attitude, Bunche felt, is unworthy of the race.

2. Avoid ghetto thinking. Bunche warned his Morgan State College audience of the "unfortunate inclination of the Negro himself to tighten the bonds of the ghetto by ghetto thinking." The life the Negro is forced to lead tempts him to make the Negro problem the center of all his thinking, as though the world revolved around the

race problem. This is "racial provincialism of the worst kind," developing "a narrowness of mind and a racial egocentrism." A corollary to ghetto thinking is the use of race prejudice as an excuse for Negro failures. "The cry of discrimination," warned Bunche, "must never be used as an alibi for lack of effort, preparation, and ability."[32]

3. Accept the responsibilities of freedom. Whatever rights and freedoms the Negro enjoys are accompanied by responsibilities and obligations, Bunche told the Morgan State graduating class. "Democracy gives no free rides. The Negro cannot be a good citizen if he concentrates exclusively on the problems of his group. All of the problems of his community and nation are his problems, and the Negro must devote his intelligent interest and effort to them. . . . The more integrated the Negro becomes, the heavier will his civic responsibilities become. Freedom is a blessing to be highly treasured; it is not license and should not be abused."[33]

4. Work hard. Even more than his white competitor, Bunche insisted, the Negro in our society must accept the necessity of hard work. He needs, Bunche said at the Fisk University commencement, "firm resolve, persistence, tenacity. He must gear himself to hard work all the way. He can never let up. He can never have too much preparation and training. He must be a strong competitor."[34]

5. Believe in yourselves. In his Fisk address Bunche described the advice of his maternal grandmother:

> Nana had traveled the troubled road. But she had never flinched or complained. Her indoctrination of the youngsters of the "clan" began at an early age. . . . Your color, she counseled, has nothing to do with your worth. You are potentially as good as anyone. How good you may prove to be will have no relation to your color, but with what is in your heart and your head. That is something which each individual, by his own effort, can control. The right to be treated as an equal by all other men, she said, is man's birthright. Never permit anyone to treat you otherwise. For nothing is as important as maintaining your dignity and self-respect.[35]

6. Support the NAACP and the Urban League. "In this hard world . . . fate helps only those who help themselves," Bunche said at Morgan State. Even though Negroes are growing stronger, economically and otherwise, and better able to use their abilities,

Bunche wondered whether "we really do as much for ourselves as we might, if we are as united and resolved as we should be." What were the evidences of united resolve?

> I doubt very much . . . that we give to our two leading organizations—the NAACP and the Urban League, which have accomplished so much for us—the support, monetary and otherwise, which they deserve. There are Negroes of considerable affluence in very many American communities—professional and businessmen—many of whom are not, by any means, giving the assistance which should be given. If they do not realize that, despite the success they may have had, they can never rise very far above their group and that their own future is tied to the future of the Negro, they are fatally shortsighted. In my view no Negro, however high he may have risen, is worth very much if he forgets his people and remains aloof from the unrelenting struggle for full Negro emancipation.[36]

What should whites do?

If concerned white citizens were to ask intelligent, informed Negroes what they should do, what would the answer be? What does the Negro wish? In "Freedom Is a Blessing" Bunche addressed himself to this question:

> The Negro asks no right to go into anyone's home, to force himself on anyone in any way. He asks only that he, as an individual, be permitted freely to make his way in a free society on the same basis as every other individual citizen; to rise or fall as his merit dictates. If the society grants him that—and nothing short of that could ever be acceptable—the Negro problem is solved. This would in no way affect the right of any person in the society to have as little or as much to do with any Negro, many Negroes, or all Negroes as he pleases.
>
> In short, the needs of the Negro citizen would be satisfied if old prejudices, like old soldiers, would just fade away.

Equal rights and equal opportunities—the Negro, according to Bunche, wishes nothing more and will be satisfied with nothing less.

At least twice in these speeches Bunche commented on the irony of segregation in most of our churches despite their protestations and teachings on democracy in race relations.[37] At Lycoming College, however, he expressed a sense of encouragement "that the organized religions in America are moving forward with increasing concern and pace in the sphere of race relations."

What did whites need to do to establish good race relations in the United States? "To perfect our design for living," said Bunche, "we need only to demonstrate that democracy is color blind."[38]

CAN WE HOPE FOR THE FUTURE?

Throughout this decade Bunche remained consistently optimistic about the future of race relations in the United States. At the beginning of the decade, speaking at Rochester in 1950, Bunche admitted that race relations "remain in a dangerous state, that they are a heavy liability to the nation, and constitute a grave weakness in our national democratic armor." Nevertheless, he was still optimistic: "Because I believe in the reason and essential goodness of human beings, because I have deep respect for and faith in my fellow men, I look to the future of race relations in our country with reasonable optimism."[39] Near the close of the decade, speaking at the Lycoming College commencement on June 8, 1958, Bunche insisted that "the direction in world racial relations is most everywhere right save for a notable exception or two, and the progress is gratifying."

Both in "The Road to Peace" (June 30, 1954) and in his speech to the NAACP in Dallas (July 4, 1954) Bunche estimated that in this field there has been more progress in the last decade than in all the years before. "The barriers of segregation and discrimination are being beaten down," Bunche told his Morgan State College audience, "and in this effort the Negro has had much help from white Americans who believe in as well as profess democracy. I think it is no exaggeration at all to say that no group of people in history has made as much progress in a comparable time as the Negro has made since his release from slavery."[40]

Speaking to an all-white audience in his final appearance on the Chautauqua lecture series, Bunche discussed "The Challenge of Human Relations" with particular emphasis on race relations. His was an optimistic appraisal. Three personal illustrations buttressed his conclusions.

First and earliest of Bunche's experiences had to do with his first day as a candidate for the freshman basketball team at UCLA. He said:

> On that same day there came out a young white boy whose family had just moved to Los Angeles from New Orleans. He too was out for the team; but he became perturbed when he saw me, and he went to the coach, who has since been a prominent lawyer in Los Angeles, and appealed to him. Quite innocently he said, "I have a problem, coach," and the coach asked him what it was. And he said: "You see, we've just come up here from New Orleans, and my folks won't like it at all if they find I'm out here playing with this colored fellow over there. I've never had that experience before, and I wish you would do something about it." And the coach listened to him very sympathetically, and he said, "Yes, it's a very simple matter to handle." And the boy looked at him expectantly, and the coach said, "Why, just go over there and turn in your suit." Well, he wanted to play basketball more than he wanted to nurture his prejudices—or, rather, his parents' prejudices—and so he didn't turn in his suit; and to drive the lesson home the coach paired him with me at guard so that we had to play in closest teamwork. We became very fast friends within a matter of weeks and have remained fast friends until this day. Within a very short time I was at his home, having meals; he was at my home; and even his parents, after the first shock, got along very well.

Another of Bunche's experiences came at the University of Arkansas lecture series. After being assured that the audience would be interracial, he accepted. Two pleasant days were spent at Fayetteville—everything interracial from first to last. On the way back to the station, however, a member of the faculty said, "Well, now that it's all over, I want to tell you how much worry that letter of yours caused me." Bunche was astonished. Everything had gone well, hadn't it? Yes, but "the university is in a county in which there aren't very many Negroes; and a few days before you were due, we were reviewing the correspondence and then saw our assurance to you and then became worried that maybe you'd get out here and find an all-white audience and figure that you had been tricked." The university was so concerned that they sent to Little Rock and Pine Bluff, both 250 miles away, to get Negroes to come to hear Bunche. Five hundred miles of Arkansas driving, Bunche replied, may be stretching democracy a little too far.

Experiences in the service of the United Nations, particularly in the UN Secretariat (which he described as an international civil service), convinced Bunche that "the most diversified assemblage of people to be found under any roof anywhere in the world . . . understand each other fully and . . . work together amicably." The staff of the United Nations, numbering in the thousands, is drawn from all races and all religions:

> In short, just about all the barriers known to human relationships are to be found in the Secretariat. . . . But we find that these barriers are remarkably fragile. All of these people, so widely diversified in origin and background, work and play together in impressive harmony. Genuine friendships cut across all lines. Social and athletic clubs are formed on the sole basis of common interests. There is an easy informality and camaraderie in relationships; and there is, of course, no little courting and marriage. It is a congenial human company enriched by its diversity.[41]

Conflicts? Those that exist seldom occur along lines of race or religion. Actually, relationships within the Secretariat involve no leap across racial or social barriers, because there is little consciousness that such hurdles exist.

The job of establishing good race relations is not so difficult as some would have us think, Bunche assured his Chautauqua audience.[42] We in America have learned that it is "not necessary to eradicate differences to achieve a single human pattern in order to enjoy democracy or to attain national unity; rather we have found that it is only necessary for people to change their attitudes and their superstitions about differences and that this can be done and is being done. Indeed, we know that differences of race, religion, and culture actually enrich the society."

But have we not been backsliding in recent years? Yes, confessed Bunche, we have.

> It is no secret that in some parts of the deep South today there are activities and practices aimed at the rights and status of black citizens which in their sinister design can only mean retrogression in race relations, in the status of the Negro, and in the growth and prestige of democracy. . . . They are certainly cause for most serious concern by every American who cherishes the American way of life. The country is in grave

danger when the law of the land comes to be openly defied and
violated with impunity.[43]

Almost a year later (1957) Bunche returned to the same problem of
retrogression in race relations, adding: "I see this as a passing phase,
an inevitable stage in the process of social change. The crisis itself is
a reaction to the changes for the good that are occurring in the status
of the Negro. In the absence of any pressure for change there would
be none."[44] In spite of the bombs and bombast, Bunche remained
optimistic.

SUMMARY AND CONCLUSIONS

During the period covered by this study — 1949-1959 — Ralph
Bunche was, in addition to his prestige as a high official of the United
Nations, almost universally accepted as a foremost Negro American
spokesman. This paper summarizes, primarily in his own words, his
ideas on race relations.

Much more is worthy of note in the speaking of Ralph Bunche.
Because he is a trained political scientist and a responsible officer of
the United Nations, his ideas on international conciliation and the
role of the UN deserve study. His extensive use of personal illustration and the personal elements of address in his language suggest
further investigation.

When Ralph Bunche spoke at his own graduation from UCLA,
he used "The Fourth Dimension of Personality" as a title and described his speech as "dripping with idealism and mysticism—so
much so, in truth, that no one, including the author, ever quite
understood what it intended to say. But the grammar was correct,
and the rhetoric soared and soared until it ended up with something
poetic from Edna St. Vincent Millay about looking up, not down,
and lending a helping hand. No one, even amidst the rampant cynicism of today, could possibly object to that."[45]

In the decade treated in this paper, however, Bunche abandoned
his earlier mysticism and soaring rhetoric. He was still optimistic,
perhaps idealistic; but in speech after speech he attacked unequivocally "our country's number-one domestic problem"[46]—race relations. On this subject, whether or not one agrees with what he had
to say, his views deserve attention.

Footnotes

1. Rewritten from a biographical sketch supplied by Dr. Bunche.
2. "Freedom Is a Blessing," delivered at the commencement exercises of Morgan State College in Baltimore, Maryland, June 4, 1951. *Vital Speeches,* XVII, 21 (August 15, 1951), 663-666.
3. Speech before the closing session of the national convention of the NAACP in Dallas, Texas, July 4, 1954. Mimeographed text supplied by Dr. Bunche.
4. (a) "The Barriers of Race Can Be Surmounted; Color Has Nothing to Do With Worth," delivered at the commencement exercises of Fisk University, Nashville, Tennessee, May 30, 1949. *Vital Speeches,* XV, 18 (July 1, 1949), 572-574.
   (b) "The Challenge of Human Relations," delivered at an Abraham Lincoln celebration sponsored by the City Club of Rochester, New York, February 11, 1950. *Representative American Speeches, 1949-50,* ed. A. Craig Baird (New York, 1950), pp. 142-153.
   (c) "Prospects for Peace: U. N. Building Firm Foundations," delivered at Stanford University in Palo Alto, California, April 28, 1951, before the first Western Conference on United Nations Affairs. *Vital Speeches,* XVII, 16 (June 1, 1951), 489-492.
   (d) "Freedom Is a Blessing," June 4, 1951.
   (e) "Toward Peace and Freedom; a Vigorous Interpretation of the United Nations," delivered before the Chicago Sunday Evening Club March 15, 1953. *The Christian Century,* LXX, 16 (April 22, 1953), 479-481.
   (f) "The Road to Peace; Learn to Live Together or Perish Together," delivered to the National Education Association at its Ninety-second Annual Convention in New York City, June 30, 1954. *Vital Speeches,* XX, 21 (August 15, 1954), 654-657.
   (g) Speech to the NAACP in Dallas, Texas, July 4, 1954.
   (h) "The Challenge of Human Relations," the last of a series of four addresses on the regular lecture series at Chautauqua, New York, August 13, 1954. Mimeographed text supplied by the office of the Director of Program and Education at Chautauqua.
   (i) Speech at the Fellowship House Family's 25th birthday dinner, Philadelphia, Pennsylvania, May 21, 1956. Carbon copy of speech manuscript supplied by Dr. Bunche for this and the next three speeches.
   (j) University of Pittsburgh commencement, February 1, 1957.
   (k) Speech at the dedication of "Ralph J. Bunche Junior High School," Compton Union High School District, Compton, California, April 10, 1958.
   (l) Speech at the Lycoming College commencement, Williamsport, Pennsylvania, June 8, 1958.
5. (a) "The United Nations as Peacemaker," Chautauqua lecture, August 9, 1954.
   (b) "The United Nations' Colonial Problem and the Under-developed Areas," Chautauqua lecture, August 10, 1954.
   (c) "The United Nations and Charter Revision," Chautauqua lecture, August 12, 1954. The lecture normally scheduled for Wednesday, August 11, was omitted because of the annual Chautauqua Recognition Day.
6. "How Far the Promised Land?" *Town Meeting,* XXI, 30 (November 20, 1955), 897th broadcast.

7. From a speech to the Periclean Club annual forum, Birmingham, Alabama, February 13, 1959.

8. See for instance "The United Nations as Peacemaker" and "The United Nations and Charter Revision."

9. Letter from Dr. Bunche, April 13, 1959.

10. Letter from Dr. Bunche, September 29, 1955.

11. "The Challenge of Human Relations," Chautauqua.

12. "Freedom Is a Blessing."

13. "The Challenge of Human Relations," Chautauqua.

14. *Ibid*.

15. To the NAACP in Dallas, 1954.

16. "Equal Justice—Under Law," an article based on an address by Dr. Bunche at a dinner given in his honor in New York City by the NAACP. *Survey*, LXXXVII, 3 (March, 1951), 115-118.

17. "The Challenge of Human Relations," Chautauqua.

18. To the NAACP in Dallas, 1954.

19. "The Challenge of Human Relations," Rochester.

20. "Freedom Is a Blessing."

21. Fellowship House dinner.

22. Rochester.

23. "Equal Justice—Under Law."

24. Lycoming College commencement. See also "Prospects for Peace," Pittsburgh commencement, Periclean Club forum.

25. "The United Nations' Colonial Problem and the Under-developed Areas."

26. "The Challenge of Human Relations," Chautauqua.

27. "The Challenge of Human Relations," Rochester.

28. "The Road to Peace." In his speech to the Fellowship House dinner he called it "a giant step forward."

29. "Freedom Is a Blessing."

30. To the NAACP in Dallas, 1954.

31. *Ibid*.

32. "Freedom Is a Blessing."

33. *Ibid*.

34. "The Barriers of Race Can Be Surmounted."

35. *Ibid*.

36. "Freedom Is a Blessing."

37. "The Road to Peace"; "The Challenge of Human Relations," Chautauqua.

38. "Equal Justice—Under Law."

39. "The Challenge of Human Relations," Rochester.

40. "Freedom Is a Blessing."

41. Fellowship House dinner.

42. "The Challenge of Human Relations," Chautauqua.

43. Fellowship House dinner.

44. Pittsburgh commencement.

45. *Ibid*.

46. Periclean Club forum.

The Reporter as Orator
Edward R. Murrow

EDWARD R. MURROW *(April 25, 1908—   ). Born at Greensboro, North Carolina; family moved to state of Washington in 1920; graduated from Washington State College in 1930; took part in collegiate forensics and dramatics; president, National Student Federation, 1929-1932; assistant director, Institute of International Education, in foreign affairs, 1932-1935; with Columbia Broadcasting System since 1935; director of Talks and Education, CBS, 1935-1937; European director, 1937-1946; vice-president, director of Public Affairs, 1945-1947; recipient of many radio and television awards, and of honorary degrees; author of* THIS IS LONDON *(1941).*

The Reporter as Orator
Edward R. Murrow

OTA THOMAS REYNOLDS *and* LESTER THONSSEN*

In his book entitled *Candle in the Dark*, the late Irwin Edman said "it may seem strange to the point of perversity" to announce that "a vivid sense of the present is one of the best antidotes of despair." He went on to say that "if men forget that the future will some day be a present, they forget, too, that the present is already here, and that even in a dark time some of the brightness for which they long is open to the responsive senses, the welcoming heart, and the liberated mind."[1]

During the last thirty years—years of conspicuous tensions and tragic happenings—American radio listeners have heard many voices announce the character of our anxieties and tribulations. Some voices have carried the message of frustration; others have spoken largely of our seemingly certain doom. Occasionally voices have even underestimated the dangers besetting mankind. On the other hand, a few analysts of public affairs have been able seriously and perceptively to survey the world scene and yet present that "vivid sense of the present" which prevents recognition of the tragic from becoming open despair. Edward R. Murrow is in this company.

In his "This Is London" series of broadcasts from 1939-1945, from which most of the illustrative material in this study is drawn, Murrow, then in his thirties, earned an international reputation as a reporter of the happenings of World War II. His job was to report

* Ota Thomas Reynolds (B.A. 1934, M.A. 1936, Ph.D. 1941, State University of Iowa) is an assistant professor of speech and chairman of the department at Hunter College of the City of New York.
  Lester Thonssen (B.A. Huron College, 1926, A.M., 1929, Ph.D. 1931, State University of Iowa) is a professor of speech at the City College of New York.

the hard news of war; this he did with penetrating insight and not a little eloquence. Without distortion of value, however, he also paused on occasion to take stock of man's enduring pleasures. Although the ugliness of war was everywhere in view, he could yet report on the beauty of a flower in early spring. Against a backdrop of world disorder and cruelty, he took time to comment on a kind deed. With the democratic order in peril, he spoke with renewed enthusiasm of individual dignity and the heritage of dissent through persuasion. This was not a sign of false optimism. He saw some light, however, where others found only unremitting darkness.

Reportorial Formula for the Speaker

Before television, the American public knew Murrow chiefly as an unseen reporter. True, he gave speeches before outside organizations, and the press took note of their delivery. Furthermore, he had addressed several hundred college and university audiences when, following his graduation from Washington State College, he served as president of the National Student Federation. But no considerable part of the American public had ever seen Murrow in a face-to-face situation. With an estimated listening audience of well over twenty million, he was a top reporter, although one without formal journalistic training—a circumstance which prompted Elmer Davis to say that veterans are "faintly scandalized that such good reporting can be done by a man who never worked on a newspaper in his life. . . ."[2] An assessment of Murrow's early speechmaking[3] must take into account the unique character of the radio commentary. Unlike most speakers mentioned in this book, the reporter usually gives not one but several talks each time he goes on the air. Each fifteen-minute presentation consists of several short speeches on a wide variety of subjects.[4] This requires capsuled, succinct treatment, as well as effective transitional links to hold the assorted themes together. Little opportunity is afforded for expansive unfolding of theses through detailed explanations, sustained reasoning, and re- cital of evidence. The audience, in turn, must occasionally accept or reject the reporter's thoughts in direct proportion to the confidence it places in the speaker. This confidence Murrow seemingly secures to an uncommon degree.

The respect a speaker enjoys derives importantly from the fundamental ideas and ideals he espouses. Murrow's basic creed seems rooted in his deep-seated belief in the dignity of the individual—a dignity which entails the individual's right to hold and express beliefs, to formulate and fulfill his own plan of living, to assume a personal responsibility in the use of his rights, and to recognize his obligation to the social units of which he is a member.

From this core emerge certain postulates supporting his social philosophy as applied to the contemporary scene: (1) Society presents many problems but little leadership to cope with them. (2) There is an ever-increasing need for the enlargement of the public's information on domestic and foreign affairs. (3) In our democracy the right of dissent and the right to suggest alternatives are essential, and threatened. (4) The need for humility in conducting our governmental transactions is urgent.

These tenets govern in part Murrow's concept of his function and obligation as a reporter. He considers himself bound by certain restrictions of the broadcasting medium, and more particularly by the network with which he is affiliated. This is not to imply that he views the restrictions as distasteful; they are in part self-imposed since he had a responsible hand in shaping the news policy of the Columbia Broadcasting System. Nevertheless, Murrow, and other CBS reporters for that matter, prepares his talks with an eye to a news formula. According to CBS policy, the network has no editorial views; neither is it disposed to advocate, directly or otherwise, anyone else's mode of viewing a subject. In short, its news analysts are expected not to air editorial positions. Obviously, such a policy limits the reporter's range of expression, though conceivably for the good.

During World War II, Paul W. White issued a statement supplementing a previous memorandum by Edward Klauber, repeating the intention of CBS to hold the news analysts to the presentation of facts "so as to inform . . . listeners rather than persuade them." Ideally, in controversial issues, White remarked, "the audience should be left with no impression as to which side the analyst himself actually favors."[5] White justified CBS's position very simply. Observing that the number of broadcast frequencies and national networks was severely limited, he said that without the no-editorializing policy "powerful and one-sided positions on serious issues

could be created for a small group of broadcasters locally, region-
ally, or nationally."[6] This, he insisted, would be detrimental not
only to radio but to the democratic system generally.

Murrow endorsed this policy. He helped formulate it and he tried
to adhere to it in his reporting. He believed that the reporter had no
right to use the microphone "as a privileged platform from which
to advocate action."[7] On controversial subjects he believed that the
reporter should supply the ascertainable facts and historical background and should point up the significant issues which would assist
the listening public in making its own decisions.

Admittedly this policy is not wholly free from ambiguity. It pre-
supposes the existence of a clear definition and standard of editorial
expression. That assumption is in part gratuitous because a speaker
can convey impressions and conclusions by subtle devices of style
and delivery which quite evade the dicta of any official memorandum.

Whether or not the policy of discouraging commentators from
editorializing, or of approving such comments only sparingly, represents the correct attitude toward the role of broadcasting is a debatable question. Periodically the problem comes up for re-examina-
tion, chiefly by the critics of radio and television. When in early
1957 an Eric Sevareid broadcast was canceled, allegedly because it
expressed a position against the State Department's ban on newsmen
visiting Communist China, the matter was reopened for extensive
airing. Among those who voiced sharp objection to the policy of
distinguishing news analysis and advocacy of view was Jack Gould,
radio and television critic for *The New York Times*. "If the networks' men are qualified for their jobs—and the CBS staff is of the
best," wrote Gould, "then listeners should have the benefit of their
independent judgments on the world's course."[8]

In a major speech before the Radio and Television News Direc-
tors' Association on October 15, 1958, Murrow himself criticized
the networks for helping to insulate the public from the hard facts
threatening man's survival. He proposed a scheme in which major
sponsors would turn over at least a few hours to the networks for
the expository presentation of material on significant public issues.
"I am not here talking about editorializing, but about straightaway
exposition as direct, unadorned, and impartial as fallible human

beings can make it. Just once in a while let us exalt the importance of ideas and information."[9] One senses in the Murrow address, however, a diminishing faith in the rightness of the "no-editorializing" policy. Surely Murrow has made partisan presentations. His "See It Now" show condemning the conduct of the late Senator McCarthy underscored his apparent conviction that there are times when a radio or television newsman should speak out. Jack Gould called the event "crusading journalism of high responsibility and genuine courage."[10] Observers generally regarded the telecast as a significant departure in the handling of controversial issues. Yet Murrow maintained: "The last thing I want to do is to take the privileged opportunity I have five nights a week on radio and two on television to attack this man. The moment I start to use my opportunity to agitate against McCarthy or against antivivisection or against anything else, then I've lost whatever standing I have as a reporter."[11]

The policy of separating news analysis sharply from advocacy requires a neutrality of mind which even such an accomplished and intelligent analyst as Murrow would scarcely approach, let alone claim for himself. Complete objectivity is as impossible of attainment as complete subjectivity would be pernicious. Murrow freely acknowledged the difficulty of realizing the CBS objective. Commenting on the problems of the wartime reporter, he said: ". . . we have tried to prevent our own prejudices and loyalties from coming between you and the information which it was our duty to impart. We may not always have succeeded. An individual who can entirely avoid being influenced by the atmosphere in which he works might not even be a good reporter."[12] And on another occasion he remarked that an approximation of objectivity is all that is humanly possible for "we are all, to some degree, prisoners of our education, travel, reading—the sum total of our experience."[13]

Editorializing results in the introduction of personal views and judgments, and possibly in recommendations for courses of action. Improperly used, it can even lead to selfish pleading. It represents a movement from exposition in the stricter sense to persuasion or advocacy. Now the distinction between these modes of discourse is tenable but elusive. Through a process of labeling, however, the reporter can, according to CBS, draw the dividing line. In one of his early speeches from London, Murrow remarked that wartime

happenings occasionally obliged the reporter "to express his personal opinion, his own evaluation of the mass of confusing and contradictory statements, communiques, speeches by statesmen, and
personal interviews."[14] He went on to say that "such statements of
personal opinion should be frankly labeled as such without any
attempt to cloak one's own impressions or opinions in an aura of
omnipotence." "What I think of events in Europe," he continued,
"is no more important than what you think, but I do have certain
opportunities for observation and study."[15] In his later radio series,
"This Is the News," Murrow used the same labeling technique; he
usually told his hearers where the reported items ended and his own
interpretation of a problem began. In general Murrow succeeded
in reporting issues without partisanship. His analyses of current
problems were carefully and fairly drawn. A reading of his early
scripts reveals that he rarely advocated a given line of action. He
consistently and persistently argued for certain principles, goals, and
ideals, but he seldom pointed to the actions which would achieve
them. Without doubt, however, he occasionally left his hearers with
a definite impression of his position and with an appeal, however
subtle and indirect, to consider or more often, to reject, a proposed
policy. There was more persuasiveness regarding lines of action in
Murrow's speaking than was indicated by the few overt endorse-
ments of policies. This persuasion was achieved partially through
choice of language, partly by the selection of historical details
affecting the credibility of those in support of opposing contentions,
and partly by the emphasis given to the pro and con of a particular
argument. Most important, however, the persuasion was induced
through the meanings conveyed by his voice. He confirmed Arthur
Krock's observation that "radio commentators are skilled in the use
of inflection and tones to produce desired effects on listeners while
adhering to a neutral text."[16] Murrow himself has spoken to the
point of this subtle persuasion. Commenting on the barring of broadcasters from Czechoslovakia, he said: "This refusal to permit broadcasters to work is a recognition of the power of the spoken word—
an admission that tone of voice, inflection, emphasis and timing can
convey meanings which cannot be controlled by any censor. Every
broadcaster who has ever worked under European censorship has

heard the complaint, 'We don't object to what you said—but the *way* you said it.' "[17]

That Murrow more frequently seemed to discredit rather than endorse actions is not strange. Measured by his highly moral code of conduct, not a few of the actions of men and governments by men are disappointing and discouraging. Since the end of World War II, he sees few of the qualities of personal greatness which emerged during the crisis and on which he reported from London. His voice is a responsive instrument which mirrors, by intonations and pauses, the distress he feels at acts which he deems unworthy. When the United Nations was considering the advisability of its members' sending ambassadors to Spain, Murrow's distaste for the action of the United States in meeting the issue was revealed even more by his voice than by his acute choice of words: "Our government has decided not to make up its mind; decided not to stand up and be counted."[18]

Murrow's concept of his own responsibility transformed the dictum of "Don't Editorialize" into a positive formula. In commenting on the job of the wartime reporter, Murrow once remarked that he had tried to give listeners "the hard news of communiqués and official statements as well as the climate in which the news has flourished, the humor, the criticism, the controversy and discussion which serve as a backdrop for the more dramatic news of the action of war."[19] This was really his reportorial prescription and he held to it with uncommon fidelity. So frequently in fact did Murrow speak to his audiences of his editorial philosophy that it became a distinctive mark of his program. Take-off and lampooning specialists seized upon this technique as an essential one in imitating Murrow's news broadcasts. Such comments as these were peculiar to his scripts: "This reporter has a certain preference for getting his dope direct from the men on the spot."[20] "This program is not concerned with who gets the nominations, or who is elected. So far as is humanly possible we shall remain neutral. . . ."[21] ". . . these words from Flaubert sum up the attitude of those of us who work on this program . . . 'Making myself known is not what is uppermost in mind . . . that can satisfy only the most mediocre vanity. . . . What I am aiming at is something better . . . to please myself.' "[22] Or, reflecting on the fiasco of the pollsters in November, 1948:

"Certainly the experience will cause many of us who write and talk to approach the task with more humility—to consider always the possibility that we may be wrong—and to search more diligently for facts upon which the reader or listener may base his opinion."[23] And there can be little doubt that the judicious restatement of these postulates contributed greatly to his reputation for honesty and reliability.

REVEALING THE CLIMATE OF OPINION

Murrow's wartime reports from London testified eloquently to the effectiveness of his reportorial prescription. Quite apart from the influence of the speaker's radio personality, they captured the spirit of a moment in history and translated it into a language that could be understood by people distantly removed from the scene of action. His reports had a certain historical perspective which less talented analysts were unable to provide. By placing happenings in large social frames, he was able to show the relation of geographically remote events to the common experiences of men and women everywhere. Without sensationalism he gave urgency and dramatic impetus to ideas and happenings which were the common concern of people throughout the world.

The secret of this accomplishment is in part a personal matter which no outsider can completely determine. But his own formula of wartime reporting offers a clue. He reported both on events and on the climate of opinion in which the news occurred. Murrow was fond of the expression "climate of opinion." He used it often. And it had a specific meaning for him. It embraced the whole backdrop, as he called it, of social, political, and economic activities in which events occurred and from which they issued. It included such things as the laughter, jokes, gripes, hopes, aspirations, fears, and quarrels of men and women in the less privileged classes as well as of those in positions of great responsibility. It included a recognition of what people believed to be true, whether it was or not. It included a respect for the traditions of a country, for the qualities that seldom come to light except in times of crisis, for the way people used their strength and assessed their weakness.

One of Murrow's characteristic techniques to reveal the climate of opinion on a given issue was to survey the controversy. On January 23, 1944, he dwelt at length on the deterioration of relations between Poland and Russia, following the latter's rejection of a Polish offer to mediate the major difficulties. In order that his hearers might appreciate the attitude of certain sections of the British public to this development, he reviewed typical comment from such liberal organs as the *New Statesman* and the *Tribune*; later he matched this with the expressions of the right-wing *Spectator*. Then he tried to articulate these variant views with Britain's position in the controversy:

> There is great sympathy for Russia amongst the masses of this country, much more probably than there is at home, for these people have more reason to be grateful. But if the British Government should accept Moscow's policies too completely, they would encounter the danger of estranging American opinion. Britain's man-in-the-street may know only vaguely that this is an election year in the States, but those who are responsible for British policy know full well that our Polish vote in New York, Pennsylvania, and Illinois will be decisive in the election and in America's willingness to participate in any international order. Most informed people here are clinging to the hope that Moscow will in the end accept Mr. Hull's offer of mediation, for if that should come about then the United States Government will have a share in the responsibility for whatever decision is taken.

Murrow made frequent use of anecdotes and humorous accounts to reveal the temper and mood of the British people, of the fighting men, and of civilian groups. Most reporters introduce some humor into their accounts. But Murrow made a distinctive use of humor; unlike many writers he chose materials which pointed up ideas and which told the listeners something about the state of mind of the people involved in the stories. The anecdotes went beyond the superficial requirement of providing interest appeal or relief from the serious. They contributed to an understanding of the mass mind, or why people responded as they did to their good or ill fortune. Yet the humor lightened but little the essentially somber and serious tone of his broadcasts.

A few samples will illustrate his technique. At the close of his speech of October 4, 1942, Murrow said: "But Hitler's new world is not to be destroyed by speeches—his or anyone else's. No more is Britain's new world to be created by oratory on behalf of the

Church or the State. It has been a week of speechmaking, and the best comment I have heard came from a wise old farmer of seventy down in the county of Kent. He had read them all—without the aid of glasses—he said: 'Don't seem to get us much nearer to winning the war, do they?' " And at the close of the talk of January 10, 1943: "During the days when invasion might have come at any hour, people were careful about what they said; but distance doesn't destroy the usefulness of information to the enemy. There's a farmer on the coast of England whose attitude might serve as an example to everyone. A friend of mine asked him directions, and the farmer demanded to see his identity card—which everyone is required by law to carry. My friend, thinking to have some sport with the local yokel, then asked to see his identity card; whereupon the farmer replied: 'No fear! I know who I be!' " The next example is from the introduction to the speech of July 16, 1944: "This attack [doodle-bug] on southern England hasn't produced anything like the humor and wisecracks that came out of the blitz. The best that I have heard deals with the experience of a sparrow. He was flying inland from the south coast, when a doodle-bug emitting its usual streak of fire went rushing past. Said the sparrow to the doodle-bug: 'What's your hurry?' and the flying bomb replied: 'If your tail was on fire you'd be hurrying too.' But the old blitz spirit has not disappeared— this is a true story. The other day a rescue squad dug a woman of sixty from under the ruins of her home. Someone offered her a cup of tea, and she replied: 'No thank you dearie, but I'll trouble you for a pint of beer!' " And a passage from the speech of October 3, 1943:

> There's a story going round over here—I've heard it four times, and seen it once in print. It is said that the story originated in France. The time is somewhere around 1950; three Frenchmen have won a lottery; the prizes are a rat, a glass of white wine, and fifteen seconds of electric power. The three men pool their winnings. They roast and eat the rat; they sip the glass of white wine; and after much debate decide to use the fifteen seconds of electric power to listen to the radio. After some slight difficulty, and just before the fifteen seconds expires, they get London just in time to hear the two words: "Patience, patience." Maybe that story is put about by so-called second front agitators, but it does reflect a deepening cynicism, and a shortage of patience.

PORTRAYING THE MEN OF ACTION

Vignettes of distinguished men are common in Murrow's reports. Regular listeners to his broadcasts can doubtless recall several such word portrayals, among them sketches of Eisenhower, Eden, Roosevelt, and Churchill. The function of these characterizations is twofold: (1) to provide human interest appeal which, in time of crisis particularly, links the news happenings and the personalities associated with the events, and (2) to serve as themes about which to assemble observations and impressions of the day's news.

Here too Murrow used the anecdote with telling effect; with it he portrayed characteristics sharply and decisively. On November 11, 1943, he reported on Cherry Brandy—really Nikolaas Gerbrandi—the Prime Minister of the Dutch government in London. He closed with this story. "The other nite he was standing in a doorway waiting for his car to pick him up. Incidentally he never possessed a car before he became Prime Minister. There was a terrific barrage going up and shrapnel was clattering down all around. Someone said, 'Surely, you're not going out in that, Mr. Prime Minister,' and Cherry Brandy replied with a chuckle, 'Yes, I go. I think I make a very small target.'" Of Jan Masaryk he said: "He had faith and he was a patriot and he was an excellent cook. One night during the blitz he was preparing a meal in his little apartment. A bomb came down in the middle distance and rocked the building. Jan Masaryk emerged from the kitchen to remark: 'Uncivilized swine, the Germans. They have ruined my soufflé.'"[24]

Like his narrative-descriptive accounts, most of the sketches showed considerable journalistic flourish. When coupled with an effective delivery, which Murrow unquestionably has, they became moving passages that illuminated ideas and happenings without introducing advocacy. On occasion they approached an oratorical display and grandeur less common today than in the nineteenth century. Perhaps here were flashes of the very style which under the title of "oratory" and "rhetoric" Murrow seems to hold mildly suspect.

One of his best sketches concerned a fellow reporter who was killed during the war. This is a quietly impressive tribute. Said Murrow:

Ben Robertson of the *New York Herald Tribune* died in a
plane crash near London. He once wrote of an earlier flight
from London to Lisbon: "The speed of that transition made
me think of Christ saying to the thief on the Cross of Calvary
. . . 'Today shalt thou be with me in Paradise.'" Out of War
into Peace. . . . There was never a night so black Ben couldn't
see the stars. This was his war from the moment he reached
London . . . he understood it for he understood the people
who were fighting it. That soft, determined South Carolina
voice was known to firemen and rescue workers in slum districts . . . and to Cabinet Ministers. He was the least hard-
boiled newspaper man I have ever known . . . he didn't need
to be, for his roots were deep in the red soil of Carolina and he
had a faith that is denied to many of us. Ben did a lot of travel-
ling and that means priorities . . . he told how familiar phrases
kept going through his head . . . he heard himself saying:
"Here is my permission . . . here is my authority"; then I
would be told . . . "But your category is only B—you must
have category A." "What must I do then; whom must I see, and
where do I see them?" "Have you priority?" "I have priority. . . ." "But for this you must have double priority." . . .
If any man I know ever had double priority for the long trip
into the Unknown . . . it was Ben Robertson.[25]

Attitude Toward the Art of Speaking

Doubtless everyone who devotes much of his professional life to
speechmaking formulates, consciously or otherwise, a general philosophy of his craft. Cicero is probably the most conspicuous example of the orator who prepared an elaborate account of his art;
Burke, Macaulay, and Disraeli, to name but a few, had definite ideas
about speakers and speechmaking, although they did not assemble
their views systematically.

Murrow's theory of public address must, of course, be inferred
from scattered remarks in his speeches. As an accomplished speaker
with an unquestioned sincerity of purpose, he obviously respects his
art. And he is sensibly conscious of the role of oral communication
in modern society. Time and again he devotes considerable space to
summarizing important speeches and assessing the skills of the
speakers.

In general, Murrow does not seem to be deeply impressed by the
current speechmaking in America. This is true not only of political
oratory, the bruising effect of which he mentions from time to time,

but of all other types as well. Only occasionally, he remarks, does he find in the mass of material—press releases, speeches, and the like— "something that seems to have merit, that combines logic and distinguished language."[26]

Obviously, there is no ideal oratory. Facts are not always allowed to speak for themselves; words are sometimes used to obscure issues rather than clarify them. Murrow shares with many others the view that oratory would be more useful if, after proper time had been given for deliberation of issues, prompt and decisive action followed. He entertains a suspicion that the language of oratory sometimes becomes a substitute, and in his opinion a poor one, for effective political action.[27] "Every sort of shouting," Joseph Conrad once remarked, "is a transitory thing. It is the grim silence of facts that remains."[28] Once the facts of political life have been assessed through discussion and the dissenters as well as the conformists have had full opportunity to speak, action should follow. Failing this, the people drift toward apathy and despair. "Speeches that are not followed by action," said Murrow, "undermine the will to act. Ambiguous announcements of policy produce disappointments, disillusionment and disunity. Rhetoric is no substitute for frankness—silence would be preferable."[29]

Murrow's use of the word "rhetoric" deserves passing notice. He seems to use it largely as a term of contempt. "Mere rhetoric" evidently signifies emptiness of thought, flourish, and form without substance. He seemingly suspects that logic is not an indivisible part of rhetoric. This interpretation is, of course, familiar to students of rhetorical theory. It is reminiscent of the dualism between rhetoric and dialectic about which much has been written. Murrow's view would apparently be largely Platonic in that it puts invention of subject matter outside the art of rhetoric, presumably in logic. It makes rhetoric largely an art of style and delivery, of the embellishment of discourse, rather than an all-embracing subject composed also of invention and arrangement. This durably persistent concept of the art of oral discourse has rendered some disservice to our field through the years.

Notes on His Style

It is surprising that Murrow should be so critical of what he calls "mere rhetoric" in much of contemporary speechmaking. Surprising, we say, because he is himself a stylist, a speaker who obviously gives considerable attention to the way in which ideas are clothed in language. But this is not a real contradiction. He does not conceive of speech style as a veneer, to be applied largely for effect. He dislikes rhetorical tricks. His first interest in language is purely functional: he wishes his words to convey an unequivocally clear, sharp impression of the meaning he has in mind. Like Hazlitt, he evidently dislikes anything that "occupies more space than it is worth."[30] Understandability is the basic requirement. Often he achieves a sharp clarity through typical journalistic techniques— elliptical units, run-on expressions, adjective-free sentences. The result is a clear, intelligible communication, effective in its simplicity. Thus on January 24, 1943, he reported from London: "I remember the picture of the approved wooden-soled shoes . . . they are to have leather treads. There is a shortage of alarm clocks in this country . . . in peacetime they were imported . . . many have broken down . . . the result is that people are late for work." No fancy words here, no frills, no embellishments; just a plain idea, plainly stated.

But Murrow can and often does express his ideas with stylistic polish. He is very much the orator. Thus we find such expressions as "flint-red, angry snap of antiaircraft bursts against the steel-blue sky";[31] "Soon we were over a cold grey sea looking like a huge grey tapestry covered with chips of marble";[32] "A lot of American and British boys are going to die before they cross those grey-brown stone mountains in North Africa and go down through the flower-flecked valleys to the sea";[33] "Here in Washington it's the eve of Inauguration . . . a big blending of patriotism, parties, politics, play and the parade."[34] Murrow is particularly fond of alliteration.

In 1947 Murrow commented: "The current crop of foreign correspondents has another fundamental problem—and the good ones recognize it. They are . . . talking from countries that are lean to a country that is fat. [There is] . . . no common denominator of experience . . . even the meaning of common words has changed."[35]

This keen awareness of the burden placed on language in translating the unfamiliar into comprehensible symbols finds expression in his sure use of figures of speech. "The flak looked like a cigarette lighter in a dark room—one that won't light. Sparks but no flame";[36] "The cookies—the 4,000 pound high explosives—were bursting below like great sunflowers gone mad";[37] ". . . the white fires had turned red. They were beginning to merge and spread, just like butter does on a hot plate."[38] And from his broadcast of May 15, 1949:

> Sitting up there in a B25 listening to the motors there was plenty of time to think of other nights and days in hostile skies —and the memories came rushing back of that indescribable warmth of companionship that always marked a good crew that fought and flew together—that feeling of being in an airborne foxhole . . . it always seemed that each man's shoulder was against the other fellow's and the understanding was complete . . . as it is between the fingers of the hand. . . . Well the bomber began to unload, five hundred pound bombs in a "string" . . . it seemed that they would never end . . . that the whole insides of the plane were tumbling out . . . the bombs began to burst on the ground . . . and still they were pouring out of the bomb bay . . . it was like a venetian blind of bombs from ship to ground . . . or like pouring seed from a tin pail . . . and it was pretty terrible. The bursts drew a straight line across the range . . . and the concussion came like a trip hammer . . . and still the bombs poured out.

Murrow's style is well-adapted to the presentation of these descriptive-narrative accounts. Doubtless it is equally appropriate to the making of explanatory analyses—the type of speechmaking for which he confesses a preference. It seems, however, that the fine balance which he establishes between simplicity of expression and rhetorical embellishment makes his style uncommonly effective in descriptive-narrative portrayal. Murrow's broadcasts from London and elsewhere during the war testify abundantly to this conclusion. Witness, for example, this passage from his speech of November 26, 1944:

> At home we fought this war in the light. Such homes as we had we still have. Our whole industrial plant is undamaged by war. Our nerves have not been tested and twisted by bombs and doodle-bugs, and things that arrive without warning. We are— we must be—less tired than the peoples of Europe. And as our

strength is greater, so must our responsibility be. There is a dim light in Europe now. The blackout is gradually lifting. And when I leave this studio tonight I shall walk up a street in which there is light—not much, but more than there has been for five-and-a-half years. You come to know a street pretty well in that time—the holes in the wooden paving blocks where the incendiaries burnt themselves out—the synagogue on the right, with the placard which has defied four winters, although it's a little tattered and smoke-stained. Tonight there'll be a street lamp just near there, and I shall be able to read the legend. "Blessed is he whose conscience hath not condemned him, and who is not fallen from his hope in the Lord." It is a street where in '40 and '41 the fires made the raindrops on the windows look like drops of blood on a mirror. It's an unimportant street where friends died, and those who lived had courage to laugh. Tonight, I suppose the air raid shelters will be empty, but it will be possible for a man to walk this street without fear of hitting a lamp post or stumbling over a curb. Five years and three months since they turned out the lights in the streets. There won't be anything brilliant about the illuminating to-night, but each shaded street lamp will, for this reporter, be like a Cathedral candle for those whose faith was greatest when the nights were darkest.

The distinction of Murrow's style derives in no small part from his selection of materials. He chooses his subject matter with good taste. He ignores, as so few have the desire or will to do, the tawdry details of the current scandals and the petty doings of the headline hunters. He respects personalities. He achieves effectiveness without sensationalism or abuse. With intelligent discernment he senses the course of historical events and reports the facts that seem to make the biggest difference in the lives of men.

Notes on His Delivery

Murrow is a skillful reader. Unlike many prominent radio per-formers, however, he does not rehearse his copy aloud before going on the air. He reads the material silently once shortly before air time. His copy carries a minimum of processing marks. Now and then he inserts a bar or parallel bars to indicate the point at which he wishes to pause; occasionally he underscores a word to remind him of the stress scheme; and on rare intervals he pencils in a scheme of pronunciation cues for difficult foreign names. But in the main his reading copy is clear. His is a personal type of punctuation supplied by changes in time, inflection, and stress. His written style favors him, of course, for it is simple, uncluttered by commas and other conventional symbols. He relies largely upon dot separations to divide the elements of his sentences.

Murrow's has been called one of the finest voices on the air. Few would disagree. The rich orotund quality is admirably suited to radio and television.

A distinctive feature of his delivery is what he calls "unorthodox timing." It commands attention from the very beginning: "This is London" or "This   is the news." For a while in 1949 Murrow shortened the pause between the first two words; to many it seemed that a distinguishing mark had been removed. Doubtless a large company rejoiced in his decision to return to the accustomed pattern.

Murrow is adept at controlling inflectional variations. The inflectional changes are used effectively to reinforce ideas. They are also used in a subtler way, but with equal incisiveness and precision, to convey impressions which, if expressed in words, would clearly amount to open editorializing and persuasion. Indeed, objective analysis may with skillful vocal manipulation become charged with advocacy.

The effectiveness of Murrow's delivery does not really flow from its conversational quality. It may even be doubted whether it has the warm, direct, and flexible features of friendly communication. Instead, it is a bit studied, aloof, mildly theatrical. Nonetheless it is an impressive, authoritative delivery.

Postscript

The news-analyst and the historian are companion workers. Both are chroniclers of events; both must select, relate, and interpret an amazing assortment of facts which for one reason or another seem worthy of remembrance. Neither can know everything that happens; nor can either, however perceptive and informed, understand everything he observes. Both must possess the supreme virtue of honesty.

To an uncommon extent Edward R. Murrow combines the best talents of the newsman and the historian in the field of popular reporting. Gifted performance as a public speaker combines with these rich endowments to make him one of America's most distinguished radio and television personalities.

Footnotes

1. (New York, 1939), pp. 73, 76.
2. Edward R. Murrow, *This Is London* (New York, 1941), p. viii.
3. Just how and where Murrow developed his skill in speaking is difficult to say. He considers the experiences during the years from 1933 to 1935, when he was in his mid-twenties, particularly important. During this time he served as secretary of the Institute of International Education. It was the function of this organization to bring prominent educators, fleeing from the European tyrannies, to America and relocate them here. Murrow found himself working in the midst of this cosmopolitan group of thinkers, all of whom were deeply affected by the march of dictatorship abroad. Murrow's apartment became a discussion center for the ever-changing group. Regular participation in these challenging seminars conducted by scholars had a three-fold effect on Murrow. His interest in academic and international problems was stimulated and deepened; his belief in the right of dissent was crystallized; and his manner of speaking was changed somewhat. In order to make himself understood by men for whom English was a foreign language, he had to cut his rate and sharpen the distinctness of utterance.

   However, he was not unaware of his speaking habits prior to these experiences. He majored in speech and history at Washington State College. He took an active part in forensics, did work in dramatics and oral interpretation, and acted in college plays. While Murrow has a warm regard for the late Ida Lou Anderson, from whom he received speech instruction at Washington State, he is not convinced that his college experience was wholly indispensable training.
4. Cf. December 27, 1942 and May 24, 1943.
5. Paul D. White, *News on the Air* (New York, 1947), p. 201.
6. *Ibid.*, p. 202.
7. September 29, 1947.
8. *The New York Times*, February 13, 1957, p. 71.
9. "A Broadcaster Talks to His Colleagues," *The Reporter*, XIX (November 13, 1958), 35-36.
10. *The New York Times*, March 11, 1954, p. 38.
11. *Newsweek*, XLIII (March 29, 1954), 51.
12. December 2, 1941.
13. September 29, 1947.
14. July 21, 1940.
15. *Ibid.*
16. *The New York Times*, July 14, 1949, p. 26.
17. March 1, 1948.
18. May 11, 1949.
19. December 2, 1941.
20. October 10, 1947.

21. March 12, 1948.
22. April 21, 1949.
23. November 5, 1948.
24. March 10, 1948.
25. February 28, 1943.
26. March 31, 1948.
27. September 20, 1942; March 26, 1944.
28. In essay on "Confidence," *Selected Modern English Essays*, 2nd series (London: Oxford University Press, 1932), p. 52.
29. September 20, 1942.
30. William Hazlitt, "On Familiar Style," in *Heath Readings in the Literature of England*, ed. by T. P. Cross and C. T. Goode (Boston: D. C. Heath and Company, 1927), p. 832.
31. September 21, 1940.
32. November 21, 1942.
33. May 2, 1943.
34. January 19, 1949.
35. *The New York Herald Tribune*, September 5, 1947.
36. December 3, 1943.
37. *Ibid.*
38. *Ibid.*